The Great Composers

THE LIVES AND MUSIC OF
50 GREAT CLASSICAL COMPOSERS

JEREMY NICHOLAS

Quercus

THIS BOOK IS DEDICATED WITH LOVE
AND GRATITUDE TO NAN AND HARRY

ACKNOWLEDGEMENTS

My sincere thanks to the following for the varying degrees of help, expertise and encouragement given to me during the gestation and writing of this book: Rob Cowan of *Gramophone* and BBC Radio 3 for introducing me to Quercus; Richard Milbank of Quercus who combines the roles of midwife, angler, diplomat, publisher and polymath with an abiding love of classical music; my editor Ben Dupré who forsook his viols and harpsichord to correct my solecisms with a gratifyingly light touch and make countless valuable improvements and suggestions; project manager Victoria Huxley; designer Austin Taylor and typesetter Geoffrey Smith; Harriet Smith and Philip Lane for their input in the early stages.

I am especially grateful to Gordon Wise at Curtis Brown for his inspiring support and astute advice; and, as always, to Jill and Rosie for simply being there.

A NOTE ON THE MUSIC

The 'Essential Works' box for each composer lists the ten or so most important and representative works for those coming fresh to the composer.

The keys in which works are written are given only when there is the risk of confusion with another work by the same composer bearing a similar title. In such cases, works in major keys are denoted thus: Fantasie in C, for example. Works in minor keys are listed with the key followed by 'minor' (Fantasie in C minor).

The date ascribed to each work is the date when the composition was completed or, if not known, when first published. The dates rarely take into account the year in which composition commenced, or those of subsequent revisions of which there may be several over a number of years. For instance, the date of Sibelius's Violin Concerto is given as 1903 (the year he finished the original composition) despite it now being universally played in the revised version of 1905.

CONTENTS

FOREWORD

To define 'a composer' is simple enough: 'one who composes music'. 'Great'? That is more problematic. When does a composer move from being merely good or talented to being 'great'? What criteria are used? Is it time and the weight of musical opinion? If so, who formulates musical opinion? Or is it just a matter of personal taste? What about those considered by their contemporaries to be 'great' but whose reputations have since shrunk to become footnotes in musical history? Can a composer be great if his or her music is relatively unknown yet acclaimed by knowledgeable, specialist devotees? The answer must surely be 'yes', but if so can they then realistically inhabit the same mountain top as the Olympian masters? Are there, in fact, grades of greatness? These were some of the conundrums to be wrestled with when compiling a list of great composers

But that was not the hard part. Choosing the Top Twenty was easy enough. Bach, Haydn, Mozart, Beethoven, Schubert, Schumann, Verdi, Wagner, Brahms, Tchaikovsky – all of them are obvious choices - but reducing the shortlist (actually, rather a long list) to the prescribed fifty took weeks of indecision while one choice was weighed against another, their various merits, popularity or relevance endlessly debated. In the end, other criteria had to intrude to reflect stylistic variety and the broad sweep of musical development, two other themes of the book. So, sadly but inevitably, the names of many indisputably great composers had to give way, on this occasion, to others, from Tallis, Lully and C. P. E. Bach to Rimsky-Korsakov, Ives and Messiaen. Some personal favourites had to go (Hummel, Fauré – by a whisker – Poulenc and Korngold) and even my publisher was unable to hang on to Josquin, Victoria, Gabrieli and Schütz.

Any 'Fifty Great' list of anything automatically invites contention ('why ever did they include X?' and 'how on earth could they think of omitting Y?'). It is a party game which, in this case, can only stimulate more interest and debate in the subject – the fascinating, bottomless treasure trove that is classical music. What is beyond dispute is the enriching, ennobling, inspiring, comforting and enduring nature of the music bequeathed to us by every one of these extraordinary geniuses. I hope this book will bring you closer to them and their unique gifts; for music, as someone once said, is a report on your inner experience.

JEREMY NICHOLAS
Wedgewood Grange, 2007

Giovanni Pierluigi da
Palestrina

Master of Renaissance polyphony

c. 1525–94

THE 16TH CENTURY WITNESSED FOUR MAJOR MUSICAL PHENOMENA: the tradition of instrumental music was established; the first opera was produced; music began to be printed; and the polyphonic school reached its peak. Polyphony is the type or method of composition in which two or more parts are combined harmoniously without losing their melodic individuality and independence. When it came to the writing of polyphonic music, the greatest master of the age was Palestrina.

There is little in the way of forceful or imaginative expression in his music, and he was neither an innovator nor particularly versatile, but some scholars regard him as the greatest composer before Bach and Handel. What Palestrina was aiming for – and achieved – was a pure beauty of sound. Rooted in medieval music, specifically in Gregorian chant (which is often directly quoted), Palestrina's music offers the finest examples of classical polyphonic writing – to the extent that even today he is held up as a model for students. 'His genius', wrote Percy M. Young, 'lay particularly in the expression of spiritual and emotional profundity through a vocabulary as simple as it is moving . . . He realised a mystical union of words and music within the liturgical opportunities of the Roman Church, so that the principal factor to emerge from performances which do not confuse propriety with lack of colour is intense spiritual insight.' Palestrina was, as Sir Donald Tovey once remarked, 'a God-intoxicated man' and is acknowledged as the Catholic Church's greatest composer and the father of the finest sacred music of subsequent eras.

EARLY YEARS

Palestrina was christened Giovanni Pierluigi but became known as Giovanni Pierluigi da Palestrina after his birthplace, a town near Rome. He was born in about 1525 (his exact date of birth is unknown) and was roughly seven years old when he began his musical career as a chorister in the cathedral of Palestrina. In 1534, when Cardinal della Valle, bishop of Palestrina, was made archbishop of Santa Maria Maggiore in Rome, he took the young Giovanni with him and entered him as a chorister there. By 1540 Palestrina was studying music at Santa Maria Maggiore and by 1544 was back in his home town as the organist and choirmaster of the cathedral of Sant' Agapit. The bishop there, Cardinal del Monte, became Pope Julius III in 1550, and with history repeating itself, he took Palestrina back with him to Rome, installing him as maestro of the Cappella Giulia. In the meantime, Palestrina had married (12 June 1547) and produced three sons.

SUCCESS AND TRAGEDY

In 1554 Palestrina dedicated a book of masses (the first of nearly 100 such settings) to Pope Julius. He was rewarded with a place in the papal choir. This caused some resentment from his fellow choristers as Palestrina had had no audition and was said not to have had a good voice. A few months later, he was given a small pension and dismissed by the new pope, Paul IV, on the grounds

'He is the real king of sacred music, and the Eternal Father of Italian Music.'
VERDI

that he was a married man. A string of appointments over the next decade followed, among them maestro at the church of San Giovanni Laterano, for which he wrote his celebrated *Lamentations*; a return to Santa Maria Maggiore; the directorship of the new Roman Seminary, where his sons were students; and a spell in the employment of Cardinal Ippolito d'Este. These peregrinations culminated in an offer from Emperor Maximilian II in 1568 to be musical director of the court in Vienna. Palestrina asked for such an exorbitant fee that the offer was quietly forgotten. In 1571 he resumed his former post at the Cappella Giulia under yet another pope, Pope Gregory XIII, where he remained for the rest of his life.

Palestrina's life took a tragic turn when in the 1570s his brother and two of his sons and then in 1580 his wife perished in three separate outbreaks of the plague. In despair, he took the first steps towards entering the priesthood but was persuaded to abandon this course when he met Virginia Dormuli, the wealthy widow of a furrier. They were married in 1581, and combining composition, a talent for real estate and an aptitude for the fur trade, Palestrina prospered until his death from pleurisy in Rome on 2 February 1594.

Essential works

MISSA PAPAE MARCELLI (1567)
MISSA ASSUMPTA EST MARIA (ND)
MISSA BREVIS for four voices (1570)
TU ES PETRUS, motet for six voices (1572)
LAMENTATIONS FOR HOLY SATURDAY (ND)
MOTETS, BOOK 4 (1584)
STABAT MATER, motet for eight voices (1589–90)

THE VATICAN STRIKES BACK

PALESTRINA WAS WORKING FOR THE VATICAN during the Counter-Reformation, that period when the Roman Church made strenuous efforts to strike back against the rise of Protestantism. The Council of Trent, which met in 25 sessions between 1545 and 1563, was formed to reconsider the Church's doctrine and to strengthen its position by clearly restating its fundamental beliefs. As far as music in worship was concerned, the Council demanded that it should eschew any secular material and avoid elaborate contrapuntal settings. Only the organ was to be used for accompanying voices or playing solos. There were to be no virtuoso theatrical vocal and instrumental displays. Palestrina knew exactly what was wanted – an ethereal cloud of sound to fill St Peter's. He was buried there himself. His coffin bore the inscription PRINCEPS MUSICAE – 'Prince of Music'.

WILLIAM
BYRD

The miracle man of music

c. 1540—1623

TO HIS CONTEMPORARIES, BYRD WAS 'THE MIRACLE MAN OF MUSIC', 'never without reverence to be named of the musicians'. This last description comes from Byrd's pupil Thomas Morley; Byrd himself was a pupil of Thomas Tallis. This unique succession formed the triumvirate that fashioned the magnificent tradition of English 16th-century music. If Tallis was the first important English composer, then William Byrd was undoubtedly the greatest of the era, not to be equalled until Purcell a century later.

Byrd's range, originality and quality made him the most complete musician of the age. Adventurous in its harmony and experimental in structure, his music had rhythmic variety and complex syncopation to an unprecedented degree. It was also freer in its melodic ideas than other contemporary works. Listening to his music, one can hear many 'wrong notes' or discords, where the independent but intertwining melodic parts clash harmonically before being resolved. Such harmonic collisions are not unusual to modern ears, but in his day Byrd was at the cutting edge of new music. In fact, such was the novelty of his writing that he was obliged to state: 'What I have written are not misprints.'

EARLY YEARS

The details of his early life are sketchy. Indeed, Byrd the man is a somewhat shadowy figure, only the outward events of his life being recorded. Like Shakespeare, his great contemporary, all that really remains is his work.

Biographers have long thought that the date of his birth was some time in 1543, but a recently discovered document suggests that it was in 1540 or late 1539. He was born in London into a staunchly Catholic family, probably the son of Thomas Byrd, a Gentleman of the Chapel Royal in London and a friend of Tallis. As a boy, William almost certainly sang in the Chapel Royal during the reign of Mary Tudor (1553–8), 'bred up to music under Thomas Tallis'. Thus his formative years were spent in the most prestigious and best-funded choir in the land, alongside some of the finest musicians of the day.

Byrd's creative life coincided with a time of great religious change in England. Obliged to attend Anglican services, Catholics were harshly treated during the reign of Mary's successor, Elizabeth I (1558–1603). Many were tortured and executed for their beliefs. Byrd managed to hold steadfastly to his faith, but remarkably his openly held Catholicism seems never to have affected his career. This began at the age of 20, when he was appointed organist of Lincoln Cathedral, a post he held until 1572. Having married one Juliana Birley four years earlier, he moved back to London to become a Gentleman of the Chapel Royal and joint organist with Tallis.

The relationship between the two men was now a partnership of equals and one that blossomed into friendship. In 1575 they co-published a collection of 34 motets entitled *Cantiones sacrae*. This was made possible by the significant royal gesture of the granting of an exclusive 21-year patent for the selling and printing of music and music manuscript paper in England. This printing monopoly was, in effect, an early attempt to establish copyright but the venture proved less remunerative than hoped. Two years later we find them petitioning the queen to allow them to lease their patent in exchange for an

A CANNY BUSINESSMAN

BYRD WAS CLEARLY AN ASTUTE BUSINESSMAN in the handling of his publishing monopoly. He was also ambitious, industrious and politically shrewd. He took over the lease of Stondon Place in Essex from its previous occupant – one William Shelley, who had been condemned to death for his part in an alleged popish plot. The estate was close to Ingatestone Hall, the home of his patrons, the Catholic Petre family. Though it took years of legal wrangling to be resolved, when the property was sequestered two years later, Byrd negotiated a Crown lease on Stondon Place that would expire only on the death of his children. There must subsequently have been a bitter family row, for Byrd's will, dated 1622, omits his eldest son Christopher from its provisions. His estate was left to his wife and three surviving younger children.

annual income of £40. Elizabeth granted them their wish. When the elderly Tallis died in 1585, the licence passed into Byrd's hands.

SECRET LOYALTIES

Byrd's religious music necessarily falls into two categories: the works in English that he wrote for the newly established Anglican rite for which he had to invent a new form and method for the setting of canticles; and the secretly composed settings of the old Latin texts for private Catholic services. The three masses (for five voices, four voices and three voices) were published anonymously during the 1590s, to be followed a decade later by two large collections (the *Gradualia*) of music required for the Catholic liturgical year. It was a risky undertaking, for the music was illegal, yet Byrd's name appeared on the *Gradualia* without him being thrown into the Tower. He wrote in the first volume: 'I have found that there is such a power hidden away and stored up in those words that . . . all the most fitting melodies come as it were of themselves, and freely present themselves when the mind is alert and eager.' Such was the power of the scriptural texts upon his imagination.

Despite his importance and fame, relatively little of Byrd's music is performed regularly today. Only a handful of the anthems, motets, services and his three mass settings are heard among roughly 150 Latin motets and over 50 English anthems. Into these he poured his prodigious invention and passionate religious conviction with an unsurpassed technical mastery. To many, Byrd's finest music is for the Anglican Church. His Great Service, scored for a 10-part choir divided into two semi-choirs, is written on a magnificent scale, with unexpected harmonies and phrase lengths, and a wonderful richness and variety of vocal colours and textures. But, remarkable as was his church music, Byrd was equally renowned for his keyboard music and songs. There was no tradition in England of writing for the virginal, harpsichord or chamber organ. In his 140 pieces, Byrd revolutionized writing for keyboard with brilliantly inventive and complex music, much of which can be found in *My Ladye Nevells Booke* (1591) and the *Fitzwilliam Virginal Book*. These rely greatly on fantasies, variations and dance movements (the pavan and galliard especially), as does his consort music – instrumental works for small ensembles written for theatres and aristocratic entertainment.

'Cultivated by many and admired by all – Master William Byrd – father of British music.'

GEORGE GAGE

In 1577 Byrd moved his family to the village of Harlington in Middlesex, where it appears his wife died. From here he carried out his duties at the Chapel Royal, composed and taught. After the successful petition to the queen, he was granted the lease of the manor of Longney in Gloucestershire. In 1593 he moved to Stondon Place (long since demolished), a large farm of over 200 acres at Stondon Massey in Essex.

The last 20 years of Byrd's life were not particularly prolific (his final compositions were four anthems published in 1614). In the end, his adherence to the Roman Church caused problems. The authorities were certainly keeping an eye on him early on, for in a list of places frequented by recusants in and about London dated 1581 is the following entry: 'Wyll'm Byred of the Chappele, at his house in p'rshe of Harlington, [Middlesex]'. In the 'Proceedings in the Archdeaconry of Essex', 11 May 1605, 'William Birde, Gentleman of the King's Majestie's Chapell' is 'presented' for 'popish practices'. We do not know what his sentence was as it seems he was in hiding at the time, but he and Ellen, his second wife, were often heavily fined for recusancy. They refused to attend the services at Stondon Massey – and when Byrd died at his home in Essex on 4 July 1623, he was buried in the churchyard in an unmarked plot of unconsecrated ground.

Essential works

GREAT SERVICE IN F
O LORD, MAKE THY SERVANT, anthem
CANTIONES SACRAE (1575)
PSALMES, SONETS AND SONGS (1588)
MY LADYE NEVELLS BOOKE, keyboard (1591)
MASS FOR FOUR VOICES (1593)
MASS FOR THREE VOICES (1594)
MASS FOR FIVE VOICES (1595)
AVE VERUM CORPUS, motet (1605)
'THE CARMAN'S WHISTLE', 'WOLSEY'S WILD' and other works from the FITZWILLIAM VIRGINAL BOOK

'WE ARE FROLIC HERE . . .'

THOUGH BEST KNOWN FOR HIS CHURCH MUSIC, BYRD COMPOSED A LARGE NUMBER OF SECULAR WORKS, proving to be a master of the solo song with polyphonic accompaniment. He preferred to use a consort of viols for accompanying rather than the lute, preferred by many of his contemporaries and successors. Among his finest songs are 'O woful Orpheus' and the exquisite 'Lullaby My sweet little darling' from Psalmes, Sonets and Songs (1588). In a letter from the Earl of Worcester to the Earl of Shrewsbury dated 19 September 1602 we read: 'We are frolic here in Court; much dancing in the Privy Chamber of country dances before the Queen's Majesty, who is exceedingly pleased therewith. Irish tunes are at this time most pleasing, but in the winter, Lullaby, an old song of Mr. Byrd's, will be more in request as I think.'

CLAUDIO
MONTEVERDI

The prophet of music

1567—1643

MONTEVERDI WAS ONE OF THE GREAT ORIGINAL MINDS OF WESTERN MUSIC. It is said that he revolutionized the art form, for he introduced entirely new methods, techniques and styles that were an abrupt break from anything that had been written before. If the honour of composing the first opera fell to Jacopo Peri, it was Monteverdi who composed the first opera with any truly dramatic concept. He was the first to realize that the orchestra could be used to comment on and add to the drama; the first to understand that certain instrumental colours projected certain moods: flutes, for example, were effective for conveying pastoral scenes, brass and percussion for portraying military episodes. Different rhythms, tempi and keys were used to project varying emotions. He introduced certain chords that no one had thought of using previously. He was the first to employ tremolando and pizzicato effects for the strings.

The fashion for polyphony had begun to fade by the end of the 16th century in favour of monody – that is, a melody confined to just one part, supported by subsidiary parts filling in the harmony, usually in the form of chords. This allowed for greater verbal clarity, and no composer made better use of this new fashion than Monteverdi. Not that he limited himself to a single style. His greatest works – the operas and the Vespers of 1610 – are an amalgam of madrigals, recitatifs, monody and diverse instrumental forms, welded together into a dramatic whole. Monteverdi's music represented a huge leap in the way it conveyed ideas and emotions. He is the culmination of the Renaissance and the beginning of the new Baroque era and beyond.

EARLY YEARS

Monteverdi's career falls into three distinct stages: Cremona, Mantua and Venice. Christened Claudio Giovanni Antonio, he was born on 15 May 1567 in Cremona, a small town in Italy's Po Valley about 40 miles from Milan. His father was a chemist and barber-surgeon whose shop was near the cathedral. Although Claudio's younger brother Giulio also became a professional musician, there is no evidence that there was a strong musical gene in the family. Young Monteverdi studied with the cathedral's conservative *maestro di cappella*, Marc'Antonio Ingegneri, and by the age of 15 he had composed a group of short religious pieces that were accomplished enough to be published in Venice. Sets of madrigals and canzonettas followed so that by his early 20s Monteverdi had a local reputation as a gifted, if conventional, composer.

FROM CREMONA TO MANTUA

In 1592 Monteverdi landed a position as viol player and singer in the court of the tyrannical, music-loving Vincenzo I, duke of Mantua (the painter Rubens was one of several important artists whom the duke employed). The director of music there was a Netherlander called Giaches de Wert, from whom his younger colleague learned much. A short time later, Monteverdi produced a book of madrigals that were quite novel in style, indicating the path his later music would take. Nevertheless, he did not publish anything further for 11 years. His patron was in the habit of taking a musical

A LANDMARK OPERA

L'INCORONAZIONE DI POPPEA was the first opera to be based on history rather than mythology; and whereas most operas had been aimed at the court audience, this one was for the general public. It marks the beginning of operas in the classical style that culminated in Handel, but it was not until Mozart, almost 150 years later, that an opera would appear with the same subtlety of characterization and dramatic force. Amazingly, *Poppea* was not heard in the United States until 1926, and in Britain until 1927.

retinue with him wherever he went, be it to Hungary to fight the Turks or to Flanders to take a water cure for gout. This allowed Monteverdi, now in charge of the duke's small band of musicians, to hear the musical trends current elsewhere on the continent – an invaluable broadening of his horizons.

In 1599, just before his 32nd birthday, Monteverdi married Claudia Cattaneo, one of the singers in the duke's retinue. Over the next five years, the couple had three children – two sons and a daughter who died in infancy. Monteverdi was made *maestro di cappella* in 1602. The duke had heard a performance of Peri's opera *Euridice* in Milan and urged Monteverdi to try his hand at this new form of dramatic expression. The result was *L'Orfeo, favola in musica* (or *Orfeo* as it is more commonly called), a lavish production that used a mixture of monody, madrigals and new instrumental forms. Among its innovations were the orchestra's five trumpets and the use of two keys simultaneously to express Orfeo's emotions when he is told of the death of Euridice. Four hundred years later *Orfeo* is the earliest opera still in the active repertory.

By now, Monteverdi's fame was spreading across Europe, he was free to write the music he wanted (with the duke paying for its publication), his fourth and fifth books of madrigals were hugely successful . . . and then everything fell apart.

In September 1607, Monteverdi's beloved wife died. It cast him into the deepest depression – he appears to have had some sort of nervous breakdown – and he left the Mantuan court to live with his father in Cremona. He was summoned back by his patron to compose a new opera, *Arianna*, to celebrate the wedding of Mantua's heir apparent. It was the greatest success of Monteverdi's career so far, yet he was now more deeply depressed than ever. It was during this unhappy period that some, if not all, of the *Vespro della Beata Vergine* (known as the Vespers of 1610) was written. Was he angling for a job to take him away from Mantua, perhaps a church job in Rome or Venice (the Vespers were dedicated to the pope)? If so, any decision was taken out of his hands when Vincenzo I died, to be

Essential works

L'ORFEO, FAVOLA IN MUSICA, opera (1607)

ARIADNE'S LAMENT, the only surviving section of Arianna (1608)

VESPRO DELLA BEATA VERGINE (1610)

Nine books of madrigals, especially Book 8, MADRIGALI GUERRIERI ET AMOROSI (1638)

L'INCORONAZIONE DI POPPEA, opera (1642)

succeeded by Francesco Gonzaga, who summarily dismissed him and a number of other artists from the service of the court.

VENICE: AN INDIAN SUMMER

Out of the blue came an invitation to become *maestro di cappella* at St Mark's, Venice, by far the most prestigious church appointment outside Rome. He accepted and journeyed with his two sons to Venice in August 1613. On the way, they were set upon by highwaymen and robbed of everything they possessed. Despite this ill-fated start, the last chapter of Monteverdi's career was, by and large, a happy one. He was paid well (and regularly, unlike in Mantua), proved to be an able administrator, improved markedly on the standards of his predecessor, and was in great demand for a variety of dramatic works. In 1632 he took holy orders but continued to produce both sacred and secular music – though at a slower pace, seemingly more content in the service of God than in that of the Venetian court.

Monteverdi's most notable achievement during this decade was a grand retrospective volume entitled *Madrigali guerrieri et amorosi* (Madrigals of War and Love) published in 1638. Though it contains much startling and progressive music, it appeared to all intents and purposes as if his most creative days were over.

'The end of all good music is to affect the soul.'

MONTEVERDI

That was before Monteverdi's Indian summer. Venice's first opera house opened in 1637. *Arianna* was revived in 1639, followed by a couple of new operas and a ballet for a court entertainment in Piacenza. Then, in 1642, he wrote what is undoubtedly his greatest masterpiece, *L'incoronazione di Poppea* (The Coronation of Poppea). The sustained power and energy of the work is remarkable for a man of 75, a feat emulated by his compatriot Verdi nearly 250 years later with his opera *Falstaff*.

A few months after the premiere of *Poppea*, in the spring of 1643, Monteverdi made a tour of his old haunts in Cremona and Mantua. He returned to Venice, where he died on 29 November. Greatly honoured, he was buried in the church of Santa Maria Gloriosa dei Frari.

THE EMOTIONS OF THE SOUL

IN DEFENCE OF HIS NEW STYLE OF WRITING, in the preface to his Fifth Book of Madrigals Monteverdi explained: 'I do not write things by accident.' In the Eighth Book of Madrigals he wrote, 'I consider the principal passions or emotions of the soul to be three, namely, anger, serenity, and humility. The best philosophers affirm this; the very nature of our voice, with its high, low and middle ranges, shows it; and the art of music clearly manifests it in three terms: agitated, soft and moderate.'

HENRY PURCELL

The English Orpheus

1659—95

HENRY PURCELL IS GENERALLY REGARDED AS THE GREATEST COMPOSER ENGLAND HAS EVER PRODUCED. There is no doubt that his early death at the age of 36 curtailed the development of an identifiable English school of music, though it is a myth to suggest, as some have done, that no great English composer emerged until Elgar and equally mistaken to think that Purcell is free of foreign influences. He himself confessed that in his sonatas he 'faithfully endeavoured a just imitation of the most famed Italian masters'. Italian music also influenced his vocal writing, as much as the fashionable French motet influenced his anthems. From Jean-Baptiste Lully, Purcell learnt how to write effective dramatic scenes and dance music for the stage.

Yet it is true that, having absorbed Lully's technique of setting French texts and poetry, 'no other composer, before or since,' in the words of J.A. Westrup, 'has succeeded so well in translating into music the accents of the English language'. John Dryden dedicated his *Amphitryon* (1690) to 'Mr Purcell; in whose person we have at length found an Englishman equal with the best abroad'. There was no area of English music that Purcell did not cultivate and enrich.

EARLY YEARS

Purcell (the name is pronounced with the emphasis on the first syllable) was born on or around 10 September 1659 in St Ann's Lane, off Old Pye Street in Westminster, London. His mother's name was Elizabeth. Scholars disagree over who his father was. Some argue forcibly for his namesake Henry, 'musician-in-ordinary for the violins and the lutes and voices, master of the choristers at Westminster Abbey'; others cite the brother of this older Henry, Thomas Purcell (scholars even dispute whether Henry and Thomas were brothers or cousins). We know for sure that both were Gentlemen of the Chapel Royal, singers in the musical service of King Charles II, that both had distinguished careers after the Restoration and that both were buried in Westminster Abbey. The older Henry died in 1664, leaving his son under the guardianship of Thomas, 'a tenor in the Chapel Royal, a member of the Private Musick, and groom of the robes and under-housekeeper at Somerset House'.

The foundations of the younger Henry's unparalleled ability to set words and music so felicitously were laid during his early years as a chorister. As one of the 12 Children of the Chapel Royal and later as a student of Matthew Locke, Pelham Humfrey (himself a pupil of Lully) and John Blow, Purcell was at the centre of English musical life from his childhood (his brother Daniel was also an organist and composer). He is said to have begun composing at nine years old, but the earliest work that can be certainly identified as his is an ode for the king's birthday, written in 1670. The 18th-century historian Dr Burney is amusingly sceptical about Purcell's studies with Blow: 'He had a few lessons from Dr Blow, which were sufficient to cancel all the instructions he had received from other masters, and to occasion the boast inscribed on the tombstone of Blow, that he had been 'Master to the famous Mr Henry Purcell'.

A RISING STAR

Purcell's rise to prominence was precociously rapid. When his voice broke in 1673, he was appointed 'keeper of the King's instruments'. At 18 he was made 'composer to the King's band' in succession to Locke. In 1676 he contributed a song – his first published work – to Playford's *Choice of Ayres*. At only 20 he succeeded Blow as organist of Westminster Abbey. Legend has it that the elder musician stepped aside in recognition of the greater genius; it is a fact that on Purcell's death Blow returned to the post and wrote a noble 'Ode on the Death of Mr Henry Purcell'.

Thereafter, Purcell was one of the busiest men in England. Apart from occasionally supplementing his official income by writing music for the Dorset Garden Theatre in the City of London, he spent almost his entire working life in the vicinity of Westminster – at Whitehall Palace, the Chapel Royal at St James's or the Abbey, all within walking distance of his home. The volume and variety of music he produced is astounding: from lewd drinking songs to ceremonial odes, from opera and incidental theatre music to chamber music, anthems and dances. His first major work was an anthem entitled *My Heart is Inditing*, composed for the coronation of James II in 1685. Four years later, when the Catholic James was overthrown, Purcell provided the coronation music for his successors, James's daughter Mary and her husband William of Orange. Purcell fell out on this occasion with the Dean and Chapter of Westminster Abbey over his right to sell tickets to the organ loft.

As the new monarchs reduced the court's musical activities, so Purcell increased his theatrical work. It was round about this time that he composed his only opera, *Dido and Aeneas*, the earliest English opera still regularly staged and, in the opinion of Gustav Holst, 'the only perfect English opera ever written'. It has long been presumed that the first performance was at Josiah Priest's school for 'young gentlewomen', Chelsea, in 1689 but recent scholarship suggests it was first heard at Court in 1683 or 1684. After these two performances and a further two in 1700 and 1704, it was not staged again till the 200th anniversary of Purcell's death in 1895. *Dido and Aeneas* is a masterpiece, and perhaps the finest example of Purcell's genius as a setter of words. Pride of place among its arias must go to Dido's famous lament 'When I am laid in earth', containing the single-note repetition of the words 'Remember me'. It remains one of the most achingly moving passages in the whole of opera.

Purcell's other stage works include four 'semi-operas' – popular entertainments that combined singing, dancing and speech with spectacular scenic effects. Among these are *The Fairy Queen* of 1692 (based on Shakespeare's *A Midsummer Night's Dream*) and *King Arthur* of 1691, with its celebrated Frost Scene.

Essential works

15 Fantasias for viols, *c.*1680

LAUDATE CECILIAM (Ode for St Cecilia's Day), 1683

MY HEART IS INDITING, anthem, 1685

DIDO AND AENEAS, opera, *c.*1689

KING ARTHUR, semi-opera, 1691

THE FAIRY QUEEN, semi-opera, 1692

TELL ME, SOME PITYING ANGEL (The Blessed Virgin's Expostulation), sacred song, 1693

COME YE SONS OF ART (Ode for the Birthday of Queen Mary II), 1694

Sonata No. 1 in D for trumpet and strings, *c.*1694

Funeral Music for Queen Mary II, 1695

In this, Purcell directs that the bass should sing with a shiver on every note, an obvious device today but daringly original over 300 years ago. Among the best-known numbers from over 50 works for the stage to which he contributed or for which he composed incidental music is the Rondeau from *Abdelazar* (1695), the tune on which Britten based his *Young Person's Guide to the Orchestra*. In 1695 his music was heard in 11 different London productions. Not even Andrew Lloyd Webber has matched that.

FINAL YEARS

If this output were not impressive enough, Purcell wrote hundreds of songs, more than 50 pieces of instrumental and keyboard music, and 24 odes for ceremonial occasions at court. The last of these include the magnificent tribute to St Cecilia, patron saint of music, *Hail, bright Cecilia,* one of many instances where the more lacklustre the text, the more imaginative Purcell became (another example is *Come Ye Sons of Art*, one of the odes he composed for each of Queen Mary's birthdays during her six-year reign). In addition to all this, the prolific Purcell composed over 100 anthems for the Chapel Royal and Westminster Abbey. When Queen Mary died of smallpox in 1694 at the age of 32, it was Purcell, as the Abbey's organist, who was responsible for the music at the lavish funeral service. What he wrote for this occasion is not only profoundly poignant and moving but, in places, remarkably advanced for its time.

'A greater musical genius England never had.'

ROGER NORTH

Less than a year later, on 21 November 1695, Purcell himself died at his house in Dean's Yard, Westminster. His wife and three of his six children survived him. The cause of his death is unclear. Most likely is that he died of tuberculosis, but there are other theories: one is that he caught a chill after returning late from the theatre to find that his wife had locked him out, another that he died from chocolate poisoning. The music he had composed for the funeral of Queen Mary was played at his own service.

HONOURED IN DEATH

PURCELL IS BURIED ADJACENT TO THE ORGAN IN WESTMINSTER ABBEY. He is one of very few composers interred there to have two memorials. The gravestone he shares with his wife Frances is inscribed (in Latin): 'Immortals, welcome an illustrious guest, Your gain, our loss . . .' Nearby is a white marble wall tablet which reads:

Here lies Henry Purcell Esq
Who left this life
And is gone to that blessed place
Where only his harmony
Can be exceeded

Antonio
Vivaldi

The Red Priest

1678 – 1741

TODAY, ANTONIO VIVALDI IS CONSIDERED ONE OF THE FOREMOST FIGURES OF THE BAROQUE ERA. A century ago, his name was almost unknown. One of Bach's ten keyboard transcriptions of his concertos might be heard occasionally; Fritz Kreisler, the great violinist, played a few works as salon pieces. In the 1900 edition of the redoubtable *Grove's Dictionary*, however, Vivaldi does not rate an entry. His birth and death dates were as uncertain as the number of works he had composed. Only in the 1930s did interest in his work revive. The now-ubiquitous *Four Seasons* was not recorded until 1947, an event which had some influence on the public's subsequent love affair with this composer, whose invention, brilliance and drama mirrored the great Venetian painters of the day.

In all, Vivaldi wrote about 770 works: 46 operas (of which only 22 are extant), 344 solo concertos, 81 concertos for two or more instruments, 61 sinfonias, and numerous secular and liturgical instrumental and vocal works. Why is he so important? As a violinist, he was the prototype of the modern virtuoso, bewitching his audiences with his technical prowess and expanding the possibilities of string sound and instrumental technique. He personalized the violin as a solo instrument, as well as exploring different methods of bowing and spreading chords. For the first time, slow movements, fashioned from the soulful arias of his operas, were given instrumental treatment. Some 230 of his concertos feature his own instrument.

> *The brilliance and fire of the great Venetian painters'*
>
> CASELLA

More significantly, Vivaldi's contribution to the development of the solo concerto was immense. The concerto – from the Italian word meaning 'to compete' – found its earliest form in the *concerto grosso* (literally 'large concerto') in which players are split into a *concertino* group (two or more players) and a *ripieno* group (the larger proportion consisting of violins, violas and cellos). Giuseppe Torelli pioneered a new form of concerto in which just one player was pitted against the rest of the orchestra. Vivaldi took the idea and ran with it. With their standard three movements (fast–slow–fast), the pacing and construction of his concertos not only anticipate the classical symphony but provide a template for the piano concertos of Haydn and Mozart. Vivaldi also developed orchestral writing and introduced the concept of programme music (that is, a musical interpretation of something that is non-musical).

EARLY YEARS

Venice was long past the zenith of its mercantile power when Antonio Lucio Vivaldi was born there on 4 March 1678, but it was the musical capital of Europe. Details of his early life and training are vague, but we know that his father was a violinist in St Mark's and that Antonio, the youngest of six children, inherited not only his gift for the instrument but also his red hair. Antonio began training for the priesthood at the age of 15, hence the nickname by which he was later known – *il prete rosso*, 'the red priest'. No sooner had he been ordained in 1703 than he was given dispensation from saying mass: he was a lifelong asthmatic and complained of chest pains, which frequently forced him to leave the altar in mid-celebration. Suspiciously, these pains never seemed to occur when he was conducting or on any of his many foreign trips. For the rest of his life, the Church remained a useful backdrop to the one area in which he shone: music.

Vivaldi's main teacher appears to have been the *maestro di cappella* at St Mark's, Giovanni Legrenzi. Vivaldi must have been an outstanding student because in 1704, in this most musical and cultured of cities, he was appointed *maestro di violino* of the Conservatorio dell'Ospedale della Pietà. Founded for the care and education of orphan girls, it was one of Venice's most famous and prestigious musical centres, where the standard of music-making was so high that many leading figures of the day would perform in concert with the foundlings.

Essential works

L'ESTRO ARMONICO, Op. 3, 12 concertos (1711)
JUDITHA TRIUMPHANS, oratorio (1716)
IL CIMENTO DELL'ARMONIA E DELL'INVENTIONE, Op. 8, 12 concertos (1725) (includes The Four Seasons)
LA CETRA, Op. 9, 12 concertos (1727)
Six concertos for flute and strings, Op. 10 (c.1728) (includes LA TEMPESTA DI MARE and LA NOTTE)
Concerto for mandolin and strings in C
Concerto for two trumpets in C
Gloria in D

AT THE HEIGHT OF HIS POWERS

In the following year, 1705, Vivaldi's first compositions were published. The next two decades saw him at his most productive, and it was during this period that he established himself as one of the foremost violinists and composers of the day. From 1713 to 1738 he produced at least one opera a year (sometimes three or four), while his instrumental works included his two most famous sets of concertos: *L'estro armonico* (Harmonic Imagination) and *Il cimento dell'armonia e dell'invenzione* (The Contest between Harmony and Invention). The first four concertos of this latter set are grouped together as

THE GOLDEN AGE OF ITALIAN MUSIC

FOR THE LAST TWO DECADES OF THE 17TH CENTURY AND FOR ALMOST THE ENTIRE 18TH CENTURY, Italy remained the dominant force in music. Arcangelo Corelli (1653–1713) from Bologna was a major figure both in the history of the violin and in the development of the concerto. Among Vivaldi's Venetian contemporaries were Tommaso Albinoni (1671–1750) and the Marcello brothers Alessandro (1684–1750) and Benedetto (1686–1739). From Padua came another great violinist-composer, Giuseppe Tartini (1692–1770) while in Naples we find Alessandro Scarlatti (1660–1725), composer of more than 114 operas, and his more famous son Domenico (1685–1757) whose nearly 600 keyboard sonatas brought unprecedented virtuosity to the harpsichord. Truly, the golden age of Italian music.

Le quattro stagioni (The Four Seasons) – No. 1 Spring, No. 2 Summer, No. 3 Autumn, No. 4 Winter. Written in 1720, though not published until five years later, they are among the first examples of tone poems. In this case, Vivaldi provided a sonnet to preface each concerto (whether they were written before or after the music is not certain), and he inserted brief captions to explain the significance of various passages, such as 'The fleeing prey', 'The barking dog' or 'The sleeping drunk'.

In 1718 Vivaldi took leave of absence from the orphanage of La Pietà to work initially for three years in the service of Prince Philip of Hesse-Darmstadt, governor of Mantua. Here he met Anna Giraud, known as La Giró, who was to take the leading role in many of Vivaldi's operas. She and her sister Paolina became Vivaldi's travelling companions. Both were said to be his mistresses, a rumour that he strongly denied. In 1723 and 1724 he visited Rome, playing before Pope Innocent XIII on one occasion. He followed this in 1728 with several audiences with the music-loving Emperor Charles VI. It is said that Charles spoke more with Vivaldi during the two weeks of their meetings than he had with ministers during the previous two years. Vivaldi's Op. 9 set of 12 concertos, *La cetra* (The Lyre), is dedicated to the Habsburg monarch.

YEARS OF DECLINE

If the 1720s saw Vivaldi at the height of his powers, the 1730s witnessed a slow decline in his creativity and a faster one in his fortunes. The Italian public showed signs of tiring of his music. His patron Prince Philip died in 1736, and the following year the church authorities banned Vivaldi from mounting any of his operas in the papal territory of Ferrara because of his lapsed priesthood and association with La Giró. Then, in 1738, the directors of La Pietà declined to renew his contract.

Vivaldi left for Vienna, possibly with the intention of seeking a post at the imperial court, but it was not to be. His friend Charles VI died in October 1740 and artistic pursuits quickly became a low priority for the new rulers, distracted with what would become the War of the Austrian Succession. The ailing Vivaldi held on, hoping for better things. Ill, poverty-stricken and quite neglected, he died on 28 July 1741. Like Mozart, just half a century later in the same city, the once-wealthy Vivaldi was buried in an unmarked grave.

VIVALDI'S 20TH-CENTURY CHAMPION

IT IS DUE ALMOST ENTIRELY TO THE TACT AND TENACITY OF ONE MAN that so much of Vivaldi's music resurfaced in the 20th century. In 1926 Alberto Gentili, a professor of music at Turin University, was approached by a boarding school in Piedmont run by Silesian Fathers. Needing to raise money, the Fathers had discovered 97 volumes of old music. Gentili was astonished to find that most of them contained Vivaldi's autograph scores. He found a private buyer and, having negotiated with the utmost secrecy, ensured that the volumes ended up in the library of Turin University. Only then did he discover that many final pages were missing and that the scores had been randomly assembled. He learnt that 25 years after Vivaldi's death, Count Giacomo Durazzo (1717–94), Austrian ambassador to Venice and a patron of Gluck, had acquired Vivaldi's scores from La Pietà. Durazzo's family had kept them secret, even stipulating that none of the works in their possession should be published or performed. Some patient sleuthing and delicate negotiations with the count's heirs led to another private buyer and a second donation to Turin University's library. Thanks to Gentili's ingenuity and discretion, 319 Vivaldi works were thus rescued for posterity and the scene was set for his restoration.

JEAN-PHILIPPE
RAMEAU

*'Singular, brilliant, complex, learned,
too learned sometimes'* DIDEROT

1683 – 1764

UNTIL THE 1970s THE ONLY MUSIC OF RAMEAU TO BE HEARD AT ALL WAS SELECTIONS OF HIS KEYBOARD MUSIC. Little was heard of his operas, the main reason for his reputation during his lifetime. Thanks to the efforts of musicians like William Christie and John Eliot Gardiner, it has been possible to re-evaluate him not only as one of the great figures of French opera, but as one of the most important and influential French composers of the 18th century. He himself regarded his work in musical theory to be his most significant and lasting contribution.

EARLY YEARS

Rameau had a strangely disjointed career. He was born some time in September 1683 in Dijon, Burgundy, the seventh of 11 children. At seven he could sight-read anything that was put in front of him on the harpsichord. Although his father was himself a musician – the organist of Dijon Cathedral – he wanted his son to become a lawyer.

Rameau, expelled from the Jesuit college at Dijon for his 'obnoxious behaviour', taught himself musical theory and became proficient on a number of instruments. For the first 40 years of his life, he was a provincial church organist moving from post to post, from Avignon to Clermont-Ferrand to Paris in 1706 (where his earliest compositions, the first book of pieces for the harpsichord, were published), back to Dijon in 1709 (to succeed his late father), then to Lyon and Clermont again. It was not until 1722 with the publication of a controversial treatise on musical theory that Rameau abandoned the organ loft to try his luck in the French capital. Though recognized as one of the country's leading organists, his progress there was slow, a characteristic that extended to marriage. He was 43 when he married Marie-Louise Mangot, the 18-year-old daughter of a court musician, herself a singer. They had four children and the union appears to have been a happy one. But it was not until 1733, when Rameau was 50, that he tasted his first real success.

MASTER OF OPERA AND BALLET

In the late 1720s, a wealthy tax gatherer and arts patron, Joseph Le Riche de la Pouplinière, backed Rameau in his attempt to change course and launch his operatic career. Only in 1732 did they find a suitable libretto (based on Racine's *Phèdre*), and *Hippolyte et Aricie* received its first private production in April of the following year. Over the next three decades, Rameau devoted himself to writing opera and ballet, producing 30 pieces for the theatre in one form or another. *Les Indes galantes* (1735), *Castor et Pollux* (1737) and *Les fêtes d'Hébé* (1739) established him as the most important composer in this area since Lully (see box, page 22). With *La Princesse de Navarre* (1745), written in collaboration with Voltaire, he diversified into opera-ballet.

In 1745 Louis XV appointed Rameau composer of his chamber music and gave him an annual pension, but for all his new-found success he remained essentially a 'learned' composer more interested in the music itself

The expression of thought, of sentiment, of the passions, must be the true aim of music.' RAMEAU

THE AGE OF ABSOLUTISM

THE ACCESSION IN 1643 OF LOUIS XIV OF FRANCE – THE SUN KING – saw the beginning of the Age of Absolutism. Virtually state-controlled for almost a century, musical life in France was dominated by the figure of Jean-Baptiste Lully (1632–87) notably in the field of ballet and opera. His conservative ghost continued to cast a deep shadow over French music, stunting its growth for some 50 years after his death. The Age of Absolutism existed, remarkably, in parallel with the Age of Enlightenment, when the freedom of thought that had originated in the Renaissance was given fresh impetus through the scientific discoveries of the period. It was in this milieu that Jean-Philippe Rameau first made his mark not with any music but with a theoretical work entitled *Traité de l'harmonie* (1722), which attempted to classify music both scientifically and philosophically. Rameau insisted that melody grew out of harmony and that therefore harmony is the basis of all musical form.

than the theatricality of a piece. At one of the rehearsals for *Les Paladins*, Rameau asked one of the singers to take a certain air much faster. 'But if I sing it any faster,' objected the artist, 'the public will not be able to hear the words.' 'That doesn't matter,' replied the composer. 'I only want them to hear my music.' He was a notably poor judge of libretti and often set inferior texts without bothering to improve them as Lully would have done. 'After 60 one cannot change,' he admitted. 'Experience points plainly enough the best course, but the mind refuses to obey.'

Throughout his operatic career, Rameau endured opposition to his ideas. In the 1730s and 1740s there was a conservative reaction against music that did not follow the path set by Lully and that employed unfamiliar harmonic devices. Rameau's innovations in harmony were allied to descriptive orchestration – music that describes action in terms of sound – and in this he anticipated many of Wagner's ideas (indeed, perhaps Rameau's greatest claim to fame is as one of the founders of classical orchestration, especially in his concern for the solo properties of wind). Audiences found his music deafening; musicians thought it complex and demanding (Wagner came in for much the same criticism a century later). In the 1750s Rameau was again attacked in a public battle of musical philosophies known as the War of the Buffoons, an acrimonious dispute over the relative merits of French and Italian music in which he saw his own standing, along with other French composers, called into question. After 1749 and his last important opera, *Zoroastre*, he produced relatively little. He died in Paris on 12 September 1764 at the age of 81.

Essential works

LES INDES GALANTES, opera-ballet (1735)
CASTOR ET POLLUX, opera (1737)
DARDANUS, opera (1739)
ZOROASTRE, opera (1749)
PLATÉE, comédie-ballet (1745)
PREMIER LIVRE DE PIÈCES DE CLAVECIN (1706)
DEUXIÈME LIVRE DE PIÈCES DE CLAVECIN (1724)
NOUVELLES SUITES DE PIÈCES DE CLAVECIN (1728)

George Frideric
HANDEL

'The greatest, ablest composer that ever lived' BEETHOVEN

1685—1759

HANDEL WAS A GREAT MAN
IN PHYSICAL STATURE, SPIRIT AND VISION.
Throughout his changing fortunes – and during his career he experienced adulation and wealth as keenly as he did derision and debt – some inner resilience forced him onwards. Nothing prevented the prodigious flow of music from his pen. In deepest grief or at lowest ebb, he had the ability calmly to separate the adversities of life from his inexhaustible creativity.

Handel wrote an enormous amount of music: 46 operas, 32 oratorios, more than 100 large-scale vocal compositions, many dramatic works and myriad instrumental pieces. There are the well-known Handel 'pops' – *Messiah, Water Music, Music for the Royal Fireworks* and *Zadok the Priest* among them; and a number of individual pieces, including 'Ombra mai fu' (better known as 'Handel's Largo') from his opera *Xerxes*, 'Arrival of the Queen of Sheba' from *Solomon*, and 'Where'er you walk' from *Semele*. But only a small proportion of the rest is ever heard regularly today. It is a mystery why such a huge body of happy, confident and melodic music is played so relatively infrequently.

Imbued with the grace of Italian vocal writing, an easy fluency in German contrapuntal technique and the English choral tradition inherited from Purcell, Handel wrote in more forms and with far more variety than any of his contemporaries. True, he borrowed a great deal from himself and others. There are numerous instances where a movement from one work reappears in a different guise elsewhere. But he was only doing what everyone else was doing – he just did it better and on a grander scale. When asked why he had lifted some material from one of his rivals, Giovanni Bononcini, he replied: 'It's much too good for him. He did not know what to do with it.'

EARLY YEARS
Handel was born in Halle, Germany, on 23 February 1685. (Just four weeks later and a mere 100 miles away, Johann Sebastian Bach was born: the two composers never met, though on three occasions Bach made special journeys to Halle to see his far more famous contemporary.) Handel's father was in his mid-60s. He was a barber-surgeon and valet to the duke of Saxe-Weissenfels – and he hated music. Somehow, the young Georg Friederich Händel, as he was christened, managed to learn the organ and spinet. One story has it that his sympathetic mother smuggled a spinet up to the attic where the strings were smothered with cloth to muffle the sound. Whatever the truth, at the age of eight he was heard by the duke playing the organ at one of the Sunday services. He insisted that Handel was allowed to study music and was put in the care of Friederich Zachow, the organist of the Lutheran church in Halle. Zachow quickly realized that he had a genius on his hands. After just three years, he confessed that there was nothing more he could teach the boy. Handel does not appear to have had any further musical instruction.

After his father's death and a brief attempt to study law, at 18 he was offered the post of organist at the cathedral of Moritzburg. Already referred to as 'the famous Handel', in 1703 he moved to Hamburg, the seat of German opera. Early works such as the opera *Almira* aroused as much enthusiasm

'Handel understands effect better than any of us – when he chooses, he strikes like a thunderbolt.'

MOZART

with the public as they did envy with his peers. After three years, he had had enough of Hamburg's cabals and petty musical rivalries. He left for Italy and continued writing operas and oratorios in Florence, Venice, Naples and Rome. Soon '*il Sassone*' ('the Saxon') was one of the most talked-about musicians in Italy, not just as a composer but as a virtuoso keyboard player.

THE MOVE TO ENGLAND

Handel's thorough absorption of the music being written in Italy was of lasting influence on his creative style and development. He moved to Hanover in 1710 to take up the post of court musician to the Elector. After a year, he was given leave to visit England, where he wrote the opera *Rinaldo* (1711), very much in the Italian manner. It was an astounding success. He went back to Hanover but soon requested a further leave of absence in order to return to London. Two years later, Handel was still absent.

When Queen Anne died in 1714, her successor was none other than Handel's German employer, the Elector of Hanover, who reigned as George I. If he was displeased with the errant composer, then forgiveness came quickly in the form of a handsome royal pension. In addition came royal commissions, among them one of Handel's most cherished works, the *Water Music*, written in 1717 to accompany a royal progression up the River Thames.

In 1717 Handel became composer-in-residence for the duke of Chandos on his magnificent estate near London. Here he composed keyboard music, anthems and other stage works including the delightful masque *Acis and Galatea*. He left in 1719 when a powerful group of opera lovers founded the Royal Academy of Music (the precursor of today's institution founded in 1822) in order to present Italian opera. The entrepreneurial Handel was appointed its artistic director. Underwritten by the nobility and cast with the finest European singers, he instigated a triumphant series of operas. He was now, unassailably, the most powerful musical figure in the land.

In 1727 Handel became a British citizen and adopted the anglicized form of the name by which he is now known. A year later, London saw the first production of John Gay's *The Beggar's Opera*. It heralded a waning of public taste for Italian opera unforeseen by Handel: he sank £10,000 of his own money into an Italian opera company and lost the lot. Bankruptcy and the debtors' prison suddenly loomed large. His health deteriorated, rheumatism set in, and he suffered an agonizing paralytic stroke. In Vauxhall Gardens, they raised a statue to him. It was as if he were dead.

THE PRIVATE HANDEL

HANDEL WAS ALMOST OBSESSIVELY SECRET ABOUT HIS PRIVATE LIFE. He never married or fathered children. Various writers have suggested he was gay on the grounds that there seems never to have been a woman in his life and that he lived for three years in the 'homoerotic milieu' of Burlington House, Piccadilly, the palatial residence of the young, homosexual Richard Boyle, earl of Burlington. There is not a shred of conclusive evidence one way or the other. Perhaps because of his very success or his foreignness or because he was dictatorial, gruff and had a violent temper, Handel was frequently exposed to attacks and ridicule. People were much amused by his comical accent, his huge bulk (he was known as 'the great bear'), his bow legs and his habit of muttering to himself as he walked the streets of London. He was known to be a glutton, and his eating habits were said to be 'repulsive'.

KING GEORGE AND MESSIAH

THE FIRST LONDON PERFORMANCE OF *MESSIAH* was given on 23 March 1743. Famously, King George II rose to his feet on hearing the 'Hallelujah Chorus' and, of course, his subjects did the same. Various theories have been put forward to explain why the monarch rose: to acknowledge a greater power than himself on hearing the words 'King of Kings and Lord of Hosts'? To salute the composer and his powerfully expressive music? Or, as one theory has it, because he had nodded off and awoke with a start? Whatever the reason, standing during this magnificent passage is a tradition that continues to this day.

A SECOND WIND

How did Handel react? After a rest cure in Aix-la-Chapelle, he returned refreshed, changed course – and wrote himself back into financial and critical success by refashioning a genre that was relatively unknown in England: the oratorio. These were dramatized stories, usually based on sacred texts, set to music in the same spirit as the operas but with massive choruses and grand orchestral writing. Nothing like them had been heard before.

In 1741, inspired by an invitation to Dublin from the duke of Devonshire, Handel wrote his most famous work, *Messiah*. An astonishing burst of creativity lasting more than 2½ hours and written in just 24 days, this 'epic in oratorio literature' (Ewen) stands as one of Western music's greatest achievements. A succession of oratorios followed, among them *Semele, Judas Maccabaeus, Joshua and Solomon*, all showing Handel at the height of powers.

Once more he ruled the musical world, only to be knocked sideways again: in 1753 he became blind. (He was operated on several times by the same surgeon who bungled the attempt to save Bach's eyesight.) Despite this, the indomitable composer continued to play the organ and conduct – he was one of the wonders of London and crowds flocked to hear him. He was directing a performance of *Messiah* there in April 1759 when he collapsed and was taken home to bed. 'I should like to die on Good Friday,' he is reported to have said. He died in the early hours of Easter Saturday on 14 April 1759.

Handel was buried in Westminster Abbey, 3000 people attending the funeral. The monument he requested to be erected in his memory shows him at his working table with the score of *Messiah* open at 'I know that my Redeemer liveth'.

Essential works

WATER MUSIC, orchestral suite (1717)

Chandos Anthems (1717-20)

ACIS AND GALATEA, masque (1718)

Harpsichord Suite No.5 in E (includes the 'Harmonious Blacksmith') (1720)

ZADOK THE PRIEST, coronation anthem (1727)

Twelve Concerti Grossi, Op.6 (1739)

MESSIAH, sacred oratorio (1741)

SAMSON, oratorio (1743)

MUSIC FOR THE ROYAL FIREWORKS, orchestral suite (1749)

Organ Concertos, Op.4 (1738) and Op.7 (1760)

Johann Sebastian
Bach

'Bach is Bach as God is God' BERLIOZ

1685—1750

'A BENEVOLENT GOD, TO WHOM MUSICIANS SHOULD OFFER A PRAYER BEFORE SETTING TO WORK SO THAT THEY MAY BE PRESERVED FROM MEDIOCRITY.' Such is Debussy's verdict on Bach, and few of Bach's successors have failed to share Debussy's sense of awe, even reverence. 'Nicht Bach,' said Beethoven famously, 'aber Meer haben wir hier': 'Not a stream [the meaning of *Bach* in German] but a whole ocean.' Schumann acclaimed him with similar sentiments: 'Music owes as much to Bach as religion to its founder.' Bach is to music what Leonardo is to art and Shakespeare to literature: one of the supreme creative geniuses of the Western world.

More than two and a half centuries after his death and knowing what we now know, it is hard to comprehend not only that Bach was essentially a self-taught musician but that in his day he was not considered particularly special. Little of his music was published or performed after his death (though it was far from ignored, as is often stated). One of his sons, Carl Philipp Emanuel, referred to him affectionately as 'old peruke' – an old fogey writing in the already unfashionable Baroque polyphonic style. He invented no new forms nor did he develop existing ones (indeed, C.P.E. has stronger claims in that area). Nor was he a sophisticated intellectual. It has often been remarked that not only do his letters betray an uneducated mind and hand, but that he knew little of anything beyond music and theology. That a man of such limited culture could produce music of such unparalleled assurance, complexity and beauty is one of the great paradoxes of music history.

EARLY LIFE

Bach came from a dynasty of professional musicians in north Germany whose roots can be traced back to the early 16th century (his own father was a respected violinist). Johann Sebastian was born on 21 March 1685 in Eisenach, Thuringia. His musical aptitude was taken for granted and he received little systematic training in his youth. It is said that at the age of nine he almost ruined his eyesight by secretly copying out by moonlight an entire library of instrumental scores to which he had been denied access.

The same year, 1694, both his parents died, and until the age of 15 he was brought up by his older brother, Johann Christoph. Then he gained a place in the choir at Lüneberg, where he was able to indulge in every possible musical pursuit – reading scores, composing, and studying the organ, clavichord and

WHAT'S IN A NAME?

BY A HAPPY COINCIDENCE, the letters of Bach's name are also musical notes in German nomenclature: our B natural is the note H in German; our B flat is known as B. Thus BACH forms the four-note motif B flat, A, C, B natural. Many composers have followed Bach's example and written works using that theme. Bach also enjoyed the fact that the cardinal numbers corresponding to the letters of his name added up to 14: B = 2, A = 1, C = 3, H = 8 (2 + 1 + 3 + 8 = 14). A chorale written shortly before his death has a theme of 14 notes; 14 is 41 inverted and the theme of the whole melody numbers 41 notes, which is also the sum of the cardinal numbers of JSBACH (9 + 18 + 14 = 41).

violin. Bach led an unadventurous life in geographical terms, but he made up for it in his thirst for musical knowledge and experience. He walked the 30 miles to Hamburg several times in order to hear the celebrated organist Johann Adam Reincken, and 60 miles to Celle in order to acquaint himself with contemporary French music. Legend has it that, having obtained leave of absence from his post as organist at Arnstadt, the 19-year-old Bach tramped the 213 miles to Lübeck to hear the famous Dietrich Buxtehude play the organ. He did not return for four months.

WEIMAR AND CÖTHEN

In June 1707 Bach moved to Mühlhausen to take up another post as organist. Four months later, at the age of 22, he married his cousin Maria Barbara, and the next year he left Mühlhausen to become court organist to Duke Wilhelm Ernst of Weimar. Bach remained here more or less contentedly for the next nine years, becoming conductor of the court orchestra in 1714 and establishing his reputation as the pre-eminent organ virtuoso of the day.

Essential works

Passacaglia and Fugue in C minor, for organ (1708–12 or later)
Fantasia and Fugue in G minor, for organ (c.1712)
THE WELL-TEMPERED CLAVIER, Books 1 (1718–22) and 2 (1738–42)
Six Cello Suites (1718–23)
Six Brandenburg Concertos (1720)
Concerto in D minor for two violins (1723)
ST JOHN PASSION (1723)
ST MATTHEW PASSION (1727)
Magnificat in D major (1728–31)
Mass in B minor (1733–8)
Christmas Oratorio (1735)
Goldberg Variations, for keyboard (1741)

His first published work, the cantata *Gott ist mein König*, had appeared in 1708, but his time in Weimar saw the stream of compositions grow to a river as music poured from his pen. Here, many of his finest organ works were composed, including the Passacaglia and Fugue in C minor and many of the great preludes and fugues.

Further advancement came in 1717 when he was offered the post of music director to Prince Leopold of Anhalt in Cöthen. Duke Wilhelm at first refused to let him go and held him under arrest for a month 'for too obstinately requesting his dismissal'. Eventually, Bach was allowed to leave and embarked on the happiest period of his professional life in the service of the musical prince. The job was well paid and he had a 17-piece band at his disposal. It was in Cöthen that he composed the bulk of his instrumental music, including the Brandenburg Concertos and the first book of *The Well-Tempered Clavier*.

This idyll was shattered in July 1720 when his beloved Maria Barbara died. Eighteen months later he married Anna Magdalena Wilcken, a daughter of the court trumpeter of Prince Saxe-Weissenfels. Bach was 36, she was 20. From all accounts it was a happy partnership, and in addition to the seven children from his first marriage, she bore him a further 13. Sadly, only 10 of Bach's 20 children reached maturity.

LEIPZIG

Exactly six months after his marriage to Anna Magdalena in December 1721, the Cantor of the Thomasschule in Leipzig died. This was one of the most prestigious musical posts in Europe and Bach applied for it. The authorities first offered it to Telemann, who declined it, then to Christoph Graupner, who was unable to take up the appointment. Third-choice Bach succeeded to the title in April 1723 and remained in the post for the rest of his life. His duties were arduous. They involved playing the organ for services, teaching music and Latin in the Thomasschule, writing music for the services at both the Thomaskirche and Nicolaikirche, and directing the music and training the musicians in a further two churches. The pay was poor (Bach fought a running battle with the authorities about this), the living conditions were cold and damp, and, initially, he was even expected to gather firewood for the Thomasschule as part of his contract.

Yet, despite all this, the music flowed – and flowed in significant amounts. When the task of gathering together and publishing all Bach's music was undertaken, the project took 46 years to complete. How did he do it while undertaking his many duties and fathering 20 children? 'I was obliged to work hard. Whoever is industrious will succeed just as well', was his ingenuous explanation. For mere industry alone

> *'He is the father, and we his children.'*
> MOZART

cannot account for some of mankind's greatest sacred music, including the Mass in B minor, the *St John* and *St Matthew Passions*, the Christmas Oratorio and well over 200 church cantatas. From this period also came the Goldberg Variations, the Italian Concerto, the Partitas for keyboard and the second book of *The Well-Tempered Clavier*.

FINAL YEARS

Towards the end of his life, Bach's vision gradually deteriorated as a result of cataracts. A British optician named John Taylor, who plied his trade in Saxony, performed an operation on Bach's eyes in the spring of 1749 – the same John Taylor who had operated unsuccessfully on Handel for the same ailment. Bach was left almost completely blind but, miraculously, his sight returned for a brief time (the cataract may have receded spontaneously), allowing him to continue work on his final composition, *The Art of Fugue*. Ten days later, he died of a cerebral haemorrhage. He was 65. The piece he was working on was a fugue in which the counter-subject was his own name in musical notes: B–A–C–H (see box, page 28).

Bach was buried in an unmarked grave in the churchyard of St John in Leipzig. His coffin was finally recovered in 1895, when his body was exhumed and his skeleton photographed. On 28 July 1949, the 199th anniversary of his death, Bach's remains were transferred to the choir room of the Thomaskirche.

THE SECRET OF GREATNESS

WHAT EXACTLY MAKES BACH SUCH A TOWERING FIGURE? As a young man he absorbed the works of earlier masters like Palestrina and Frescobaldi, and studied the more recent works of Albinoni, Vivaldi, Froberger, Pachelbel and (especially) Buxtehude. He was also well acquainted with the work of contemporary German composers. In his command of counterpoint, the combined ingenuity and unforced complexity of which are unique, he had no equal. His superior harmonic sense and greater daring in the treatment of his material set him apart. In other words, with all his mature works written in the half century between 1700 and 1750, Bach is the miraculous culmination – indeed, the accumulation – of all Baroque styles. He combines in one person with unsurpassed skill and inspiration the contrapuntal German school, the melodic, vocal Italian school and the elegant, dance-based French school.

CHRISTOPH WILLIBALD
GLUCK

Great pioneer of operatic reform

1714 – 1787

OF ALL THE INDISPUTABLY

GREAT COMPOSERS, GLUCK HAS THE SMALLEST NUMBER OF WORKS IN TODAY'S ACTIVE REPERTOIRE. He wrote almost exclusively for the opera. His six sonatas for two violins and nine symphonies were rare excursions into other areas and are hardly ever performed. Of his roughly 50 operas, only one is regularly revived – *Orfeo ed Euridice*. Few will have encountered anything else from his remaining output beyond some ballet music and selected arias. But Gluck, though he did not consciously set out to be so, was one of the great revolutionaries in music. Some claim that *Orfeo* provided the single most abrupt change in the history of opera.

The story of his early life can be quickly told. Christoph Willibald Gluck was born on 2 July 1714 in Erasbach, in what is now Bavaria in southern Germany. His father was a forester and huntsman in the service of the aristocracy, and during Gluck's childhood the family moved frequently. The details of his youth are sketchy, but it seems probable that he was educated at the Jesuit school in Komotau between 1726 and 1728 and entered Prague University in 1732. We know he was in the Czech capital until 1736, making a living playing the violin, cello and keyboard. His father had entered the employment of Prince Lobkowitz in 1729, and it was this connection that brought Gluck to Vienna in 1736 as a chamber musician in Lobkowitz's household. In 1737, financed by Prince Melzi, he left for three years study in Milan with the famous Giovanni Battista Sammartini (1701–75). He stayed in Italy for eight years and saw the first of a series of early operas produced there in 1741.

EARLY CAREER

Following the characteristically peripatetic life of the successful opera composer of the time, Gluck drifted to Paris, then to London. Here he met Handel, who liked him but had little regard for his musical ability, remarking that 'My cook understands more about counterpoint than he does' (which may have been true, as Handel's cook at the time, Gustavus Waltz, was a professional musician). In any case, Gluck seems not to have taken Handel's jibe too seriously: the two composers maintained a friendly relationship and, later in life, Gluck had a portrait of Handel hanging in his bedroom.

For the next three years, Gluck travelled round Europe conducting and composing. Back in Vienna in 1749 he met and married Marianne Pergin, the daughter of a wealthy banker. It was a match that made Gluck an unusual example at the time of a financially independent composer. Through his post as conductor of the private orchestra of Prince Hildburghausen in Vienna, he became known to Empress Maria Theresa. A production of his *Le Cinesi* led to him being made musical director to the court by Count Durazzo, director of the imperial theatres.

Up to this point Gluck, now aged 40, had written about 20 operas all in the traditional and immensely popular Italian style. Many had libretti by the Italian poet Pietro Metastasio (1698–1782), the imperial court poet of Vienna. The texts of Metastasio's 27 musical dramas were set by 18th-century composers over 1000 times, some of them by as many as 70 different composers. The well-constructed texts were based on mythology and ancient history, and consisted of a formulaic succession of solos and duets sung by singers who would routinely interpolate their own

improvisations and ornaments into the music, stepping forward over the footlights to show off their vocal fireworks. Recitatives were accompanied by a chord or two on the harpsichord; characters were cardboard cut-outs; singers lauded it over composers with their empty displays of vocal gymnastics. That was the accepted Italian style, but there was growing opposition to it.

THE REFORM OF OPERA

Gluck arrived in the right place at the right time. In him, Durazzo met a man whose operatic ambitions matched his own. Another Italian, a dancer named Gasparo Angiolini, was also keenly interested in reforming his own art. In 1760 Gluck came across a book by another dancer, the French ballet-master Jean-Georges Noverre. This proposed that the most important elements of a ballet or an opera should be the story and the feelings of the characters within that story; the music and singing must contribute to the plot and the understanding of the personalities. Then, in 1761, a third collaborator arrived in Vienna. This was the remarkable Raniero de Calzabigi, playwright, critic, lottery organizer for Madame de Pompadour in Paris, and, according to Casanova himself, 'a great lover of women'. Calzabigi was entirely in tune with Gluck's reforming ideas. He provided the scenario for a ballet, *Don Juan*, based on Molière's play; Gluck composed a faithful realization of the text in music; and Durazzo ensured that the ballet was properly produced. It was a work that broke free from convention, offering a more human, truthful and dramatic work than anything else available at that time. *Don Juan* was the first work of this 'reform group'.

There is no musical rule that I have not willingly sacrificed to dramatic effect.'

GLUCK

If *Don Juan* caused a stir when it was first seen in October 1761, it was nothing to the bewilderment that greeted *Orfeo ed Euridice* almost exactly a year later. No ornamented vocal lines, no spectacular pageant scenes, no harpsichord in the recitatives (Gluck used the orchestra); the chorus and ballet sequences were made an integral part of the action; there were just three main characters. The plot of the Greek legend, the poetry and the music were all reduced to an elevated 'noble simplicity and calm greatness', as the contemporary art historian Johann Joachim Winckelman described it.

Soon audience bewilderment was replaced by enthusiasm, but it took the reform group another

TYRANT OF PODIUM AND TABLE

AS A CONDUCTOR, GLUCK WAS A SHORT-TEMPERED MARTINET, the Toscanini of his day. He would insist on players repeating a passage as many as 20 or 30 times until he was satisfied. They detested him cordially. A vivid description of him comes from Johann Christoph von Mannlich, a court painter in Paris: 'Anyone meeting Gluck . . . would never have taken him for a prominent person and a creative genius,' he wrote. He was 'stocky, strong and muscular without being stout. His head was round, his face ruddy, broad and pockmarked. The eyes were small and deeply set. He called things by their name and therefore, twenty times a day, offended the sensitive ears of the Parisians used to flattery. He was a hearty eater, never denied being grasping and fond of money, and displayed a goodly portion of egotism, particularly at table, where he was wont at sight to claim first right to the best morsels.'

five years before they came up with Orfeo's successor, *Alceste* (1767). A third Calzabigi–Gluck collaboration, *Paride ed Elena*, was produced in 1770. In the preface to *Alceste*, Gluck wrote: 'I have tried to restrict music to its true role of backing up poetry by means of expression and by following the situations of the plot, without holding up the action or stifling it with a useless superfluity of ornaments.' Gluck was one of the first composers to use clarinets, cors anglais and trombones in his opera scores (when Mozart later included trombones in *Don Giovanni* it was still considered unusual), as well as cymbals, triangles and bass drum.

Now a rich man (he had given up his court appointment in 1764), Gluck decided to try his luck in Paris. He and his wife had adopted his ten-year-old niece, Marianna Hedler, who promised to be a fine singer. In 1773 all three arrived in the French capital, where Gluck set about composing his next opera, an adaptation of Racine's *Iphigénie en Aulide*. The rehearsals were long and arduous, for the perfectionist Gluck had to correct acting and vocal styles that had changed little since the days of Lully. His acute ear would not tolerate sloppy playing, and his dictatorial demands and abrupt manner caused a furore among French musicians, critics and rival composers. Gluck was not above calling on royalty to promote his cause – the Austrian princess Marie-Antoinette had been one of his pupils before her marriage to the Dauphin (the future Louis XVI) and came to the defence of her old teacher's music and methods.

Despite this support and successful French premieres of *Orphée et Eurydice* (a revised version of *Orfeo*) in 1774, *Alceste* in 1776 and *Armide* in 1777, Gluck's enemies arranged to import one of Italy's most skilful and popular composers to assist their cause. The arrival of Niccolò Piccinni (1728–1800) heralded an intense rivalry between the two opposing factions, Gluckists and Piccinnists. This state of affairs, unimaginable today, was resolved when both composers were contracted to write an opera on the same subject, *Iphigénie en Tauride*, using different librettos. Gluck's version was heard on 18 May 1779. It was a triumph. Piccinni had not completed his score in time and the production was a disaster.

That same year, Gluck, now the imperial court composer in Vienna, decided to retire from the French scene and returned home, though without his beloved adopted daughter, who had died prematurely in 1776. He suffered the first of several 'apoplectic seizures' at the end of October and in 1781 had a serious stroke which left him partially paralysed. His declining health kept him in Vienna for the remaining six years of his life. He composed no more, but it was as the acknowledged leading master of music that he died from a final stroke on 15 November 1787 after an agreeable lunch with two friends from Paris.

Essential works

ORFEO ED EURIDICE, opera (1762); includes 'Dance of the Blessed Spirits' and the arias 'Che puro ciel!' and 'Che farò senza Euridice'

PARIDE ED ELENA, opera (1770); includes the aria 'O del mio dolce ardor'

IPHIGÉNIE EN AULIDE, opera (1774)

ALCESTE, opera (1767 and 1776); includes the aria 'Divinités du Styx'

ARMIDE, opera (1777)

IPHIGÉNIE EN TAURIDE, opera (1779)

JOSEPH
HAYDN

'Genius, goodness, propriety, benevolence, rectitude' CHARLES BURNEY

HAYDN'S PERSONALITY,

REFLECTED SO ACCURATELY AND VIVIDLY IN THE MUSIC HE WROTE, fitted like a glove the age in which he lived: civilized, good-natured, logical, emotionally restrained, well-balanced, religious (but not immoderately so), experimental (but not dangerously so). He was born when Handel was at the height of his powers; he was a close friend of Mozart; by the time of his death, Beethoven had already written the 'Eroica' Symphony and 'Appassionata' piano sonata, music as far removed from Haydn's as Haydn's was from Bach's.

Haydn was one of music's most prolific composers and he wrote in every form. Reference books list 104 symphonies, nearly 90 string quartets, 62 piano sonatas, dozens of concertos, oratorios, masses and choral works, 23 operas, many songs, and a huge amount of instrumental and chamber music. He has been called 'the Father of the Symphony', not because he invented the form but because he developed it to a higher degree and provided a template that would survive through the entire 19th century.

EARLY LIFE

There were no musical antecedents in Haydn's ancestry. Neither was he any kind of child prodigy. His father was a wheelwright and the local sexton in the town of Rohrau, on the border of Austria and Hungary. Franz Joseph, born on 31 March 1732, was the second of 12 children. Until his late 20s, Haydn knew nothing but abject poverty. Despite his peasant upbringing and a miserable childhood ('More floggings than food,' he remembered), his musical gifts emerged at the age of six when he was sent to Hainburg by a cousin. While learning to read and write, he was given instruction in wind and string instruments. Though he never became a virtuoso on any instrument ('but I knew the strength and working of all'), he recalled that 'Our Almighty Father had endowed me with such fertility in music that even in my sixth year I stood up like a man and sang masses in the church choir and I could play a little on the clavier and violin.' He never enjoyed a formal musical education.

Having spent nine years eking out a living playing at social functions, teaching, arranging music and composing, Haydn's first break came in 1759 when he was appointed music director and composer for Count Maximilian von Morzin at his estate in Lukavec. The following year he made what was perhaps the biggest mistake of his life. He had been in love with one of his pupils in Vienna. When she became a nun, he married her sister Maria Anna Keller. She was three years older than Haydn, ill-tempered, with no love of music and no appreciation of his talent (she used his manuscripts for hair-curlers). He quickly became disenchanted with 'that infernal beast', as he called her, and for most of his life they lived separately. He sent her money, but although they corresponded, it is said that he never opened her letters. He handled his many affairs with gentlemanly discretion.

ESTERHÁZY PERIOD

In 1761, just two years after his disastrous marriage, Haydn lost his job when Morzin was compelled to disband his musical establishment. Then came the single most significant event in his career. Prince Paul Anton Esterházy had heard one of his symphonies at Lukavec and invited him to

become second Kapellmeister to the elderly Gregor Joseph Werner at his estate in Eisenstadt. Esterházy was the head of the richest and grandest family in Hungary, a famed patron of art and music. When Paul died the following year, he was succeeded by his brother Nikolaus. Nicknamed 'Nikolaus the Magnificent', he was a fanatical music-lover who entertained on an awesomely lavish scale and set about building a new palace near Süttör beside the Neusiedlersee. Eszterháza, as he named it, was rivalled in magnificence only by Versailles. With a 400-seat theatre for opera and a private orchestra at his disposal, Haydn must have thought he had died and gone to heaven. He remained in the service of the Esterházy family for the next 30 years.

When he became Kapellmeister after the death of Werner in 1766 (the same year in which Eszterháza was completed), Haydn's genius blossomed just as his onerous duties multiplied. In addition to two daily performances of chamber music, Haydn and his orchestra had to present two operas and two concerts every week; he had to compose and act as librarian, administrator, copyist and arbitrator. But his salary was generous and he was encouraged to compose as he wished. He recalled: 'As a conductor of an orchestra I could make experiments, observed what produced an effect and what weakened it, was thus in a position to improve, alter, make omissions, and be as bold as I pleased. I was cut off from the world, there was no one to confuse or torment me, and I was forced to become original.'

In this Arcadian setting far removed from Rohrau, Haydn now lived in one of the most splendid palaces in Europe. He had a maid, a coachman, a carriage and horses, and absolute control over a hand-picked band of musicians. These varied between 20 and 23 in number. His players adored him, referring to him fondly as 'Papa Haydn' as a tribute to the strict but level-headed, caring way he looked after them. In the early 1770s the contract with the Esterházys that banned the sale of Haydn's compositions was relaxed, and his works soon appeared in print in London and Amsterdam. Throughout Europe, Haydn was hailed as a genius, honoured by all.

Haydn made only brief annual visits to Vienna between 1780 and 1790, but during one of these he met Mozart for the first time. Twenty-five years old and a quarter of a century younger than Haydn, Mozart deeply admired Haydn's music and dedicated his first six string quartets to him. After a performance of these, the ever-generous Haydn remarked to Mozart's father: 'I tell you before God and as an honest man, that your son is the greatest composer I know, personally or by reputation.' Their mutual admiration had musical benefits: Mozart learned a great deal about

Essential works

Symphonies Nos. 93–104, the 'London' symphonies (1791–5); including No. 94 'The Surprise' or 'Paukenschlag' ('Drumstroke'), No. 100 'The Military', No. 101 'The Clock', No. 103 'The Drum Roll' and No. 104 'The London'
Piano Concerto in D (c.1784)
Cello Concerto in D (1783)
Trumpet Concerto in E flat (1796)
Piano Sonata No. 62 in E flat (1794)
Six String Quartets Op. 20 (1772)
Six String Quartets Op. 76 (1797–8)
Piano Trio No. 25 in G 'Gypsy' (1795)
THE CREATION, oratorio (1796–8)
Nelson Mass (1798)

'He alone has the secret of making me smile and touching me at the bottom of my soul.'

MOZART

structural organization from Haydn, while Haydn wrote more expressively and profoundly after exposure to his young friend.

FINAL YEARS

In 1790 Prince Nikolaus died. His son Paul Anton, who succeeded him, was more interested in paintings than music. The orchestra was disbanded, but as a reward for Haydn's loyalty, the new prince awarded him an annuity of 1000 florins as nominal Kapellmeister of Eszterháza, while allowing him to live permanently in Vienna. The same year, the enterprising impresario Johann Peter Salomon commissioned Haydn to compose six symphonies and invited him to London for a series of concerts. Feted wherever he went, the composer returned to Vienna 18 months later, in June 1792, with a small fortune. He travelled by way of Bonn, where he met Beethoven, who later that year arrived in Vienna to study with Haydn. The lessons ended when Salomon issued a return invitation to London and commissioned a further six symphonies. The 12 'London' symphonies represent the apex of Haydn's endeavours in this field.

The second trip was equally successful and strenuous. Back in Vienna, Haydn learned that Paul Anton had died. His son, another Prince Nikolaus, revived the Haydn orchestra. As Kapellmeister, Haydn now turned his attention to choral works, producing a further string of masterpieces. From this period come the Nelson Mass, *The Creation*, *The Seasons*, and the Austrian national anthem, first performed on the emperor's birthday, 12 February 1797.

In his mid-60s Haydn's health began to fail. When he resigned as Kapellmeister in 1802, Prince Nikolaus increased his pension to 2300 florins and paid all his medical bills, ensuring that Haydn should suffer no financial burden. At his final public appearance in 1808, a concert given in his honour was conducted by Salieri. The next year, when Vienna capitulated to Napoleon, the French emperor ordered a guard of honour to be placed round Haydn's house. He died on 31 May 1809 and was buried in the Hundsturm churchyard. At his funeral service, the music played included Mozart's Requiem, and it is Mozart who perhaps best summed up the qualities of his friend: 'He alone has the secret of making me smile and touching me at the bottom of my soul,' he wrote. 'There is no one who can do it all — to joke and terrify, to evoke laughter and profound sentiment — and all equally well: except Joseph Haydn.'

A BELATED REUNION

AFTER HAYDN'S DEATH, Joseph Rosenbaum, a friend of Haydn and secretary to the second Prince Nikolaus, persuaded the prince to let him decapitate the composer in order to examine it for phrenological purposes, promising to return it in a matter of weeks. It was not until 1820, when Esterházy honoured his intention of transferring Haydn's corpse to a specially built mausoleum at Eisenstadt, that it was discovered that the composer was a head short. After a complicated plot of theft, double-dealing and court cases, the skull ended up in the Vienna Gesellschaft der Musikfreunde in 1839. Here, the skull was put on display in a glass case sitting on a piano, where it remained until 1954. On 5 June that year, Haydn's head made the 30-kilometre journey from Vienna (via his birthplace) to Eisenstadt, to be reunited with his trunk 145 years after they had been parted.

WOLFGANG AMADEUS
MOZART

'O Mozart, immortal Mozart!' SCHUBERT

1756–91

MOZART WAS ARGUABLY THE MOST NATURALLY GIFTED MUSICIAN IN HISTORY. His inspiration is often described as 'divine', and he was certainly born with musical gifts that mere mortals can only dream of. Nevertheless, he worked assiduously to become not only a great composer but also a conductor, virtuoso pianist, organist and violinist. In other words, he was supreme in all areas of musical endeavour. His compositions (over 600 of them) embrace the very different demands of opera, symphony, concerto, chamber, choral, vocal and instrumental music. In every form he touched he produced an astonishing number of imperishable masterpieces. Though he had little interest in establishing new musical structures, he brought to perfection those already in existence with 'music more beautiful than it can ever be played', as the great pianist Artur Schnabel once aptly described it.

It comes as a relief to know that Mozart was mere flesh and blood like the rest of us. He was tactless, arrogant and impulsive and had a scatological sense of humour. Far from physically glamorous, his head was too big for his body and he had protruding eyes, a yellowish complexion and a face pitted with smallpox scars. His death was particularly unpleasant. It is partly his very human fallibility that lends the music its miraculous quality, for as another pianist, Lili Kraus, put it: 'there is no feeling – human or cosmic – no depth, no height the human spirit can reach that is not contained in Mozart's music.' Of all the great composers, none is regarded with such universal approval as Mozart, and many of the greatest composers themselves revered him as their idol.

A CHILD PRODIGY

From where does such genius come? Mozart's father, Leopold, was an ambitious composer and violinist in the service of the Prince Archbishop of Salzburg. Wolfgang – or Johannes Chrystostomus Wolfgangus Theophilus Mozart, as he was baptized – was born on 27 January 1756. He and his elder sister Maria Anna (nicknamed 'Nannerl') were the only two of Leopold's seven children to survive infancy. Both were musically talented, and when Leopold realized that Wolfgang, at the age of four, was a child prodigy, he spared no effort in ensuring that his son would become a great musician and that the world would know about him. He exploited his children's gifts to the full, and as early as 1762 he set off with them on a tour of European courts. The following year, Mozart's first compositions were published in Paris; his first symphonies appeared the following year. The critic and journalist Baron Melchior von Grimm wrote after hearing the nine-year-old Mozart improvise on the harpsichord: 'I cannot be sure that this child will not turn my head if I go on hearing him often; he makes me realise that it is difficult to guard against madness on seeing prodigies. I am no longer surprised that St Paul should have lost his head after a strange vision.'

After the wunderkind period, in 1766 the Mozarts arrived back in Salzburg, where Wolfgang applied himself to the serious study of counterpoint under his father's tutelage. His first opera (*La finta semplice*) was produced in Vienna in 1767. He then spent nearly two years in Italy with his father studying with the Italian composer Padre Martini. Returning to Salzburg in 1772, Mozart discovered

FEAT OF MEMORY

LEGEND HAS IT THAT DURING HIS STAY IN ROME between 1769 and 1771 Mozart wrote out the entire score of Allegri's *Miserere* from memory after hearing it sung just once in the Sistine Chapel. Copyright of the papal choir's music was jealously guarded and infringement risked excommunication. Alas, the tale is an exaggeration, for Mozart had almost certainly seen the score beforehand and, in any case, returned for a second performance to check the accuracy of what he had written down.

that as a now fully mature musician he had lost the capacity to captivate an audience and was compelled to enter the service of the archbishop of Salzburg to eke out a living. Though his first important works were produced during this period, including the five violin concertos and the 'Haffner' Serenade, it was a miserable time, for his employer treated him as menial servant, subjecting him constantly to personal abuse. The success of his first important opera, *Idomeneo* (1780), convinced him to leave Salzburg for good. His final meeting with the archbishop ended with Mozart being literally kicked out of the door by Count Arco, the archbishop's secretary.

THE GOLDEN YEARS

Mozart moved to Vienna in 1781, the city that would remain his base for the rest of his life. It marked the beginning of his golden years as a composer. Looking at the list of works produced during this time, it is staggering to realize that this period lasted a mere decade – for that is all that Mozart had left to him. His first lodgings in Vienna were with the Weber family, with one of whose daughters, Aloysia, he had earlier fallen in love. It was not long before he had fallen equally hopelessly for Aloysia's flighty younger sister Constanze. On a commission from the emperor, Mozart wrote his opera *Die Entführung aus dem Serail* (The Abduction from the Seraglio). Its success gave him the confidence to marry Constanze in August 1782. A string of fine works appeared: the 'Haffner' and 'Linz' Symphonies; five string quartets dedicated to his close friend Joseph Haydn; and in 1786 his comic opera *Le nozze di Figaro* (The Marriage of Figaro).

The Mozarts' marriage appears to have been genuinely happy. Constanze was easy-going, free-spending and usually pregnant (though, sadly, only two of the couple's six children survived). Their finances were always perilously poised despite many commissions and concert appearances. No court appointment materialized, and though not exactly on the breadline, Mozart felt poor enough to write begging letters to various friends, many to his fellow mason, the Viennese banker Michael Puchberg. The loans he received were never repaid and Mozart seems to have had no scruples about not paying his debts. Despite these anxieties, between 1784 and 1786 he composed nine of the greatest piano concertos in the literature. Three of them were written at the same time that he was composing *The Marriage of Figaro*! The year 1787 saw the death of his father and the premiere (in Prague, not Vienna) of his second operatic masterpiece, *Don Giovanni*. He also secured an appointment as *Kammercompositor* in Vienna in

'When the angels sing for God, they sing Bach; but I am sure that when they sing for themselves, they sing Mozart – and God eavesdrops.'

KARL BARTH

41

Essential works

Serenade No. 10 in B flat, 'Gran Partita', for 13 wind instruments, K361 (1781–4)

Piano Concerto No. 24 in C minor, K491 (1786)

THE MARRIAGE OF FIGARO (LE NOZZE DI FIGARO), opera, K492 (1786)

DON GIOVANNI, opera, K527 (1787)

Symphony No. 40 in G minor, K550 (1788)

Symphony No. 41 in C, 'Jupiter', K551 (1788)

COSÌ FAN TUTTE, opera, K588 (1790)

THE MAGIC FLUTE (DIE ZAUBERFLÖTE), opera, K620 (1791)

Requiem in D minor, K626 (1791)

Clarinet Concerto in A, K622 (1791)

succession to Gluck, but whereas Gluck's stipend had been 2000 gulden, Mozart had to settle for a paltry 800.

Though bad luck and lack of money were constants in his life, Mozart was able to rise above his immediate circumstances and compose with a fluency and organization that are given to few. He could score a complicated piece while planning another in his head, an ability that is beyond the comprehension of most of us. What makes him stand apart? His melodies sing, his harmonies are full of emotion and personal expression, his handling of the technical aspects such as counterpoint and orchestration are effortless (listen to the last movement of the 'Jupiter' Symphony where, famously, he handles five separate themes simultaneously). Instruments such as the horn and clarinet are allowed to flower in their own right, while the brass section is given weighty dramatic roles. The keyboard (harpsichord and then piano) was Mozart's main instrument, and it is in the later piano concertos that we hear him express himself most personally and to a greater degree than any composer up to that time. Lastly, his writing for the voice has rarely been matched. He composed with specific singers in mind, exploiting their particular abilities to write music of true dramatic expression. In his operas we encounter real people with real emotions, and music that simultaneously evokes pathos and comments on the unfolding drama.

PROLIFIC TO THE END

The succession of immortal works that Mozart composed in the last four years of his life almost beggars belief: *Eine kleine Nachtmusik*, the Clarinet Quintet, *Così fan tutte*, three piano trios, the 'Coronation' Piano Concerto, two piano sonatas, three string quartets, and the final three of his 41 symphonies, each one highly contrasted with the others: No. 39 all sunshine and smiles; No. 40 all gloom and despair; and No. 41, the 'Jupiter', the crowning glory of symphonic writing in the 18th century. As he toiled, his health began to fail, assailed as he was by chronic nephritis, fainting fits and periods of depression. The phenomenal work rate slowed. Somehow he rallied and in 1791 alone composed two operas (*La clemenza di Tito* and *The Magic Flute*), the Requiem (left unfinished at his death), the autumnal final piano concerto (No. 27 in B flat), the String Quintet in E flat and the sublime Clarinet Concerto. Any one of these would have been enough to make a composer's reputation. But all by the same man? In one year?

In July 1791 a mysterious visitor delivered an unsigned letter asking Mozart whether he would be willing to write a Requiem mass. Mozart believed that the stranger had come from another world and that the Requiem would be for his own soul. The request had in fact come from an eccentric nobleman, Count Franz von Walsegg, who intended the work for his late wife and wanted to pass it off as his own. Mozart accepted the commission but did not live long enough to complete it. On 5 December 1791 just before one o'clock in the morning, a few weeks before his 36th birthday, he succumbed to a hideous litany of physical failures: streptococcal infection, Schönlein–Henoch syndrome, renal failure (which caused fever, polyarthritis, swelling of the limbs and vomiting), cerebral haemorrhage and terminal broncho-pneumonia.

Tradition has it that a blizzard or heavy rainstorm on the day of the funeral prevented any mourners attending the burial and that the composer was buried in a pauper's grave. Neither is true. The weather reports for Vienna that day confirm there was no blizzard or rainstorm. Constanze could afford only the cheapest of funerals. After the service at St Stephen's Cathedral, held in the open air (a consequence, probably, of the putrid state of Mozart's corpse), none in the party chose to accompany the coffin to the cemetery of St Marx, a good hour's walk from the city centre. When the family failed to pay the mandatory dues, Mozart's remains seem to have been moved from their original unmarked location to another. The result is that the precise final resting place of one of music's greatest geniuses is unknown.

MOZART'S SURVIVORS

IN 1809 CONSTANZE MARRIED A DANISH DIPLOMAT, Georg Nikolaus von Nissen, and went to live in Copenhagen. After his death in 1826, she lived comfortably in Salzburg until her own death on 6 March 1842, having outlived Mozart by 50 years. Of Wolfgang and Constanze's two surviving children, the elder, Karl, became a civil servant for the Austrian government in Milan and died there in 1859. The younger, Wolfgang Amadeus Franz Xaver, became a respected pianist and composer, though (as one writer put it) 'his name alone was sufficient to preclude his rising to eminence'. He died in Carlsbad on 30 July 1844.

LUDWIG VAN
BEETHOVEN

'A colossus beyond the grasp of most mortals' YEHUDI MENUHIN

1770—1827

WHO IS THE GREATEST

COMPOSER? FOR SOME IT IS BACH. FOR OTHERS IT IS MOZART. For a large number of people it is Beethoven. It is very much a matter of personal taste. But Beethoven has a strong claim to be the most important great composer, the defining figure in musical history. Just as the French Revolution had so recently overthrown the established order and spread a wave of rebellion throughout Europe, so Beethoven, with equal decisiveness and defiance, overturned accepted musical form and traditional harmony and structure. His credo was exactly similar to that espoused by Rousseau, Voltaire and the other philosophers of the Enlightenment, which stated that the creative ego has the right to express itself in its own way without fear and hindrance.

Beethoven was not without the necessary self-confidence to achieve this. In a letter to Prince Lichnowsky written as early as 1806, he wrote: 'Prince, what you are, you are by the accident of birth; what I am, I am of myself. There are and there will be thousands of princes. There is only one Beethoven.' He truly felt that he was both sent by God and inspired by God. 'Music is a higher revelation than all wisdom and philosophy', he is quoted as saying. 'It is the wine of a new procreation, and I am Bacchus who presses out his glorious wine for men and makes them drink with the spirit.'

Beethoven's career falls conveniently into three distinct periods. The first, extending from the 1790s, when his first compositions appeared, to about 1800, shows him still clearly under the influence of the Classical period, in the world of Mozart, Haydn and *Zopfmusik* ('pigtail music') – though even here, in the early sonatas for piano and the first two piano concertos, we can hear a distinct new voice emerging. In the second period, coinciding with the onset of his deafness, Beethoven becomes ever more adventurous in his breaking of accepted musical forms and harmonies – the era of the 'Eroica' Symphony, the 'Appassionata' Sonata and *Fidelio*. Then, from about 1818, his music enters a third phase as distinct from the second as the second is from the first: a period marked by daring modulations, harmonic progressions and unorthodox structures so original and puzzling that many of his contemporaries agreed with his fellow composer Carl Maria von Weber that he was 'quite ripe for the madhouse'. Beethoven could not have cared less. A genius must write what he must without reference to lesser mortals.

ORIGINS

Beethoven's family was of Dutch descent (the name means 'beet garden'). He had a thoroughly miserable childhood. Perhaps his indomitable spirit was a result of it. Born on 15 or 16 December 1770 in Bonn, Germany, he was the son of Johann van Beethoven, an alcoholic brute and a singer in the Electoral Chapel.

'You make upon me the impression of a man who has several heads, several hearts and several souls.'

HAYDN

Determined that his son should become a second Mozart, this monster would keep him slaving at the piano all night, raining blows on him whenever he made a mistake or dragging him from his bed to entertain his drunken companions. Beethoven was an unprepossessing-looking child; he was clumsy and had no friends. The only warmth he knew came from his mother.

Despite or because of this start, Beethoven's prodigious innate gifts allowed him to master the violin, piano, organ and horn and have his first work (Variations on a March by Dressler) published at the age of 11. His first significant lessons were from Christian Neefe, the court organist, who recognized and nurtured his exceptional talent. At 14, Beethoven was made deputy court organist.

In 1787 his mother died. His father's alcoholism cost him his job, and Beethoven was obliged to earn money to keep himself and his siblings (he had two younger brothers) by playing the viola in a theatre orchestra. Five years later he moved to Vienna, his home for the rest of his life. He studied briefly but unprofitably with Haydn, who, while intolerant of Beethoven's crude manners and disregard for convention, once made the quite wonderful remark to him: 'You make upon me the impression of a man who has several heads, several hearts and several souls.'

After three further years of lessons in counterpoint with Albrechtsberger and in composition with Salieri, Beethoven made his public debut in Vienna, probably playing his Piano Concerto No. 2 in B flat. His reputation as a composer and virtuoso pianist spread rapidly. It was the following year, 1796, when Beethoven was only 26, that he became aware of impending deafness. Part of the cause was otosclerosis, an abnormal growth of honeycomb bone in the inner ear, accompanied by tinnitus. A contributory factor was congenital syphilis. The effects of this show up in the life mask made in 1812 and in the photograph of his skull taken in 1863, when his body was exhumed.

MIDDLE PERIOD

Beethoven's predicament spurred him to a furious spell of creativity. Over the next six years he produced the Piano Concertos Nos. 3, 4 and 5 (the last of these is the 'Emperor'); the 'Kreutzer' Sonata for violin and piano; the 'Moonlight', 'Waldstein' and 'Appassionata' Piano Sonatas; Symphonies Nos. 3 ('Eroica'), 4, 5 (with perhaps the most familiar opening of any piece of music) and 6 ('Pastoral'); the first version of his opera *Fidelio*; the three 'Razumovsky' String Quartets; the Violin Concerto and the Triple Concerto – to name merely the best known among many other works. Many of these were not merely masterpieces but were revolutionary, none more so than the 'Eroica' Symphony, one of the true landmarks in the development of Western music. Written on an epic scale, its emotional content was startlingly raw, coloured by harmonic dissonances and brutal

THE RAPTURE OF COMPOSITION

'I CARRY MY THOUGHTS ABOUT ME FOR A LONG TIME BEFORE I WRITE THEM DOWN. Meanwhile my memory is so tenacious that I am sure never to forget, not even in years, a theme that has once occurred to me. I change many things, discard and try again until I am satisfied. Then, however, there begins in my head the development in every direction and, insomuch as I know exactly what I want, the fundamental idea never deserts me – it arises before me, it grows – I see and hear the picture in all its extent and dimensions stand before my mind like a cast, and there remains nothing but the labour of writing it down, which is quickly accomplished when I have the time, for I sometimes take up other work, but never to the confusion of one with the other.'

BEETHOVEN IN A LETTER TO LOUIS SCHLÖSSER, 1823

accents of a kind never heard before.

Beethoven's belief in himself and the importance of what he was doing was immense. He knew he was breaking new ground. 'With whom need I be afraid of measuring my strength?' he once boasted. Though financially insecure, he turned down well-paid posts in order to continue what he was doing on his own terms. As he became increasingly deaf, so he grew more petulant, irritable and sensitive: not an easy man to live with, as many of those he fell in love with must have realized. He seems never to have had a full-blown, passionate love affair, though he made his feelings plain to the string of young, beautiful and quite unattainable ladies he fell for. Music, in the end, had to come first. Those who were unsupportive were banished forever, including some of his closest friends. Many others were prepared to put up with his foibles and showed him immense loyalty, among them Prince Lobkowitz, Countess Erdödy and especially the Archduke Rudolph.

Essential works

Piano Concertos Nos. 1–5 (1795–1809)
32 Piano Sonatas (1797–1822)
Symphonies Nos. 1–9 (1800–24)
Septet in E flat for winds and strings (1800)
'Kreutzer' Sonata for violin and piano (1803)
FIDELIO, opera (1804–14)
Three 'Razumovsky' String Quartets (1805–6)
Violin Concerto (1806)
MISSA SOLEMNIS (1823)
The five Late Quartets (1824–6)

LATE PERIOD

Beethoven, like many deaf people, began to retreat into himself and shun society. After Symphonies Nos. 7 and 8, during the five years between 1812 and 1817, there was a marked decline in the amount of music that he produced as well as in its adventurousness. In 1818 Beethoven became totally deaf, but in the same year he began a third and final phase of composition with a vengeance, starting with the mighty 'Hammerklavier' Piano Sonata. 'As long as a symphony, as difficult as a concerto', the technical and musical demands of this 45-minute work are considered by most pianists to make it one of the most challenging in the repertoire.

During this final decade of his life, deprived of the wife and family he longed for, Beethoven found a surrogate son in the person of his nine-year-old nephew Karl, whose father (Beethoven's younger brother, also named Karl) had died in 1815. Beethoven regarded Karl's mother as unfit to bring up the boy and, in a series of sordid and bitter court battles, eventually succeeded in 1820 in winning sole custody from his sister-in-law. For the next six years he stifled Karl with avuncular affection in an attempt to win his love. In return, Karl regarded his uncle with something like contempt, piled up enormous debts and finally attempted suicide, before joining the army and going on to have a normal life.

During this period, Beethoven's composing slowed to a trickle. When he did return to full-time composition, his music had undergone a further transformation with works including the Ninth Symphony ('Choral'), the *Missa Solemnis* and the late string quartets. The 'Choral', whose last movement is a setting of part of Schiller's *Ode to Joy*, is a great celebration of the human spirit. The *Missa Solemnis* is regarded as one of the pinnacles of religious music, along with Bach's B minor Mass and Mozart's 'Great' Mass in C minor. The final quartets are different again, mystical and frequently demanding even to modern ears, in which traditional development of themes is abandoned to be replaced by fragments of ideas, sometimes repeated, interrupted or varied. The music is elevated to a spiritual plane not found in Beethoven's other works. Many consider them to be his greatest music in any form.

JUST ONE DAY OF PURE JOY

IN A DOCUMENT DISCOVERED ONLY AFTER HIS DEATH, Beethoven wrote poignantly of his deafness, which for many years he kept secret from everyone but his doctor. In this so-called 'Heiligenstadt Testament' (written in the village of Heiligenstadt just outside Vienna in 1802), he revealed that 'I was on the point of putting an end to my life – The only thing that held me back was my art'. In a postscript he pleads: 'Oh Providence – do but grant me one day of pure joy ...'

Living in his own world, deprived of any external sounds and only able to communicate by means of conversation books, the defiant Beethoven must have struck a pathetic figure in his last years. At the beginning of 1827, already ill, Beethoven caught a cold while visiting his surviving brother. The cold developed into pneumonia, and jaundice and dropsy set in. He died on the afternoon of 26 March in the middle of a violent electrical storm. His last words were reported to have been: 'I shall hear in heaven.' All Vienna mourned, schools closed and people stayed away from work as he was taken for burial at the Währing Cemetery. In 1888 his body was moved to the Central Cemetery.

Carl Maria von
Weber

Pioneer of German Romantic opera

1786—1826

WEBER IS THE FATHER OF GERMAN ROMANTIC OPERA, a label due almost entirely to a single work, *Der Freischütz* (The Marksman). So influential and successful was this opera that it has overshadowed the remainder of his output. This includes some of the most important (and delicious) works for the clarinet and a large body of piano music that remains shamefully undervalued and which exerted a strong influence on the young Schumann, Chopin and Liszt.

Carl Maria Friedrich Ernst von Weber was born on 18 November 1786 in the small town of Eutin, near Lübeck, in northern Germany. If his background was fairly humble (despite the spurious aristocratic 'von'), it was entirely musical. His father, a violinist, was Kapellmeister to the prince bishop of Lübeck, while his mother was a talented singer. A cousin of Mozart's wife Constanze, the young Weber spent much of his childhood on tour with his parents, for soon after his birth his father became the director of a travelling theatre company. He could play the piano and sing by the age of four, before he was able to walk properly (he was handicapped by a congenital disease of the hip), and to the satisfaction of his father, he showed every indication of becoming an infant prodigy like Mozart, despite any systematic education. He spent some time studying with Joseph Haydn's brother Michael in Salzburg, where his first compositions were published when he was just 11 years old.

EARLY SUCCESSES

Soon after, Weber began a career as a concert pianist. Though of slim build and a sickly consumptive, he had unusually large hands and was able to cover a twelfth on the keyboard. The music he wrote was, naturally, tailored to his own abilities and the enormous stretches involved put many pages beyond the reach of the average pianist. In 1800 his first opera *Das Waldmädchen* was produced in Freiberg; the manuscript has not survived and may have been destroyed by the composer himself, who was quoted as saying 'puppies and first operas should be drowned'.

Aged only 17, Weber secured the post of Kapellmeister at the theatre in Breslau, the first of a number of positions which led to the directorship of Prague Opera in 1813, where he stayed for three years. In addition to this work and his successful concert tours, during this period Weber composed his two piano concertos, the two clarinet concertos (inspired by his friend, the magnificent clarinettist Heinrich Bärmann), two symphonies, a bassoon concerto and the concertino for horn. Then in 1817 the king of Saxony invited him to take charge of the German Opera Theatre in Dresden. It was a prestigious position and one he held for the rest of his life.

Essential *works*

Clarinet Concerto No. 1, Op. 73 (1811)
Clarinet Concerto No. 2, Op. 74 (1811)
Bassoon Concerto (1811)
Piano Sonatas Nos. 1–4 (1812–22)
Clarinet Quintet (1815)
Concertino for horn (1815)
Grand Duo Concertant for clarinet and
   piano (1816)
DER FREISCHÜTZ, opera (1821)

CARL MARIA VON WEBER

A SHORT BUT BRILLIANT CAREER

As a conductor, Weber was fiercely demanding of his singers and musicians, ordered German translations to be made of all the important operas, corrected errors in the scores and generally raised standards to a new level – a latterday Gluck. These endeavours to develop a German national opera were not achieved without opposition from the court and the presiding master of opera in German, Gaspare Spontini, who dictated the Italian-French musical tradition from the Berlin Opera. All that changed with *Der Freischütz.*

Composition of the opera took three years. When Weber conducted the first performance in Berlin on 12 June 1821, the curtain rose not only on a self-contained masterpiece but on the new Romantic movement in music. Instead of the classical ideals of order and balance with acknowledged structures of form and expression, the door was opened on a world which relied more on the experience, fantasy and inner feelings of the composer. The same year saw the composition of a pioneering work for piano and orchestra, a one-movement piano concerto entitled *Konzertstück.* While full of virtuoso effects for the soloist, the actual music portrayed a story of medieval knights and crusaders. In the little time left to him, the increasingly frail Weber never hit such heights again.

> 'Weber seems to whisper in my ear like a familiar spirit, inhabiting a happy sphere where he awaits to console me.'
>
> BERLIOZ

After the moderate success of his next opera, *Euryanthe,* with its chaotic libretto, Weber took himself off to Marienbad to seek a cure for his tuberculosis, returning to write *Oberon* to a commission from London's Covent Garden. It, too, suffered from an all but unstageable libretto (both operas are best experienced on record), though it met with huge success when he conducted the premiere in April 1826.

By then, Weber knew he was a doomed man. He died in London on 5 June the day before he was due to return home. He was buried in Moorfields Chapel, but 18 years later his remains were transferred to Dresden. When the ship carrying his coffin arrived in Hamburg, all the vessels in the port dipped their colours in tribute. It was Wagner, Weber's great successor in Dresden, who gave the graveside oration – an appropriate gesture for, as the writer R.A. Streatfield wrote, 'Without Weber, Wagner would have been impossible.'

GERMAN NATIONAL OPERA

Before Weber, there had been very little German opera. Mozart's *The Magic Flute* was the only major success in the language, while Beethoven's *Fidelio*, though much admired, had not led to any German school to rival the current French-Italian craze. In Dresden, Weber befriended a writer and lawyer, Friedrich Kind, who suggested the idea of a libretto on a German subject. *Der Freischütz's* highly dramatic, allegorical theme suffused with folkloric and supernatural events in a world populated by ordinary human beings proved highly attractive to the public.

Weber's melodic genius and mastery of the orchestra allowed him to break with the traditions of the past. Many of his ideas, such as recurrent motifs to achieve musical and narrative unity, anticipate Wagner's by 30 years. The opera's overture was the first of its kind not only to include thematic material from the opera but to quote complete melodies.

GIOACHINO
ROSSINI

Italian opera's comic genius

1792—1868

GIOACHINO ROSSINI IS ONE OF THE 'SUNSHINE COMPOSERS'. Like Mendelssohn and Saint-Saëns, his music puts a spring in your step with its vitality, untroubled spirit and inexhaustible flow of melody. A character in Thomas Pynchon's novel *Gravity's Rainbow* (1973) commented: 'a person feels good listening to Rossini. All you feel like after listening to Beethoven is going out and invading Poland . . . There is more of the sublime in the snare-drum part of *La gazza ladra* than in the whole Ninth Symphony.'

Rossini was indecently prolific, writing with an extraordinary fluency from an early age. If he was not always as self-critical as he should have been, his almost unbroken string of successes between 1813 and 1829 made him the leading opera composer of the first half of the 19th century. He made Italian opera famous throughout the world, and his contribution to its development was far-reaching – where he led, Donizetti and Bellini followed. The extraordinary thing is that, at the height of his powers in 1829, Rossini withdrew completely from the field he dominated and for the remaining 39 years of his life composed almost nothing.

EARLY LIFE

There was never any question about Rossini's career – no doubting parents, no dabbling in other, more secure professions before taking the plunge. His father, Giuseppi, was a trumpet player in Pesaro, Italy, as well as being a municipal inspector of slaughterhouses; his mother was a gifted opera singer. Born on 29 February 1792, Gioachino, an only child, was four years old when his father was jailed for expressing his political opinions. His mother secured a singing role in Bologna, where they remained until Giuseppi was released. Here, Rossini had his first music lessons and made his first attempt at writing an opera – aged eight.

By the time he had reached his teens, Rossini could not only play the piano, viola and horn but was noted for his beautiful singing voice. He entered Bologna's Liceo Communale at the age of 15. When he left just three years later, he had already composed a huge amount of music, including five accomplished string quartets. But opera was his goal. Commissioned to write a one-act *opera buffa* (a form of comic opera), Rossini came up with the first of six one-acters he wrote within the following year: *La cambiale di matrimonio* (1810) was an instant success at its premiere in Venice. In late 1812, La Scala mounted his two-act opera *La pietra del paragone*. After that, his career took off in spectacular style. His first full-length opera, *Tancredi* (1813), was a triumph – it included the aria 'Di tanti palpiti', which achieved the same kind of success as one of today's pop hits. This was followed by the even more successful *L'Italiana in Algeri*, also produced in Venice. By the age of 21, Rossini was a national celebrity.

YEARS OF PLENTY

After Venice, Rossini moved on to Milan, thence to Naples and Rome. He could write at astonishing speed, the whole process from finding a libretto, setting

'Delight must be the basis and aim of this art. Simple melody – clear rhythm!'
ROSSINI

THE BARBER OF SEVILLE

ACCORDING TO ROSSINI, HE COMPOSED THE 600-PAGE SCORE IN 13 DAYS. Even if the true period was 19 (according to his biographer, Stendhal), and even with a number of self-borrowings, this remains one of the most astounding examples of sustained, rapid musical creation in history. Donizetti was once asked, 'Do you really think Rossini wrote the opera in 13 days?' 'Why not?' came the reply. 'He's so lazy.'

The premiere of *The Barber* was a fiasco. One of the singers tripped and had to sing with a bloody nose, a cat wandered onto the stage and distracted the audience's attention, while the partisan first-nighters in Rome hissed their disapproval of the choice of subject. The second performance, however, was a triumph. Rossini fever swept Italy.

it to music, rehearsing the singers and mounting the production taking sometimes as little as six weeks. Yet this did not preclude innovation. His 1815 opera *Elisabetta, regina d'Inghilterra* is notable for being the first to have the vocal ornamentation fully written out, thus preventing the prima donnas from introducing their own embellishments and set pieces, as was then the habit. Another innovation was the 'Rossini crescendo'; in this, excitement mounts as a musical theme is repeated, each time at a higher pitch and with larger orchestral accompaniment.

At the same time, such prodigious fecundity was boosted by a certain amount of self-plagiarism, a practice indulged in by composers great and small through the ages. The best-known example of this is the famous overture to Rossini's greatest comic masterpiece, *The Barber of Seville* (*Il barbiere di Siviglia*). It was a straight lift from an earlier flop, *Aureliano in Palmira* (1813), whose overture Rossini had also used for *Elisabetta*.

Based in Naples, Rossini began an affair with the prima donna Isabella Colbran, for whose florid, dramatic style of singing he created a number of roles in the more elevated style of *opera seria*.

Essential works

Overtures to LA SCALA DI SETA (1812) and IL SIGNOR BRUSCHINO (1812)
THE BARBER OF SEVILLE, opera (1816)
LA CENERENTOLA, opera (1817)
LA GAZZA LADRA, opera (1817)
SEMIRAMIDE, opera (1823)
WILLIAM TELL, opera (1829)
STABAT MATER (1842)
PETITE MESSE SOLENNELLE (1863)

Among these, *Otello* (1816), *Armida* (1817) and *Ermione* (1819) stand out as demonstrations of Rossini's innate instincts as a dramatist. To satisfy his audience's demands for more *opera buffa*, he produced *La Cenerentola* (1817), based on the Cinderella fairy-tale and including the brilliant aria 'Non piú mesta'. It is second only in popularity to *The Barber*. Also from 1817 comes *La gazza ladra* (The Thieving Magpie) with its dazzling overture; from 1818 *Moses in Egypt*; from 1819 *La donna del lago*; from 1822 *Zelmira*; and from 1823 the glorious *Semiramide*. All in all, Rossini operated on a scarcely believable level of creativity. Between 1808 and 1829 he produced no fewer than 40 operas. 'Give me a laundry list,' he is supposed to have said, 'and I will set it to music.'

Having married Colbran in 1822, Rossini moved to Vienna, where he visited Beethoven (the great man congratulated him on *The Barber of Seville*), then on to London, where he was fêted by public and royalty alike (George IV sang duets with him). Now hailed as one of the greatest living composers, he settled in Paris, where the French government gave him a yearly pension and the titles of Royal Composer and Inspector General of Singing. Adapting his style to French tastes, he wrote the sparkling *Le Comte Ory* (1828). This was followed by his grand opera masterpiece, *William Tell* (1829), with perhaps the most celebrated of all Rossini's overtures. Though many people may be unfamiliar with the complete *William Tell*, *La gazza ladra* (rarely staged today), *La Cenerentola*, *Semiramide* or even *The Barber of Seville*, concert performances of their overtures remain the most frequently played of any opera curtain-raisers.

EARLY RETIREMENT

No one has yet come up with the definitive explanation of why Rossini simply stopped composing after *William Tell*, even though he was only 37 years of age. It seems likely that at first he intended merely to take an extended holiday, but as the years went by and fashions changed, he became ever more remote from the new music his successors were producing. Perhaps it was the prolonged bouts of neurasthenia from which he suffered. Whatever the reason, he was certainly true to the old stage adage 'Leave them wanting more'. The fact is that apart from his magnificent *Stabat mater* (1831–42) and *Petite messe solennelle* (1863), he wrote nothing substantial again.

In 1832 Rossini took Olympe Pélissier, a great Parisian beauty, for his mistress. They left Paris for Bologna in 1836, and when Isabella Colbran died in 1845, they married. From 1848 to 1855 they made their home in Florence. It was during this period that Rossini suffered increasingly from depression, a condition ameliorated only after his return to Paris, the composer's home until his death.

Rossini had become immensely wealthy, of course, and so could entertain on a lavish scale, his home becoming the focal point for many of the great artists of the day. He was renowned as much for his generosity as for his hospitality, and an invitation to his table was one of the most sought after in the city. Fat, amiable and bald (he had seven toupees, one for every day of the week), he was legendary for his wit. 'Wagner,' he once said, 'has lovely moments but awful quarters of an hour.' Of Berlioz's *Symphonie fantastique* he commented, 'What a good thing it isn't music.'

Having been born on a leap day (29 February), Rossini took great delight in celebrating his 19th birthday in 1868. Like many Italians, he was extremely superstitious, especially of Friday 13th, so it was strangely ironic that he should die on 13 November 1868 – a Friday. In his funeral procession there were 6000 mourners, four military bands and a chorus of 399 who sang the Prayer from his *Moses in Egypt*. He was buried in the Paris cemetery of Père Lachaise, but 19 years later his remains were taken to be re-interred in the church of Santa Croce in Florence.

BON VIVEUR

ROSSINI WAS A NOTED GOURMET AND GOURMAND. His love of food is commemorated in the many dishes named after him (most memorably Tournedos Rossini), the majority including foie gras, truffles and a demi-glace sauce. Fine wines were another pleasure. When Baron James Rothschild sent Rossini some superb grapes from his hothouse, the composer thanked him: 'Splendid though your grapes certainly are, I don't take my wine in pills.' The baron took the hint and sent Rossini some of his famous Château-Lafitte.

Franz
Schubert

'The first lyric poet of music'

Harold Schonberg

1797—1828

FRANZ SCHUBERT

'A LUMP OF FAT,' SAID ONE OF HIS ACQUAINTANCES, 'SHORT, SOMEWHAT CORPULENT, WITH A FULL ROUND FACE, but with eyes so sparkling that they revealed at once the inner fire.' Schubert was just 5 feet 1½ inches tall, nearsighted and almost always wore glasses. Some say he even kept them on his bed so that he could start composing the minute he woke in the morning. 'If you pay him a visit,' reported his friend, the poet Franz von Schober, 'he says "Hello, how are you? – Good!" and goes on working, whereupon you go away.'

Every description one reads of Schubert reveals the affection in which he was held by everyone who knew him. Almost universally, his music provokes the same reaction. Who could not warm to the miraculous fountain of songs (more than 600 of them), the heart-easing piano music, the melody-soaked chamber music and symphonies? Such a reaction is doubtless intensified by the sad facts of Schubert's life – a life that fits the cinema's ideal of the musical genius living in poverty whose music is heard by only a few during his lifetime, and who, in the best romantic tradition, dies tragically young and almost unknown. But such was Schubert's fate.

Exceptionally for such a fecund composer, there are comparatively few second-rate works. Musicologists will point out that his knowledge of counterpoint was weak, that in longer forms (the symphonies, say, and some of the sonatas) the themes are not properly developed in the traditional manner. Rather, the same material is presented in a different guise with a change of key or instrument when, frequently, fresh ideas emerge. His instincts and innate feel for musical shape were enough. It was in the smaller forms that his genius flowered and in his songs he was in a class of his own. With him, melody, however striking, was of subsidiary importance to the text, while the accompanying piano part, when considered independently of both, was a thing of beauty in its own right.

EARLY LIFE

Schubert's father was a schoolmaster in the suburbs of Vienna and a keen amateur musician. His mother was a cook. Of their 11 children, only three survived infancy. Franz Peter was born on 31 January 1797, and though his natural musical talent was encouraged, it was simply assumed that he would eventually follow into the teaching profession. But his precocious gifts soon put him beyond the modest accomplishments of his father and the local choirmaster. By the age of ten he could play the piano, organ, violin and viola and was accepted into the Imperial Court Chapel in Vienna, all his education, board and lodging paid for. Among his teachers was Antonio Salieri, Mozart's old rival. 'You can do everything,' he is said to have announced to the timid, diffident little boy, 'for you are a genius.'

In 1810 Schubert completed his first work, a fantasy for piano duet; on 30 March 1811 he composed 'Hagars Klage', the first of his songs; by 1813 he had produced several orchestral overtures and his first symphony. His father had remarried after the death of his wife in 1812, and Schubert, rather than complete the final year of his education, bowed to paternal wishes and took up a position as an assistant teacher at his father's school. Here he stayed for three years, loathing every minute of it. All he wanted to do was write music. And write it he did. During this period he completed five symphonies, four masses, several string quartets, stage music, an opera and some of

57

his most famous lieder: 'Gretchen am Spinnrade', a song with many of the methods and techniques of Schubert's later songs, was composed when he was 17, while 'Erlkönig', a masterpiece of the art-song form, was written at 18. In 1815 alone he composed more than 140 songs. On 15 October of that year, he composed eight in one day. In 20 years he wrote as much music as Brahms did in 50.

In 1816 Schubert abandoned teaching to take his chances as a full-time composer, sharing lodgings with his close friend Franz von Schober, a law student and amateur poet. Their evenings were often spent with other friends, Schubert presiding at the piano improvising and entertaining in convivial gatherings that came to be known as Schubertiads. He supplemented his meagre income by teaching the daughters of Count Esterházy at his summer estate in Zelésk, Hungary, but unlike Haydn before him there was no permanent post there; and unlike Beethoven, his lifelong idol, Schubert never found a rich patron.

THE FLUENCY OF GENIUS

NOT FOR SCHUBERT THE INNER STRUGGLES OF BEETHOVEN OR THE FRETTING INDECISION OF CHOPIN. He rarely revised his work. His ideas came tumbling out like water from a spring. His gift of melody has, quite probably, never been equalled. It is not merely the beauty of the ideas but their variety of character that is truly astonishing, encompassing every emotion and mood. What makes him so original is the way in which he harmonizes his melodies, offering surprises yet taking his listeners exactly where they hope to go – 'the element of the unexpected that is yet so inevitable', as one writer put it.

ABUNDANCE IN DESPAIR

By 1820, of the more than 500 works that he had composed, only two had been heard in public – the Mass in F in 1814 and a solitary song in 1819. He was commissioned to write music for two operettas (which were critical flops), but it was not until 1821 that any of his music was published – a volume of songs, the cost of which was paid for by his friends. The lack of recognition began to bite hard. Living in obscurity, with no money and relying on the charity of friends, made him increasingly despondent. Added to this, he had to cope with the effects of syphilis. 'Each night when I go to sleep,' wrote Schubert, 'I hope never again to waken, and every morning reopens the wounds of yesterday.' Yet in the midst of this his intrinsically sunny disposition shines through, for in 1822 he began (amongst many other works) his Symphony No. 8 in B minor – begun but never finished – one of his most beautiful creations; the majestic 'Wanderer' Fantasy for piano; the airy, light-hearted Octet for strings, clarinet, bassoon and horn; the singular Arpeggione Sonata; and one of his finest song cycles, *Die schöne Müllerin*. Given Schubert's circumstances, such endeavour and inspiration is almost miraculous.

Yet there was more to come – much more – despite his failing health and frequent periods of despair. Almost as though he knew he had only a short time left, Schubert produced music in ever greater quality and quantity, including what is perhaps his most famous song, 'Ave Maria', one of his settings of poems from Sir Walter Scott's *The Lady of the Lake*. A few more of his works were published but brought him little income, and in 1826 he petitioned the emperor for the position of Vice Musical Director to the Court Chapel. The post went to one

'His soul being steeped in music, he put down notes when another man would resort to words.'
SCHUMANN

Josef Weigl. Schubert is reported to have responded: 'Much as I should have liked to have received the appointment, I shall have to make the best of the matter since it was given to so worthy a man as Weigl.'

By February 1827 he had composed the first half of his great song cycle *Die Winterreise*. Three months later he visited the dying Beethoven and, a few days afterwards, was one of the torch-bearers in his hero's funeral procession. Over the next 12 months, Schubert composed some of his most divine music: the String Quintet with its heart-breaking slow movement, the 'Great' C major Symphony, the sublime last three piano sonatas and most of the piano impromptus, the Mass in E flat, the two piano trios, and the 14 songs that would be gathered together after his death to form the cycle *Schwanengesang*.

On 26 March 1828 in the Musikverein of Vienna, for the first and only time in his life, a concert was given consisting entirely of works by Schubert. It was put on by friends, of course, and was well received, but it clashed with concerts given by Paganini and so was never even reviewed. Less than eight months later, babbling of Beethoven, Schubert died from a combination of typhoid poisoning and tertiary syphilis. He was 31 years old, and at his own request he was buried as near to Beethoven as was practicable. The epitaph on his monument, written by his friend Grillparzer, reads: 'The art of music here entombed a rich possession, but yet fairer hopes.' He left absolutely nothing at all — except his manuscripts.

Essential works

Piano Quintet in A, 'The Trout' (1819)
Symphony No. 8 in B minor, 'Unfinished' (1822)
Fantasy in C, 'Wanderer', piano (1822)
DIE SCHÖNE MÜLLERIN, song cycle (1823)
String Quartet in D minor, 'Death and the Maiden' (1824)
Symphony No. 9 in C, 'Great' (1825)
DIE WINTERREISE, song cycle (1827)
String Quintet in C (1828)
Eight Impromptus, piano (1828)
Piano Sonatas in C minor, D958; A major, D959; and B flat major, D960 (1828)
SCHWANENGESANG, song cycle (1828)

FORGOTTEN TREASURES

RECOGNIZED TODAY AS THE EQUAL OF HAYDN, MOZART AND BEETHOVEN in the pantheon of great composers, the neglect of Schubert during his lifetime seems incomprehensible. It was only by chance and through the diligence of other musicians that the piles of manuscripts, left forgotten, bundled up in cupboards and publishers' cellars, came to light. Schumann came across the score of the 'Great' Symphony in C (No. 9) when visiting Schubert's brother in 1838; the 'Unfinished' Symphony was found in a chest and not heard until 1865; and in 1867 George Grove (creator of the famous dictionary) and the young Arthur Sullivan (of Gilbert and Sullivan) unearthed in a publisher's house in Vienna Symphonies 1, 2, 3, 4 and 6, the music for Rosamunde, and 60 songs.

GAETANO
DONIZETTI

Prolific master of Italian opera

1797—1848

ROSSINI, DONIZETTI AND BELLINI FORM THE GREAT TRIUMVIRATE OF ITALIAN OPERA COMPOSERS DURING THE FIRST HALF OF THE 19TH CENTURY. After Rossini's early retirement and Bellini's premature death, it was Donizetti who pointed the way forward to Verdi. He was a practical man of the theatre who understood the requirements of the box office, how to make the best use of the musical forces at his command, and the benefits of writing with a particular artist in mind. It was the vocal opportunities he gave to his singers (especially sopranos) that have contributed to the enduring popularity of the greatest of his operas: *Lucia di Lammermoor*, *L'elisir d'amore*, *Don Pasquale* and *La fille du régiment*. Those that had fallen by the wayside, such as *Anna Bolena*, *La favorite*, *Linda di Chamounix* and *Emilia di Liverpool*, were revived in our own time as vehicles for singers of the calibre of Maria Callas, Joan Sutherland and Montserrat Caballé.

Donizetti's career falls into three parts: the apprentice years when he imitated Rossini's methods and techniques; a middle period which, significantly, began in 1830, the year after Rossini stopped composing – a time when Donizetti proved his independence by his mastery of vocal ensemble writing, brilliant coloratura arias, flair for comedy and a gift for lyricism that was quite the equal of Bellini's; and a third period that saw him adapting his Italian methods to French ways, producing serious operas of great splendour and comic operas of sparkling sophistication.

Rossini could write at incredible speed but he is a mere slouch when compared with Donizetti's fecundity. Entire operas – libretto and music – were written from start to finish within a fortnight. Most of the last act of *La favorite*, it is said, was sketched in a couple of hours. During his 'Rossini period' he served up four operas in 1822, another two in 1823, two in 1824, at least three in 1826, four in 1827 and a further four in 1828.

The musical result was, inevitably, formulaic and trite. Lack of self-criticism in a composer frequently goes hand in hand with such facility, and it is for that reason that most of his more than 70 operas have been consigned to oblivion. But, as Cecil Gray noted, 'When he chose to take trouble, he was able to touch greatness.' We must remember that only a genius in complete control of his craft could have written something like the Sextet from *Lucia di Lammermoor*.

EARLY YEARS

Gaetano Donizetti was born in Bergamo on 29 November 1797. His father, a weaver and later a pawnbroker, would not countenance a musical career for his son. He apprenticed the boy to an architect. That was soon abandoned. He was then instructed to study law. That, too, fell by the wayside. All Donizetti was interested in was poetry, painting and writing music. Finally his father reluctantly consented for him to attend the Bergamo School of Music. Here he discovered the opera scores of Rossini, who – though only five years his senior – became Donizetti's idol. His dream was to be able to write operas in the same mould.

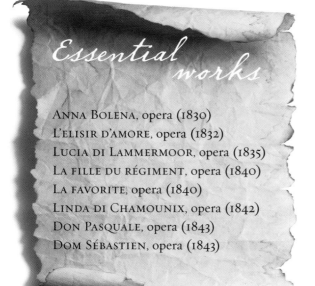

Essential works

ANNA BOLENA, opera (1830)
L'ELISIR D'AMORE, opera (1832)
LUCIA DI LAMMERMOOR, opera (1835)
LA FILLE DU RÉGIMENT, opera (1840)
LA FAVORITE, opera (1840)
LINDA DI CHAMOUNIX, opera (1842)
DON PASQUALE, opera (1843)
DOM SÉBASTIEN, opera (1843)

There was still, however, his father to contend with. Having accepted that his son must be a musician, he decided that he must become a church musician and sent him to the Liceo Filarmonico in Bologna, which was noted for such training. Here, one of Donizetti's teachers was Padre Mattei, who had taught Rossini – a relationship which only made him more determined in his ambition. His father once again intervened, insisting that if he was not going to compose church music, then he must abandon music altogether and become a teacher. Donizetti's answer was to join the Austrian army.

Following three earlier one-act farces, Donizetti completed his first opera proper, *Enrico di Borgogna*, in 1818, during his military service. It was favourably received, but it was not until 1822, with the premiere in Rome of his fourth full opera, *Zoraïde di Granata*, that he had his first great success – so emphatic that the government released him from further military duty in order that he could compose full time. The 23 apprentice works that followed, though written by the hand of Donizetti, had the voice of Rossini.

OUT OF THE SHADOW OF ROSSINI

It was only in 1830 that he broke the umbilical cord and produced a work that was not so clearly in debt to the Rossini idiom. This was *Anna Bolena*, first performed in Milan that year, and, though rarely revived now, considered by Donizetti's contemporaries as his *magnum opus*. It made him internationally famous, a reputation consolidated in 1832 by one of his finest comic operas, *L'elisir d'amore* (The Elixir of Love). His 40th opera, the music for which was written in just 14 days, contains one of opera's best loved arias, 'Una furtive lagrima' – one reason why every tenor aspires to the role of Nemorino. Donizetti's next notable successes followed three years later with *Maria Stuarda* and *Lucia di Lammermoor*, his greatest masterpiece, based on Sir Walter Scott's novel *The Bride of Lammermoor*. The title role provides one of the supreme showpiece vehicles for coloratura soprano, climaxing in the famous Mad Scene (Act 3), while Act 2 has the celebrated Sextet, the finest of its kind in all opera.

In 1828 Donizetti had married his adored wife Virginia Vassellani, little knowing that he had already contracted syphilis when a student in Bologna. She gave birth to three children: the first boy was born deformed and survived for only two weeks; the second child, a girl, was stillborn; a second son died shortly after birth. Tragically, Virginia herself died after her third labour in 1837, at the age of just 29. Donizetti never fully recovered from this loss. He could not write her name in letters and could not even enter the room in which she died.

That same year, Donizetti was appointed director of the Naples Conservatory but left the post – and indeed left Italy – after a bitter controversy with the censors over his opera *Poliuto*, which depicted on stage the martyrdom of a saint. He set off for Paris. Revivals of his earlier operas and a string of new successes such as *La fille du régiment* and *La favorite* quickly made him as popular there as in

Italy. On a visit to Vienna in 1842 for the first performance of *Linda di Chamounix*, he was given a hero's welcome and made Court Composer and Master of the Imperial Chapel by the emperor. Riding the crest of the wave and continuing his colossal self-imposed workload, Donizetti was back in Paris the next year for the premiere of his comic tour de force *Don Pasquale* and the five-act grand opera *Dom Sébastien, roi de Portugal* – not a success at the time but a work that contains some of his finest music. In 1844 we find him in Naples for what would be his last opera, *Caterina Cornaro*. But then the relentless workaholic routine came grinding to a halt.

'His talent is great, but even greater is his fecundity, which is exceeded only by rabbits.'

HEINRICH HEINE

A WRETCHED END

Donizetti seems to have been an amiable, well-liked man with a sense of his own place in musical history, aware that he was the musical heir of Rossini but aware too when his time was up: 'My heyday is over,' he wrote in a letter of 1844, 'and another must take my place . . . Others have ceded their places to us and we must cede ours to still others . . . I am more than happy to give mine to people of talent like Verdi.' It was about this time that Donizetti's mental condition began to deteriorate. For some time he had complained of depressions, hallucinations and violent headaches; he then became cantankerous and, according to more than one source, compulsively addicted to sex. His deranged letters and strange behaviour eventually led to confinement in an asylum at Ivry, outside Paris, where he spent all of 1846 and half of 1847. According to the critic and poet Heinrich Heine, who visited him there, Donizetti would dress daily in full court regalia adorned with all his decorations, then 'sat immobile, his hat in his hand, from early in the morning till late in the evening. But that too has stopped. He recognises no-one. Such is the fortune of poor mankind.'

In October 1847 Donizetti was put into the care of his brother and taken back to Bergamo, where he died on 8 April 1848 from a combination of a fever and a series of strokes common in the terminal stage of syphilis.

NO END OF MISERY

POOR DONIZETTI WAS NOT ALLOWED TO REST IN PEACE AFTER HIS WRETCHED DEATH. His body was exhumed in 1875, when it was revealed that the cap of his skull had been removed. This was recovered from the director of a nearby asylum, but instead of being returned to the body it was placed in an urn in the Museo Donizettiano. It was not until 1951 that the Bergamo Municipal Council decided that the cap should rejoin the skull. The body was exhumed for a second time and the cap reverently fitted back onto the skull, secured with three pieces of transparent adhesive tape. The remains were then wrapped in fresh linen and the coffin resealed.

VINCENZO
BELLINI

The master of Italian bel canto

1801–35

IN HIS SHORT LIFE AND CAREER, VINCENZO BELLINI CHANGED THE FACE OF ITALIAN OPERA, laying the foundations for the later works of Verdi and Puccini. Unlike his near contemporaries Rossini and Donizetti, who could complete three or four operas a year, Bellini struggled with each one, shaping, structuring and experimenting. He wrote only ten operas in all, each one an advance on the previous one.

If he did not present his singers with enormous acting challenges, Bellini reviewed the dramatic content of the libretto and matched the emotion in the music to the moments when the characters and the story demanded it – a significant move away from the predominantly decorative vocal displays of earlier Italian opera. Singers were now asked to act in character and sing like birds. Nevertheless, while the vocal lines may have been less ornate than those of Rossini or Donizetti, few have composed such brilliant, agile music for the voice or such long-breathed decorative phrases. 'Long, long melodies, such as no one has written before', was how Verdi put it. Of course beautiful melodies had been written by opera composers before, but they had never been matched to the intensity that Bellini brought to his work.

EARLY YEARS

Bellini was born on 3 November 1801 in Catania, Sicily. Though he came from a family of musicians (both his father and grandfather were organists of Catania Cathedral and *maestri di cappella*), a musical career was opposed. Such was his ability, though, that friends of the family exerted pressure on his father to relent, and when the duke and duchess of San Martino offered to fund his studies at the Real Collegio di Musica di San Sebastiano in Naples, his father gave in. From 1819 Bellini was taught harmony, counterpoint and composition there, and in addition he made a close study of the works of Pergolesi, Jommelli, Paisiello and Cimarosa as well as the German classics. He proved to be a diligent student, writing several sinfonias, two masses, a cantata – *Ismene* in 1824 – a tuneful oboe concerto and his first opera, *Adelson e Salvini*. This was produced at the Conservatorium with such success that the San Carlo Opera of Naples commissioned him to write a one-act opera as a follow-up. What they got was a short two-act opera, *Bianca e Gernando* (1826), later revised and retitled *Bianca e Fernando* (1828).

The last of these was no mere apprenticeship work, as the critic Charles Osborne has pointed out, but 'the earliest of Bellini's operas in which his mature musical personality and style are readily apparent. Bianca is one of the great female characters worthy to stand beside Norma, Adina or Beatrice in his later operas *Norma*, *La Sonnambula* and *Beatrice di Tenda*.' Donizetti attended the premiere. It elicited from him a heartfelt if somewhat inaccurate response: 'the first production of our Bellini – bella! bella! bella! – especially as it is the first time he has composed anything.'

'Opera must make people weep, feel horrified, die through singing.'

BELLINI

GOLDEN YEARS

Bianca e Gernando led to another commission, this time from Italy's most prestigious house, La Scala. In April 1827 Bellini left Naples to live in Milan. Working with the experienced librettist Felice Romani, he wrote the work that secured his reputation internationally – *Il Pirata*, first performed in October 1827. It was a sensational success and productions were mounted soon afterwards in London, Vienna, Dresden, Madrid and elsewhere. Though popular with the public, Bellini's vocal writing was not immediately appreciated by his early interpreters, who were used to more showy, athletic arias. One, Adelaide Tosi, demanded that Bellini give her something more demanding and effective to wow the audience. Bellini refused, insisting that the music be sung as written. One wonders if Rossini or Donizetti would have done the same.

In 1828 Bellini fell in love with Giuditta Turina, the daughter of a wealthy silk merchant. She was beautiful, adoring, rich and married. The affair, tolerated by Giuditta's husband as long as it remained discreet, lasted five years, a relationship which, in Bellini's words, 'protected [him] from marriage'. Passionate though their relationship was (at least in the early stages), its duration coincided with his next three operas, which, though not failures, were relatively unsuccessful. *La Straniera* (first produced at La Scala in 1829) developed further the notion of placing the music wholeheartedly at the service of the drama. *Zaira* (Parma, 1829) was written in a hurry, circumstances in which Bellini did not produce his best work. *I Capuleti e i Montecchi*, first seen at La Fenice, Venice, in 1830, was based on one of the earlier Italian sources of the same story which Shakespeare used for *Romeo and Juliet*.

His next opera, however, premiered at Milan's Teatro Carcano in 1831, was a masterpiece. *La Sonnambula* (The Sleepwalker), his seventh opera, was a gentle romance set in a Swiss village which concerned the sleep-walking habits of the heroine, Amina. If Romani's story is proof that opera lovers do not go to the opera because of the plausibility of the plot, the role of Amina has always attracted the great coloratura sopranos, from Giuditta Pasta, the first Amina, Jenny Lind and Patti, to Galli-Curci, Callas and Sutherland.

By the time *La Sonnambula* was complete, Bellini's relationship with Giuditta Turina had faded and he was contemplating marriage with Clelia Pasta, the 13-year-old daughter of his inspiring leading soprano. In 1834, when Clelia was 16, he approached the Pastas to ask for her hand. The refusal was 'most polite but icy', and she was married off to one of her cousins soon afterwards. Despite affairs with other women, two proposals of marriage and three other prospective partners, none of whom could provide the minimum dowry of 200,000 francs he demanded, Bellini never married.

La Sonnambula was followed by the greatest of all Bellini's operas, *Norma*. The story of a Druid priestess (Pasta again created the title role) who breaks her vow of chastity and self-immolates on a pyre could not have been in greater contrast to *La Sonnambula*. The orchestration, too, reveals a greater independence, the music has more vigour, the choruses are more magnificent – and the title role is an Everest of the soprano's repertoire, immensely long and

A TEARFUL AFFAIR

'PASTA AND RUBINI SANG WITH THE MOST EVIDENT ENTHUSIASM to support their favourite composer. In the second act the singers themselves wept, and carried their audience along with them, so that . . . tears were continually being wiped away in boxes and stalls alike. Embracing Shterich in the Ambassador's box, I too shed tears of emotion and ecstasy.'

THE RUSSIAN COMPOSER GLINKA AFTER THE FIRST NIGHT OF *LA SONNAMBULA*

vocally taxing. One famous Norma, Lilli Lehmann (1848–1929), said she would rather sing three Brünnhildes than one Norma. Her aria 'Casta diva' has a claim to be the most popular of all soprano operatic arias. The first night at La Scala was a disaster – Bellini was in tears after the performance – but it quickly established itself for what it was: 'A great score that speaks from the heart,' in Wagner's words, 'A work of genius.'

A SUDDEN END

During the composition of his next opera, *Beatrice di Tenda*, Bellini and Romani quarrelled, and it was received with only luke-warm enthusiasm at its premiere at La Fenice, Venice, in March 1833.

Essential works

Oboe concerto (c.1825)
IL PIRATA, opera (1827)
I CAPULETI E I MONTECCHI, opera (1830)
LA SONNAMBULA, opera (1831)
NORMA, opera (1831)
I PURITANI, opera (1835)

Afterwards Bellini set off for London and then to Paris, where he remained for the last two years of his life. There he befriended Rossini and Chopin.

His partnership with Romani at an end, Bellini's final opera, *I Puritani*, had a libretto by Count Carlo Pepoli, an Italian exile living in Paris. Its four leading characters were sung by the four leading singers of the day, Grisi, Rubini, Tamburini and Lablache. The first performance was on 25 January 1835 at the Théâtre Italien. Eight months later, Bellini was dead. A few weeks short of his 34th birthday, he was stricken with a fatal inflammation of the large intestine exacerbated by an abscess of the liver. He died at the home of an English friend at Puteaux, on the outskirts of Paris, on 23 September. Bellini was buried in the cemetery of Père Lachaise, but in 1876 his remains were removed to the cathedral of Catania.

BEL CANTO

BELLINI'S WRITING EPITOMIZES THE ITALIAN *BEL CANTO* ('beautiful singing') school of singing, a somewhat imprecise term used to describe the style of vocalization that emphasizes beauty and evenness of tone (sound), fine legato (smooth) phrasing and perfection of technique. *Bel canto* contrasts with the German tradition of a more dramatic approach and greater emotional expression, and had a strong influence on both Berlioz and Chopin. Tellingly, Bellini once remarked to a friend after listening to Pergolesi's *Stabat mater*: 'If I could write one melody as beautiful as this, I would not mind dying young like Pergolesi.' It was a hauntingly prescient comment: his first opera was produced in 1825, his last just ten years later.

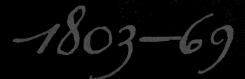

Hector
BERLIOZ

The high priest of Romantic fervour

1803—69

BERLIOZ IS THE ARCHETYPAL ROMANTIC COMPOSER, his music a product of impulse and instinct unfettered by convention and rules. His life, like his music, was all you would expect of a romantic: ecstatic and melancholic by turn, turbulent, passionate, eccentric, excessive and egotistic. Everything is extreme about Berlioz, a revolutionary writing in revolutionary times. The poet Heinrich Heine described him in a wonderfully resonant phrase as 'like an immense nightingale, a lark as great as an eagle . . . the music causes me to dream of fabulous empires filled with fabulous sins.'

Not all Berlioz's contemporaries were as complimentary. To some, his music sounded very strange with its irregular rhythms and complex orchestration. Mendelssohn met Berlioz in Italy in 1832 and thought him 'a regular freak without a vestige of talent'. Chopin was convinced that 'he composes by splashing his pen over the manuscript and leaving the issue to chance'. Schumann was one of those who got the point: 'Berlioz does not try to be elegant,' he wrote. 'What he hates, he grasps fiercely by the hair; what he loves, he almost crushes in his fervour.'

EARLY YEARS

Medicine was Berlioz's intended career – at least, the career intended for him by his father. Berlioz père was a cultured, well-to-do country doctor practising in La Côte-Saint-André near Grenoble in south-eastern France. Louis-Hector (but always known as Hector) was born there on 11 December 1803, one of five children only three of whom survived into adulthood. He toyed with the flute and guitar as a youngster, but his instrument was to be the orchestra, his inspiration love and literature. Berlioz is almost unique among the great composers in being unable to play proficiently a single musical instrument.

In 1821 Berlioz went off dutifully to Paris to study medicine, simultaneously taking private music lessons from Jean-François Le Sueur. Three years later, in opposition to his parents, he abandoned medicine and enrolled at the Conservatoire with Le Sueur (for composition) and Anton Reicha (counterpoint and fugue). Le Sueur had lost the directorship of Notre Dame 30 years earlier for making his sacred music too 'dramatic' and 'descriptive'. This was exactly what Berlioz would set about doing with a vengeance.

In a single blow Berlioz was struck by two inspirational forces in September 1827. He went to see the celebrated Anglo-Irish actress Harriet Smithson as Ophelia in a production of *Hamlet*. If Shakespeare became his idol, Berlioz was completely infatuated with Harriet. He rented rooms near her, bombarded her with love letters, put on a concert of his work to impress her – all to no avail. Over the following three years, Berlioz worked on an orchestral symphony, an autobiography-in-music of his feelings for Miss Smithson. He arranged the first performance of the completed work, the *Symphonie fantastique*, to coincide with her return to Paris. Though the work was received with great acclaim, Miss Smithson was not present.

'Love cannot express the idea of music, while music may give an idea of love.'

BERLIOZ

69

UNDYING LOVE

BERLIOZ WAS 12 WHEN HE FIRST FELL IN LOVE. The girl was Estelle Duboeuf, seven years older than himself, and although it was a platonic holiday romance and he saw her only twice more, he remained entranced by the idealized memory of his feelings for her for the rest of his life. When he was 20, he wrote a little opera about love called *Estelle et Némorin*. When he was 60 and she a widow of 67 with six children, he sought her out again. She did not remember him. He proposed marriage. She turned him down, but they corresponded until his death. That would have pleased Berlioz, never happier than when in the grip of unrequited love and romantic misery.

LOVER, COMPOSER, CONDUCTOR

During the period of composition of this masterpiece, Berlioz had tried three times unsuccessfully to win the prestigious Prix de Rome, which entitled its recipient to study free in Rome for four years. Tired of waiting for Miss Smithson, Berlioz transferred his affections to a second-rate pianist named Marie-Félicité-Denise Moke. After a passionate (of course) affair, the two became engaged. When, at the fourth attempt, he finally won the Prix de Rome in 1830, Berlioz left Paris and his fiancée for the Eternal City, only to find that he disliked both the food and the music of Italy as well as the musical instruction. To make matters worse, he learned that Marie had begun an affair with an older lover, her fellow pianist Camille Pleyel who later took over his father's piano manufacturing business and made a fortune. Incandescent with rage, Berlioz set off for Paris disguised as a lady's maid and armed with a brace of pistols intent on killing Marie Moke and her mother, Camille Pleyel and then himself. While in Genoa, however, he mislaid his disguise. By the time he had found a replacement, he had calmed down and returned meekly to Rome.

Back in Paris in 1832, Berlioz took an apartment in Rue Neuve-Saint-Marc only to discover that, by coincidence, it had been vacated the previous day by none other than Harriet Smithson. To Berlioz, this was Fate calling. He arranged a second performance of the *Symphonie fantastique*. This time the bewildered actress answered the call, heard, saw and was conquered, though her feelings may have been swayed by the fact that her career had stumbled and that she was also, perhaps not coincidentally, bankrupt. Despite the violent opposition of both their families, the couple were married in October 1833. Almost inevitably, the marriage was not a success. After he had won the object of his affections, the chase was over. He spoke no English and she no French. A son, Louis, was born in August the following year, but after several volatile

Essential works

SYMPHONIE FANTASTIQUE (1830)

HAROLD IN ITALY, viola and orchestra (1834)

REQUIEM (GRANDE MESSE DES MORTS) (1837)

ROMÉO ET JULIETTE, dramatic symphony (1839)

LES NUITS D'ÉTÉ, six songs (1841)

THE DAMNATION OF FAUST, dramatic cantata (1845–6)

TE DEUM (1849–50)

L'ENFANCE DU CHRIST, oratorio (1850–4)

years in poverty – Harriet turned out to be a shrew and an alcoholic – they decided to live apart. By then, Berlioz had already taken up with an old-established mistress, a mediocre singer called Marie Reci, and the year after Harriet died in March 1853 aged 53, he married Marie. To his credit, Berlioz supported his first wife until her death and always gratefully acknowledged her inspiration. Alas, his second marriage proved equally unhappy. It lasted for eight years until Marie, too, died.

Berlioz had a unique ability to transfer literary and dramatic works into musical form. Shakespeare dominates (there are overtures or operas based on *Hamlet, King Lear, The Tempest, Romeo and Juliet,* and *Much Ado About Nothing*), but Scott is there too (the overtures *Waverley* and *Rob Roy*), as are Virgil (*Les Troyens*), Byron (*Childe Harolde, The Corsair*), Goethe (*Faust*) and many others. Another feature of Berlioz's Romantic spirit was his love of the grandiose. For his *Grande messe des morts* (Requiem), he suggested 700 to 800 voices where possible, with an orchestra of 150 stringed instruments, woodwind, brass, 16 kettledrums and four brass bands. For his celebratory cantata *L'impériale* in 1855, he assembled an orchestra, military band and chorus of 1200. These he conducted, keeping the mighty forces in time by holding his baton in his right hand and, in his left, an 'electric metronome' which passed on the tempo to five sub-conductors.

It was not merely a demand for huge forces that made Berlioz's music exceptional. Nobody previously had studied the refinements of orchestral sound as thoroughly as Berlioz, and if melody, harmony and form were of secondary consideration, his skill as an orchestrator was truly fresh and innovative, advancing the potential of the orchestra to an undreamt-of degree. Liszt, Wagner and the Russians were the immediate beneficiaries of his genius. He left a famous treatise on orchestration which continues to influence composers to the present day.

END IN DESPAIR

Yet, unlike Liszt and Wagner, Berlioz had no cult following during his lifetime. He wrote no solo works as a result of which his name might have appeared regularly on concert programmes, and he had enormous difficulty mounting his operas and stage works. He himself began to believe he was a failure and the last seven years of his life were miserable, overshadowed by illness and resentment at his country's inability to recognize him for what he was. After Marie died of a heart attack in 1862, he spent three years finishing his memoirs (published at his own expense, but still among the most entertaining and vivid of all composer autobiographies). In 1867 he suffered the cruellest blow of all: the death of his seafaring son Louis from yellow fever while in Havana. 'It is Shakespeare that is our father,' he wrote despairingly, ' our father in heaven, if there is a heaven. I say hourly to Death: "When you will." Why does he delay?'

Berlioz was consigned to bed in January 1869, sank into a coma and died on 8 March. He was carried to his resting place in Montmartre by Charles Gounod, Ambroise Thomas and other famous French musicians to the accompaniment of his own funeral march from the *Grande symphonie funèbre et triomphale*.

LINK THROUGH TIME

THOUGH BERLIOZ WAS BORN OVER 200 YEARS AGO, he lived recently enough to be photographed. There is even a gramophone recording – only one, mind you – which has a direct link to Berlioz. In 1928 the elderly French pianist Francis Planté recorded his own piano transcription of the Serenade from *The Damnation of Faust,* an arrangement he had played 60 years earlier to the composer's enthusiastic approval.

Felix
MENDELSSOHN

The Mozart of the nineteenth century
SCHUMANN

1809–47

OF ALL THE GREAT COMPOSERS, NONE LED SUCH A HAPPY, UNTROUBLED EXISTENCE AS FELIX MENDELSSOHN. 'Felix' is Latin for 'happy' – an auspicious choice, for it reflects exactly the character of the man and the music he composed. His family was enormously affluent and cultured. Praised, constantly encouraged throughout his life (though not spoilt) – at no point did he have to give a second thought to where the next meal was coming from. This alone is enough to diminish him in the eyes of some critics, who feel that, had he known hardship, his talent would have developed more than it did and the emotional range of his music would have broadened. As a result, to paraphrase the conductor, composer and pianist Hans von Bülow, Mendelssohn would not have 'begun as a genius and ended as a talent'.

Mendelssohn had an astonishing melodic gift and the powerful ability to express youthful exuberance, triumph, poetic fantasy, tenderness, serenity and life's joys in a way that few have ever equalled. He was one of musical history's most astonishing prodigies, on a par with Mozart, Saint-Saëns and Korngold. Indeed, Mendelssohn wrote music of far greater maturity when he was 16 than Mozart had written at a similar age. The string Octet, composed when Mendelssohn was just 16, is unquestionably one of the supreme masterpieces of chamber music. The Overture to *A Midsummer Night's Dream*, written a year later, is doubly miraculous as the work of an adolescent. His style seems to have been pre-formed, for his adult voice is already there with its unique 'light, aerial, fairy' touches.

EARLY YEARS

Jakob Ludwig Felix Mendelssohn was born on 3 February 1809. His father Abraham was a powerful Hamburg banker. By talent, toil and opportunism, he had raised the family from Berlin's Jewish ghetto. Lea, Abraham's wife, came from a family of brilliant Berlin Jews. She was a gifted artist, could read Homer in the original, and spoke French, German and Italian. Both Felix and his sister Fanny were exceptionally talented, studying violin, piano, languages and drawing from an early age (their younger sister Rebecca sang and younger brother Paul played the cello). As soon as it was clear that music was to be their children's future, Abraham and Lea decided to convert them from the Jewish faith to Protestantism – a pragmatic step, for many paths in the musical world were closed to Jews. Later, both parents followed suit, adding 'Bartholdy' to their name to distinguish them from other Mendelssohns (Felix later dropped the addition).

By the age of nine, Felix was a good enough pianist to appear in public; by 12 he had composed several string symphonies, two operas, fugues for string quartet and other works. He learnt from Bach (fugal techniques), Handel and Mozart (harmony, form, textures) and Beethoven (orchestral and instrumental technique). He was content to use traditional structures like the symphony and sonata but invested them with his own Romantic inclination: literature and geographical and historical subjects were his inspiration.

Mendelssohn was made to rise every day at 5 o'clock for a period of study. To the family's work ethic and comfortable existence was added a continual influx to the Mendelssohn house of the distinguished and influential. In the summer of 1825, the family moved in Berlin from the Neue Promenade to

3 Leipzigerstrasse, a palatial mansion of 40 or so rooms set in seven acres of parkland. A garden house seated two or three hundred people for concerts. Regular visitors, who included the composers Weber, Spohr, Cherubini and Moscheles, and the poets Heine and Müller (two of Schubert's collaborators), were incredulous at the talents of the young Mendelssohn. When the 12-year-old was taken to Weimar to be introduced to the mighty Goethe, then 70 years old and a living legend, the two became firm friends.

INCESSANT WORK

The Octet and the Overture to *A Midsummer Night's Dream* were enough to establish Mendelssohn's name internationally. Extraordinarily, however, it was only after he had completed three years of study at Berlin University that he decided on a career in music. When he was just 20, he conducted a performance of Bach's *St Matthew Passion* (albeit in a shortened version) at the Berlin Singakademie. It was the first time the work had been performed in public since Bach's death in 1750 (it is said that 1000 people had to be turned away) and it led to a general revival of interest in Bach's music. Not long afterwards Mendelssohn made the first of ten visits to Britain during which he gave the first English performance of Beethoven's 'Emperor' Concerto. From London he travelled to Scotland, a visit during which he met Sir Walter Scott and one that inspired his *Fingal's Cave* (*Hebrides*) Overture and the 'Scottish' Symphony.

In May 1830 Mendelssohn embarked on a grand tour of Europe. Of the six countries he visited, Italy impressed him most, giving rise to one of his most popular works, the 'Italian' Symphony. After a brief spell as musical director of the Lower Rhine Festival in Düsseldorf, in 1835 Mendelssohn was made conductor of the prestigious Leipzig Gewandhaus Orchestra. Over the next five years, he turned the orchestra into the world's finest. His care over preparation and interpretation proved to be a turning point in the evolution of conducting.

Mendelssohn was a most eligible bachelor. Despite being somewhat priggish, he was an athletic, good-looking man with a high forehead and dark-brown curly locks; and he was, naturally, always expensively dressed in silk and cashmere cravats and beautifully tailored frock coats. Fanny was Felix's mother confessor, sounding board, yardstick and inspiration. It has been said that the correspondence between the two reads like a series of love letters.

In 1836, having been by all accounts oblivious to the charms of the opposite sex until then, Mendelssohn met and fell in love with Cécile Jeanrenaud, the 17-year-old daughter of a French Protestant clergyman. When they married the following year, Fanny could hardly conceal her jealousy (neither she or her mother could bring themselves to attend the wedding), but it was a union that proved to be idyllically

Essential *works*

Octet for strings (1825)
Overture to A MIDSUMMER NIGHT'S
  DREAM (1826)
FINGAL'S CAVE (HEBRIDES) Overture
  (1830)
Piano Concerto No. 1 (1832)
Symphony No. 4 'Italian' (1833)
Symphony No. 2 'Hymn of Praise' (1840)
VARIATIONS SÉRIEUSES, piano (1841)
Violin Concerto (1844)
SONGS WITHOUT WORDS, piano
  (1829–45)
ELIJAH, oratorio (1846)

happy and one that produced five children.

In 1843 Mendelssohn fulfilled a long-held ambition by founding a new conservatory of music in Leipzig, a project in which he was assisted by Robert and Clara Schumann. All this time he had been working at a furious pace, composing, conducting, teaching, giving concerts and raising a family. His health began to decline, and he suffered headaches and recurrent bouts of abnormal fatigue. In August 1846 he visited Birmingham for the triumphant premiere of his oratorio *Elijah*, and in the spring of the following year he made his final visit to England, where he had become firm friends with Prince Albert and Queen Victoria, both fervent and long-time admirers. A British acquaintance noted that the composer looked old beyond his years, tired and drawn 'like someone entering middle-age'.

> *'Even the smallest task in music is so absorbing, and carries us so far away from town, country, earth, and all worldly things, that it is truly a blessed gift of God.'*
>
> MENDELSSOHN

KILLED BY GRIEF

It was in May 1847 that Mendelssohn received news that his beloved sister had died (from a paralytic stroke mid-rehearsal, it is said, while conducting one of her brother's works). Fanny's loss had a devastating effect on him, causing him to faint and rupturing a blood vessel in the brain. Inconsolable with grief, he returned to Germany. On medical advice, he moved his entire family to Switzerland in an attempt to stabilize his physical and mental health. Suffering terrible depressions and agonizing pain, he returned to Leipzig in late September, determined to retire from public life and concentrate on composing. But he never recovered and, after a steady decline, died in his sleep at 9.24 pm on 4 November 1847. To all intents and purposes, Felix Mendelssohn had died with his sister.

Following a massive funeral service in Berlin, Mendelssohn was laid to rest in the family plot in the Dreifaltigheits Kirchhof next to his sister. Memorial services were held not only in most of the major cities of Germany but also in London, Manchester, Birmingham and Paris.

HERE COMES THE BRIDE . . .

MENDELSSOHN'S MUSIC IS FAMILIAR TO MANY WHO WOULD SCARCELY RECOGNIZE HIS NAME. His Wedding March (1842), from the incidental music to *A Midsummer Night's Dream,* has sent countless thousands of happy couples down the aisle since the tradition was established by the fashionable royal wedding of Queen Victoria's daughter, the Princess Royal, in 1858. One of our most popular Christmas carols, 'Hark! the Herald Angels Sing', is sung to music by Mendelssohn. The tune, far from being conceived as a carol, is in fact the second section of his choral work *Festgesang* (1840), written in praise of the invention of printing. It was adapted by an English organist, W.H. Cummings, to fit verses by Charles Wesley and first appeared in 1856 in the form in which we know it today. 'O for the Wings of a Dove', from the motet *Hear My Prayer* (1844), became one of the gramophone's first million-sellers through its inspirational recording in 1927 by the Temple Church Choir and treble soloist Ernest Lough.

FRÉDÉRIC
CHOPIN

The poet of the piano

18-10—49

CHOPIN DIFFERS FROM MOST OTHER GREAT COMPOSERS in three main respects: he wrote no symphonies, no operas, no ballets, very little chamber music and no church music; his chief claim to immortality does not rely on large-scale works but on miniature forms; and every single composition, regardless of form, involves the piano. For him, the piano was his entire *raison d'être*.

A high percentage of Chopin's relatively modest musical output has remained consistently popular with artists and audiences alike. Two factors have contributed to this: first, the extraordinary fecundity of his melodic, harmonic, rhythmic and structural ideas; secondly, his hypersensitive self-criticism – very few works he authorized for publication fall below his own high standards. He was responsible, more than any other composer, for the development of modern piano technique and style, and his influence on succeeding generations of writers for the instrument was profound and inescapable. When music is described as being 'Chopinesque', we know at once what it will sound like.

EARLY LIFE

For all his enduring fame, Chopin's life and character reveal a mass of contradictions and paradoxes. Though considered the greatest of all Polish composers, his father was French. Nicolas Chopin had gone to Poland as a young man and become a tutor to the family of the Countess Skarbek at Zelazowa Wola, a small village about 20 miles west of Warsaw. His mother, descended from minor Polish nobility, was the countess's lady-in-waiting. Fryderyk Franciszek Chopin was born on or around 1 March 1810 (the exact date is uncertain). His dual nationality was, consciously or not, reflected in his music: the legacy of his homeland and its culture tempered by the refined elegance of the French.

'My universe will be the soul and heart of man.'
CHOPIN

The family moved to Warsaw when Chopin was a few months old. He had his first piano lessons aged six from Adalbert Zywny and in 1825 became a student of Jósef Elsner at the Warsaw Conservatory. It is largely due to Zywny and Elsner that Chopin matured into an original creative personality, for they saw his exceptional gifts and allowed them to flourish in their own way. 'Leave him in peace,' replied Elsner to someone who had reproached the young Chopin for his disregard of conventional musical rules. 'His is an uncommon way because his gifts are uncommon.'

Chopin first found his voice in a set of variations on Mozart's 'Là ci darem la mano' (from *Don Giovanni*) which he introduced to Vienna in 1828, prompting the youthful Robert Schumann (just four months Chopin's junior) to famously pronounce in print: 'Hats off, gentlemen! A genius.' The fading attractions of Warsaw persuaded him to seek his fortune away from Poland, and in 1831 he moved to Paris, which was to become his home for the rest of his life.

LIFE IN PARIS

At first Chopin struggled to find his feet but that all changed when he was introduced to the salon of Baron Jacques de Rothschild, a member of one of the wealthiest and most influential families in Paris. In this environment, Chopin triumphed. The rich, privileged world of the nobility not only

CHOPIN LIVE

What was it like to listen to Chopin playing the piano? There are many contemporary descriptions, few more vivid than the 17-year-old Charles Hallé, later founder of the famous Manchester orchestra. On 2 December 1836 he wrote to his parents:

'I heard – Chopin. That was beyond all words. The few senses I had have quite left me. I could have jumped into the Seine. Everything I hear now seems so insignificant that I would rather not hear it at all. Chopin! He is no man, he is an angel, a god (or what can I say more?). Chopin's compositions played by Chopin! That is a joy never to be surpassed . . . There is nothing to remind one that it is a human being who produces this music. It seems to descend from heaven – so pure, so clear, so spiritual. I feel a thrill each time I think of it.'

appealed to his instincts but also provided the perfect ambience for his music and particular style of playing. While his friend Liszt was the epitome of the dashing, romantic virtuoso, Chopin was the tasteful, undemonstrative poet. His perfect manners and aristocratic bearing made him an irresistible attraction to the world he had entered, and within a matter of months he had moved into a luxury apartment, boasted his own carriage and manservant, and was dressed in the height of fashion. Regarded as one of the stars of the pianistic firmament, his music attracted publishers (and high prices) and he was in constant demand as a teacher. Fryderyk Franciszek became Frédéric François.

After his two magnificent piano concertos of 1829 and 1830, Chopin never again used the orchestra in any of his works but instead concentrated on producing the inimitable compositions that came to define him: the two sets of études in which, for the first time, technical exercises were subsumed into the poetry of sublime music; the first of the series of 62 mature mazurkas, a dance form that Chopin elevated to concert status; the first of his 21 nocturnes; the first of 19 extant waltzes; the first of the four ballades, and the four scherzi, both forms of short tone poems for the piano which Chopin invented; and the continuing series of polonaises (some 16 in all, the earliest of which he had written as boy of eight).

Chopin was a sensitive, fastidious, physically frail man who never enjoyed robust health. Until 1835 his only recorded love interest – unrequited – had been a young soprano in Warsaw. All his emotions were poured into his music. In the summer of 1835 Chopin fell in love with Maria, the flirtatious daughter of Count Wodzinska, whose family he had known well in Warsaw. His lukewarm courtship coincided with a period of worse than normal health, and one in which Chopin suffered the first of many bouts of bronchitis and coughed up particles of blood, the early symptoms of what would prove to be tuberculosis. The Wodzinska family, determined that Maria should not marry anyone with so fragile a constitution, terminated the affair.

Chopin's next relationship, in stark contrast, was with the intellectual novelist and socialist George Sand, the pseudonym of Amandine Aurore Lucie Dupin, Baronne Dudevant (1804–76). As notorious for her colourful love life as she was for wearing men's clothes and smoking cigars, she did not impress Chopin initially. 'What a repellent woman she is,' he reacted. 'Is she really a woman? I'm ready to doubt it.' But her brilliant mind and dynamic personality fascinated him and a relationship developed that lasted for ten years during which Chopin wrote some of his finest music. She knew she had captured a genius and provided the stability for which he yearned, a mother figure who catered to all his needs. From her letters, we know that the physical side of the relationship was embraced with less than whole-hearted enthusiasm by the composer.

to eight children as well as having several pregnancies that did not reach full term. Yet, beneath the veneer, there were conflicts and tensions. For Robert to work in silence – silence punctuated, one assumes, by the shrieks of young children – Clara had to forego her daily practice routine so that the ambitions she housed for her husband could be realized. For any professional instrumentalist, that is an almost inconceivable sacrifice. Somehow, however, this extraordinary woman managed to maintain her playing career while being almost constantly pregnant, mothering her children, and supporting her husband. Clara was far more famous as a performer than Robert was as a composer, and he disliked being in her shadow. How galling for him, during a concert tour that took the couple to Russia in 1844, to be introduced as 'the husband of Clara Schumann'. At one musical soirée in St Petersburg, a nobleman asked Robert: 'Are you, too, a musician?'

'Everything beautiful is difficult, the short the most difficult.'
SCHUMANN

More contentiously, not all of Clara's ambitions for her husband were fitted to his temperament or technique. Schumann's genius flowered most imaginatively when uninhibited by formal structures. Though his four symphonies are much loved, critics have always pointed to their many defects in texture and orchestration. His choral music is rarely heard, while his operatic writing is the least successful part of his output: having little sense of theatre, his intense labours on his one opera *Genoveva* have not been repaid by popularity.

A DOWNWARD SPIRAL

After his return from Russia Schumann, suffering many symptoms of nervous breakdown, resigned from the editorship of the *Neue Zeitschrift für Musik* and from the teaching post that Mendelssohn had created for him in 1843 at the new Leipzig Conservatory. The couple moved to Dresden in the hope that Schumann's mental equilibrium could be restored. Music poured from him: the Piano Concerto was completed here, as were the Second Symphony and more vocal music and works for solo piano. But from the late 1840s it was clear that he was becoming increasingly unbalanced.

In 1850 Schumann accepted the post of Director of Music in Düsseldorf. It proved to be a disaster, for Schumann (though both he and Clara refused to admit it) was no conductor. Wagner and Liszt found him boring. He became increasingly depressed, unable to communicate and unaware of his surroundings, and after one particularly calamitous concert in October 1853 he was forced, humiliatingly, to resign. One benefit of his time in Düsseldorf was his meeting and subsequent friendship with the 21-year-old Brahms. A brief, touching note in his diary records their first encounter: 'Brahms to see me (a genius).'

In Düsseldorf, on 27 February 1854, wearing only his dressing gown and bedroom slippers, Schumann rushed from his house and jumped from a bridge into the freezing waters of the Rhine. He was rescued by two fishermen and then taken to a private asylum at Endenich near Bonn where he remained for the rest of his life. Though Brahms was a welcome visitor (he once disturbed Schumann obsessively making alphabetical lists of towns and countries), the next time Clara saw her husband was two-and-a-half years later, a few days before his death. She hardly recognized him, he had aged so much. He died in her arms at 4.00 in the afternoon of 29 July 1856. He was 46. The following day he was buried in the Alter Friedhof cemetery in Bonn. Opinions differ on the cause of his final illness, but whether it was tertiary syphilis, sclerosis of the brain (his own doctor's verdict), dementia praecox or starvation induced by psychotic depression, it was the least romantic of ends for this most romantic of composers.

FRANZ LISZT

'Mephistopheles disguised as an Abbé'

18-1-1-86

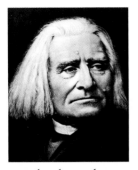

FRANZ LISZT WAS ONE OF THE SEMINAL FIGURES AND MOST SIGNIFICANT COMPOSERS OF THE 19TH CENTURY. His detractors see little but grand gestures, superficiality and vulgarity. It is true that some of his music has these traits, but even a brief acquaintance with his achievements shows how such criticism is itself superficial. Liszt worked in almost every field of music, and to each he contributed a significant development. The descriptive orchestral one-movement symphonic (or tone) poem was his invention. He developed the idea of 'thematic transformation', a device particularly associated with Wagner's operas, in which brief phrases are used to create subtle evocations of mood, character and events. He experimented, too, with harmony, unprepared modulations into unrelated keys, and even with atonality and dissonance.

The piano was Liszt's principle means of expression. As a performer, he was one of the very greatest pianists in history. None of his contemporaries could compete with his power, brilliance and sheer volume, let alone personal magnetism (he was a strikingly handsome man). He invented the concept of the solo piano recital, and was among the first to play complete programmes from memory. He made the piano sexy and the music he wrote for the instrument was equally liberating, adventurous and experimental. Liszt was a colossus as a man, as a performer and as a composer, generous with the wealth of music he left us and with all those who came into contact with him.

EARLY YEARS

He was born Ferenc Liszt on 22 October 1811 at Raiding, near Ödenberg in Hungary. His father, an excellent musician, was an official on the Esterházy estate. The young Liszt was a *wunderkind*: at the age of nine he played Hummel's difficult B minor Piano Concerto in public and extemporized on themes submitted by the audience. His musical education was arranged by Prince Esterházy and other aristocrats, allowing him to study in Vienna with the revered Carl Czerny, who, however, refused to accept any payment for the pleasure of teaching him. Liszt studied composition with none other than Antonio Salieri, who had played such a significant role in Mozart's life. He played for Beethoven ('Devil of a fellow!' exclaimed the great man as he kissed the boy's brow. 'Such a young rascal!') and saw the first of his compositions published.

Still aged only 12, Liszt took off for Paris. Failing to gain admission to the Conservatory (the director, Cherubini, disliked child prodigies and foreigners), he continued with private studies while establishing a reputation as one of the foremost living pianists. In 1827 Liszt's father died suddenly. For the next few years, exhausted by touring, he bowed out of the limelight, teaching, reading everything he could lay hands on and embarking on the first of his many affairs with the 16-year-old daughter of the French minister of commerce. For a time he

'The most important germinative force in modern music.'

CECIL GRAY

MUSICAL PROPHET

THE FAMOUS CHORD WITH WHICH WAGNER'S OPERA *TRISTAN UND ISOLDE* OPENS (the so-called 'Tristan chord', cited as the first indication that music could dispense with tonality) was used, with one small difference, by Liszt in a song written in 1845, years before *Tristan* was conceived. Wagner, writing in 1839, admitted that, 'since my acquaintance with Liszt's compositions, my treatment of harmony has become very different to what it was.' As early as 1837, Liszt incorporated the whole tone scale into the Dante Sonata, and his late piano pieces contain experiments with atonality. In these and his little-known oratorios his unconventional devices anticipate the methods of Debussy, Bartók and Schoenberg.

considered changing career, first to religion, then to philosophy and literature. But then he encountered three musicians who were to change everything: Chopin, Berlioz and Paganini. Chopin's refined, tasteful, poetic style was a revelation to him, as were the orchestral sonorities and large-scale conceptions he encountered in Berlioz's music. But it was the electrifying stage presence of Paganini and the spectacular demands of his music that immediately fired his imagination. For two years, from 1832 to 1833, he shut himself away to achieve his objective of emulating on the piano what Paganini wrought on the violin.

LISZTOMANIA

Liszt's re-emergence on the concert platform was a major artistic event. Those who heard him at the time were left speechless, for even the most seasoned observers had never witnessed such power and skill at the keyboard. 'For him,' wrote one, 'there were no difficulties of execution, the most incredible seeming like child's play under his fingers.' From 1833 to 1847 his life was dominated by composing and touring all over Europe, a period in which he amassed a huge fortune. In 1834 Liszt met and fell in love with the beautiful Comtesse Marie d'Agoult. Though married with three children, within a year she had left them to live with Liszt. Their first child, Blandine, was born in December 1834 (she died in 1867), followed by Cosima in 1837 and Daniel in 1839. Daniel, too, died young at the age of only 20, but Cosima, destined to become the wife of Richard Wagner, survived until 1930.

The relationship with Marie d'Agoult gradually disintegrated, but while on a

Essential works

Piano Concerto No. 1 (1849, rev. 1853 and 1856)

Piano Concerto No. 2 (1839, rev. 1849–61)

TOTENTANZ, piano and orchestra (1849, rev. 1853 and 1859)

ANNÉES DE PÈLERINAGE, books 1, 2 and 3, piano solo (1848–77)

12 ÉTUDES D'EXÉCUTION TRANSCENDANTE, piano solo (1851)

19 Hungarian Rhapsodies, piano solo (1846–85)

Piano Sonata (1853)

RÉMINISCENCES DE DON JUAN, piano solo (1841)

Fantasia and Fugue on AD NOS, AD SALUTAREM UNDAM, organ solo (1850)

A FAUST SYMPHONY (1854–7)

LES PRÉLUDES, symphonic poem (1848)

concert trip to Kiev in 1847 he met the Polish-born princess Carolyne Sayn-Wittgenstein, a cigar-smoking, unhappily married intellectual. This was Liszt's last great love, and their shared love of religion and mysticism propelled the princess to abandon her husband and 30,000 serfs to join Liszt in Weimar, where he had been made Kapellmeister to the grand duke.

Turning his back on the life of the travelling virtuoso, Liszt spent the 11 years between 1848 and 1859 transforming Weimar into a world centre for music. Here he conducted symphonic works and operas both of the standard literature and by his contemporaries. These included a revival of Wagner's *Tannhäuser* and the world premiere of *Lohengrin* – works by a political revolutionary sought by the authorities – and the first German performances of many of Berlioz's works. Piano students flocked to him from all over the world. How he also, during these years, managed to compose the bulk of his music is quite mystifying. The amount he produced was simply staggering: 12 symphonic poems, the Faust and Dante Symphonies, two concertos and Totentanz for piano and orchestra, the B minor Piano Sonata (one of the great works of the instrument's literature), to name merely some of the best known, as well as literally hundreds of other new pieces and revisions of music he had written in the 1830s and 1840s.

FINAL YEARS

In 1859 Liszt resigned from his musical duties in Weimar. Attracted again by the religious life, from 1861 for the next decade he and the princess made their home in Rome. From 1871 until his death, he divided his time between the Eternal City and teaching piano in Pesth (now Budapest) and Weimar. He reviewed concerts, gave concerts, continued to compose, and wrote a voluminous number of letters every day in French and German. He taught (without taking a fee) students from all over Europe and America, numbering among them such keyboard lions as Carl Tausig, Hans von Bülow (the first husband of his daughter Cosima) and others who lived well into the 20th century, including d'Albert, Rosenthal, Lamond, de Greef and von Sauer. In addition, Liszt offered unstinting encouragement and advice to young composers. His influence, directly or indirectly, on the following generation of composers is hard to exaggerate: Borodin, Balakirev, Rimsky-Korsakoff, MacDowell, Smetana, Debussy, Saint-Saëns, Fauré, Grieg and Brahms all benefited in some way from Liszt's wisdom.

In 1886, though now frail and suffering from dropsy, Liszt made a final tour, visiting Pesth, Liège, Paris and London, where his engagements included a private recital at Windsor Castle for Queen Victoria. In July he travelled to Bayreuth for the festival but had to be taken from the auditorium during a performance of his son-in-law's *Tristan und Isolde*. Dropsy had developed into pneumonia. He died there on 31 July.

A MASS OF CONTRADICTIONS

PART OF THE FASCINATION OF LISZT LIES IN HIS CONTRADICTORY PERSONALITY. He could be as arrogant and egocentric as, at other times, he was humble and self-effacing; he was profoundly spiritual, yet delighted in the pleasures of the flesh – he had at least 26 major love affairs and fathered several illegitimate children; he was attracted to the life of a recluse, yet loved luxury and the adulation of the public; he practised at the highest level of his art, yet could indulge in meretricious theatrics; he was a Casanova, yet having taken orders in the Catholic Church in 1865 he became an abbé.

RICHARD
WAGNER

Giant of German opera who changed the course of music

18—13—83

NO COMPOSER HAS HAD SO MUCH WRITTEN ABOUT HIM, none has had so deep an influence on the course of his art before or since, none has polarized opinion quite so violently as Richard Wagner. He knew he was a genius and, with one of the most massive egos in musical history, was not backward in proclaiming the fact: 'I am being used as the instrument for something higher than my own being warrants . . . I am in the hands of the immortal genius I serve for the span of my life and that intends me to complete only what I can achieve.'

A philosopher, man of letters, first-rate conductor and one of the key composers in the Western European tradition: there is no doubt that Wagner was one of the most remarkable men of the 19th century. There is also no doubt that he was one of the most unpleasant. Notoriously, he was a racist and a virulent anti-Semite, and in his private and professional life he was utterly ruthless, allowing nobody to stand in his way. He was adept at using people unscrupulously, borrowed money without the slightest intention of repaying it, and was indifferent to the pain he caused other people; yet he became neurotically obsessed with the pain anyone caused him.

More than one writer has noted the parallels of Wagner's life with that of a deity: the mystery of his birth; the gospel of Wagner in words and music; the fanatical disciples; the temple he built in Bayreuth in which his works could be celebrated and he himself worshipped; the rejection of all who did not believe in him.

EARLY LIFE

Wilhelm Richard Wagner was born in Leipzig on 22 May 1813. Although his mother was married to a police registrar, Karl Wagner, the composer's natural father was – with some irony in the light of future events – a Jewish actor and painter named Ludwig Geyer. Richard was only six months old when Karl died, and though Geyer himself died only eight years later, he was brought up in a world of books, paintings and the theatre. He was 11 when he wrote his first drama, which was drawn from Shakespeare and the Greeks. While his latent passion for music was aroused by a performance of Weber's *Der Freischütz*, when he heard Beethoven's *Fidelio* for the first time, it became an obsession. He began to absorb scores and compose. Before he had had any formal training he produced two orchestral overtures, both of which were performed in Leipzig.

To all intents and purposes, Wagner was virtually self-taught. A born rebel, Wagner was expelled from the Thomasschule in Leipzig, spent most of his time at the university there drinking, gambling, duelling and womanizing, and only in 1831 settled down to study counterpoint with the cantor of the Thomaskirche, Thomas Weinlig. After six months Weinlig admitted that there was nothing more he could teach him. He spent the next ten years learning his trade on the hoof, accruing gambling debts, conducting at minor opera houses, composing unsuccessfully and, in 1836, marrying a pretty young actress named Wilhelmine Planer. Minna, as she was known, eloped – twice – the following year with an actor called Dietrich but each time returned to Wagner. It was not the best of starts to a marriage. Far worse was to come, for throughout their married life Minna had to

A NATURAL NAZI

WAGNER, AS IS WELL KNOWN, WAS THE FAVOURITE COMPOSER OF THE NAZIS. What is not as well known is that half a century before Hitler's rise to power, in 1881, Wagner was advocating 'racial cleansing' (*Rassenreinigung*). His polemical book *Das Judenthum in der Musik* was written because of his deep-seated resentment of any Jews who achieved success in his field. Even Hitler's concept of the Final Solution was adapted from Wagner's term *Die grosse Lösung*, though Wagner called only for the expulsion of Jews from Germany. Chillingly, he also suggested that during a performance of Lessing's pro-Jewish play *Nathan der Weise*, the theatre should be filled with Jews, locked and burnt down. The Nazi slogan '*Deutschland erwache!*' ('Germany awake!') was coined by Wagner – Hitler was merely quoting. The faeces-coloured uniform worn by Hitler's brown-shirt thugs was, most appropriately, inspired by the title of Wagner's diary, *The Brown Book*.

endure her husband's serial infidelity, usually with married women. Dismissed from his opera post in Riga, hounded by creditors and with his passport confiscated, he and Minna were forced to flee the country via a smuggler's route, eventually landing up in Paris.

The couple lived in poverty (on two occasions, Wagner was imprisoned for debt), but then came his first successes, the operas *Rienzi* (1842) and *The Flying Dutchman* (1843). At the age of 30 Wagner got into his stride, and from then on there was no stopping him.

GROWING STATURE

Now famous throughout Germany, Wagner was made director of the Dresden Opera. His six-year tenure raised performance standards to unprecedented heights. Highlights included the premiere in October 1845 of his own *Tannhäuser*, which tells of the love of the knight Tannhäuser for Elizabeth and contains the famous overture and the Pilgrims' Chorus. For three years he worked on his second early masterpiece, *Lohengrin*, but by 1849 he had become embroiled in radical republican politics, and when the hoped-for revolution in Saxony came to nothing, he was forced to flee Germany. For the next 13 years he lived in exile in Zurich.

During this period Wagner wrote many influential essays, among them *The Artwork of the Future* and *Opera and Drama*, in which he laid out his theories of *Gesamtkunstwerk* (see box, page 92). He finalized the libretto for the cycle of four music dramas which were eventually to become *Der Ring des Nibelungen* (The Ring of the Nibelung), a project that took him a quarter of a century to complete.

But Wagner being Wagner, there was also time for a succession of extramarital affairs. The first of these, in 1850, was with the 21-year-old English wife of a wine merchant. She, exceptionally, saw the light and returned to her husband. In 1856, while working on *The Ring*, Wagner lived in the luxurious villa belonging to a wealthy silk merchant, Otto Wesendonck, and his wife Mathilde. Wesendonck's kindness and generosity were repaid by Wagner having a passionate affair with Mathilde. Much of his next opera, *Tristan und Isolde*, was written under her influence – she may even have been the inspiration for this reworking of the Arthurian legend (its most celebrated passage is the rapturous and sensuous 'Liebestod'). Be that as it may, the work is one of the most important of the 19th century. Its harmonic innovations were an immense influence on the future of classical music. Indeed, many consider *Tristan* to be the starting point of modern music.

Eventually Wesendonck had had enough of being cuckolded and provided funds for Wagner and Minna to travel to Paris. Soon Minna, who spent most of the 1850s following Wagner around with a dog and parrot in tow trying to lure her husband back, had to endure a third married woman

in his life. This time it was different. This was the woman Wagner had been searching for all his life. Cosima von Bülow was the daughter of his champion and friend Franz Liszt, the wife of the distinguished pianist and conductor Hans von Bülow, and an independent-minded woman of great intelligence. Wagner and Cosima had two illegitimate daughters (Isolde and Eva) before Minna conveniently died in 1866. Only then did Cosima leave her husband and set up house with Wagner. No better illustration of the mesmeric power and blind loyalty that Wagner inspired is that, throughout this public humiliation, von Bülow remained devoted to both Cosima and Wagner, finally writing to his wife: 'You have preferred to devote your life and the treasures of your mind to one who is my superior. Far from blaming you, I approve your action from every point of view and admit you are perfectly right.'

MUNICH AND BAYREUTH

Wagner's greatest days were still before him. Having been allowed to return to Germany after a political amnesty, he was invited to Munich by the young, homosexual King Ludwig II of Bavaria and promised unlimited support for all his projects. Thus Munich saw the premieres of *Tristan und Isolde, Die Meistersinger von Nürnberg, Das Rheingold* and *Die Walküre*, the latter two forming the first completed sections of *The Ring*. Here, supported by his infatuated patron, Wagner conceived his ultimate ambition: to build an opera house to his own specification in which nothing but his own works would be mounted and performed in ideal conditions. Ludwig's lavish funding of Wagner was such that the Bavarian cabinet, scandalized by the composer's morals and political dabbling, advised the king that the whole economy of his country would collapse if his largesse continued on such a scale. Wagner retreated with Cosima to a palatial estate on Lake Lucerne (paid for by Ludwig). Following her divorce in July 1870, the couple married the following month.

Instead of Munich, the backwater Bavarian town of Bayreuth offered a site for Wagner's own opera house. It was a huge undertaking which Wagner tackled with characteristic vigour and determination, raising money from wealthy patrons (Ludwig contributed 100,000 thalers) and by conducting concerts. The cornerstone was laid in May 1872; the Bayreuth Festival Theatre opened on 13 August 1876. Four thousand visitors, including many crowned heads and

Essential works

TANNHÄUSER, opera (1841–5)
LOHENGRIN, opera (1845–8)
TRISTAN UND ISOLDE, opera (1856–9)
DIE MEISTERSINGER VON NÜRNBERG, opera (1845 and 1861–7)
DER RING DES NIBELUNGEN (1848–74)
    DAS RHEINGOLD, opera (1851–4)
    DIE WALKÜRE, opera (1851–6)
    SIEGFRIED, opera (1851–2, 1857, 1864–5 and 1869)
    GÖTTERDÄMMERUNG, opera (1848–52 and 1869–74)
PARSIFAL, 'stage-consecrating festival play' (1857, 1865, 1877–82)
SIEGFRIED IDYLL, for chamber orchestra (1870)

> '*I am not like other people. I must have brilliance and beauty and light. The world owes me what I need.*'

RICHARD WAGNER

composers such as Tchaikovsky, Saint-Saëns, Gounod, Grieg and Liszt, were crammed into the small town for the first complete performance of *The Ring* cycle, with *Siegfried* and *Götterdämmerung* receiving their premieres. Today, the Bayreuth Theatre remains a living shrine to Wagner's music and vision.

Living in the luxurious villa Wahnfried (meaning 'free from delusion') a short walk from the Festival Theatre, Wagner settled down to other things, including a final fling with a married woman, the beautiful daughter of the poet Théophile Gautier and wife of the poet Catulle Mendès. Judith Mendès actually moved into Wahnfried for a time (Cosima turned a blind eye) before returning to her husband in 1878. Wagner then set about completing his final opera, or 'consecrational play', *Parsifal*. Though he had no religious belief, he had a long-held ambition to compose a sacred work and the legend of the Holy Grail greatly attracted him.

Six months after its premiere in 1882, Wagner took Cosima and their children to Venice for an extended holiday. While there, on 13 February 1883, he suffered a massive heart attack. His body was brought back to Bayreuth for burial in a vault in the garden of his villa. After his death, the imperious Cosima, born in 1837, became the guardian of the Wagner shrine until her death in 1930.

WAGNERIAN INNOVATION

WAGNER'S INNOVATIONS WERE ON TWO LEVELS, AESTHETIC AND MUSICAL. Ever since the time of Gluck, German opera had been leading to the ideal of *Gesamtkunstwerk* – 'total art work': a synthesis of poetry, music, drama, lighting, design and acting in a single indivisible entity. To achieve this, Wagner became his own librettist, adapting the epic sagas on which his operas are based into poetic, if prolix and dramatically dull, utterances. The music evolved organically from the libretto. There were no more showpiece arias to gratify the taste of the public or the whims of a soloist. The music became the story as much as the story became the music. To underpin the whole score, Wagner introduced short, descriptive tunes (leitmotifs) associated with various characters and moods, which would appear throughout an opera and even in separate works that featured the same characters (*Das Rheingold* and *Götterdämmerung*, for instance). The orchestra became an equal partner in the drama, no longer merely accompanying the story but commenting upon it and developing the narrative.

GIUSEPPE
VERDI
Master and hero of Italian opera

1813—1901

THE TWO DISTINCT VOICES

OF VERDI AND WAGNER DOMINATED THE OPERA WORLD IN THE SECOND HALF OF THE 19TH CENTURY. Both were motivated by the same desire to create a musical art form that had dramatic truth and artistic validity. Both achieved this aim, but in different ways. The broad generalization might be made that Wagner, born just five months earlier than Verdi, relied on symphonic methods, while Verdi emphasized the vocal part. Both were revolutionaries in their own way: Wagner was the theoretician and idealist; Verdi worked on instinct and pragmatism with one eye on the box office. 'There is hardly any music in my house,' he wrote in a letter of 1869. 'I have never gone to a music library, never to a publisher to examine a piece. I keep abreast of the better contemporary work not by studying them but by hearing them occasionally at the theatre . . . I repeat, I am the least erudite among past and present composers.'

A number of factors set Verdi apart and, with his musical heir Puccini, make him the most popular of all operatic composers: the unending string of glorious melodies; an innate understanding of the stage; and an ability to write for the human voice, to express himself directly, unhampered by academia, and to score with technical brilliance, colour and originality.

EARLY LIFE

Verdi was born in Le Roncole, near Busseto in the Duchy of Parma, on 9 October 1813. His father was the village innkeeper. Christened Giuseppe Fortunino Francesco, Verdi began his long career as an organist, taking over the duties at the local church when still a small child. A wealthy merchant, Antonio Barezzi, paid for his musical education in Milan, where he acquired a thorough knowledge of counterpoint. In 1833 he settled in Busseto, became director of the Philharmonic Society and, in 1836, married Margherita Barezzi, daughter of his patron. He completed his first surviving opera, *Oberto*, in 1839, which was mounted with some success at La Scala in Milan when he was 26.

But immediately tragedy intervened. His two infant children died, and in 1840 his beloved young wife died of encephalitis. *Un giorno di regno*, a comic opera completed in the face of this devastation, was a fiasco. He was convinced that he should abandon his operatic ambitions, and that might have been the end for the provincial musician, with his taciturn, moody, intense character. Instead, he was persuaded by the impresario Merelli to undertake a third work, this time using a biblical subject. The new opera, *Nabucco* (1842), was a turning point in Verdi's career – and also for Italian opera. It caused a sensation. Overnight he became one of the most idolized composers of his time. No one is sure whether Verdi was conscious of the parallels between the enslaved Hebrews of his opera and the plight of his fellow Italians under Austrian oppression, but 'Va, pensiero', the chorus of the Hebrew slaves, was taken up as the Italian anthem for independence and Verdi himself became a symbol of the resistance.

MIDDLE PERIOD

Other successes followed, but nothing to match the triumph of *Nabucco*. In fact the next landmark in his career was not until 1851, the year in which we may say that Verdi's early period ended. The start of his 'middle period' arrived with one of the most popular operas ever written – *Rigoletto*, based on a Victor Hugo novel. Soon every barrel organ was playing 'La donna è mobile', the teasing aria of the lecherous duke. So sure was Verdi that this number was going to be a hit tune that he kept it under wraps until the dress rehearsal for fear that someone would steal it.

Had Verdi composed only *Rigoletto*, he would have been assured a place in musical history as a one-hit wonder. What followed, though, was nothing short of miraculous, for his next opera, completed in the astonishingly short time of 30 days, was *Il trovatore*, the most popular opera of the 19th century (despite its improbable and imponderable plot). It was first performed in January 1853 in Rome. Less than two months later, it was followed by the premiere in Venice of a third imperishable masterpiece, *La traviata*. Based on the play of the novel *La dame aux camélias* by Alexandre Dumas *fils*, it tells the story of courtesan Violetta, the fallen woman of the title, who sacrifices everything for love and is thereby redeemed. Today, it is a much-loved part of the standard opera repertoire, but in its day it was a revolutionary piece: the realism of the text and music anticipate the later *verismo* movement of opera (*Carmen, Cavalleria rusticana, Pagliacci*), while its sympathetic treatment of a courtesan was unique.

Les Vêpres siciliennes (1855), *Simon Boccanegra* (1857) and *Un ballo in maschera* (1859) followed, but though hugely successful in their day, they have never achieved quite the same level of popularity with the public. The year 1859 also marked the marriage of Verdi to the soprano Giuseppina Strepponi, who had created the original role of Abigaille in *Nabucco*. Now the most acclaimed of living opera composers, he and his new wife spent the summers on their vast farm in Sant' Agata enjoying a simple peasant existence. The winters were spent in their palatial home in Genoa.

Verdi's frequent foreign travels included a special trip to St Petersburg in 1862 to see the first performance of his latest creation *La Forza del destino*, a commission from the Imperial Opera. The next milestone came five years later with his flawed masterpiece *Don Carlos*. With another impenetrable plot, this colossal, sprawling epic, subject to many revisions and cuts, was seen by many as the zenith of grand opera. In reality, Verdi was just limbering up for his next project, the grandest (yet most intimate) of all grand operas – *Aïda*.

Commissioned for the staggering sum of $20,000 by the khedive (viceroy) of Egypt, it was intended to be performed at the new Cairo opera house to mark the opening of the Suez Canal. In fact,

NATIONAL HERO

VERDI WAS A FERVENT SUPPORTER OF THE RISORGIMENTO, the movement for the reorganization of the numerous small Italian states into one country. The theme of resurgent nationalism in his early operas, the frequent clashes with the censor (who suspected him of revolutionary tendencies), his political career in the 1860s when he sat reluctantly for five years in the new Italian parliament – all these things endeared Verdi to the general public. The symbolic leader of the nationalist movement was Victor Emmanuel, the future king of Italy – Vittorio Emmanuel, Re d'Italia. Thus all over Italy the initials V.E.R.D.I. were to be seen, the cries of 'Viva Verdi' heard as vociferously in the opera house as they were in the street. After the premiere of *Falstaff* in 1893, Victor Emmanuel, by then king of a united Italy, offered to ennoble Verdi, but he declined. 'I am a peasant', he told the king.

Aida did not receive its world premiere there until over two years later, on Christmas Eve 1871. The occasion was an international event, though Verdi, who loathed glitzy occasions and travelling by sea, did not attend. Instead, the khedive's assistant wired him from Cairo, telling him that the reaction had been one of 'total fanaticism . . . we have success beyond belief'. In *Aida* we see every element of Verdi's genius: the stunning large-scale choruses, pageantry, dance, spectacle and exoticism. The work confirmed him as one of opera's greatest musical dramatists.

'What I have done is the best I can do.'
VERDI

Aida brought to a brilliant conclusion Verdi's second creative phase, though in 1873, prompted by the death of the Italian poet and patriot Manzoni, Verdi wrote his great Requiem. It is his only masterpiece not intended for the stage, aptly described by Hans von Bülow as 'Verdi's latest opera in church vestments'.

AN INDIAN SUMMER

After the Requiem Verdi wrote nothing more for 13 long years. He simply retired to live the country life. Then in 1887 he was tempted back to work on a new project, a fine adaptation of Shakespeare's *Othello* by the librettist and composer Arrigo Boito. It marked the beginning of the third period of Verdi's creative life. After this further triumph, at the age of 79, he embarked on a final opera, again based on Shakespeare and adapted by Boito. *Falstaff*, one of the high points of Italian opera, shows that far from his powers waning, Verdi was developing. It ends with a perfectly poised fugue and shows that he had assimilated some aspects of Wagnerian music drama while remaining true to himself. In this glorious comic opera, wrote R.A. Streatfield, 'He has combined a schoolboy's sense of fun with the grace and science of Mozart.'

Essential works

NABUCCO, opera (1842)
RIGOLETTO, opera (1851)
IL TROVATORE, opera (1853)
LA TRAVIATA, opera (1853)
UN BALLO IN MASCHERA, opera (1859)
LA FORZA DEL DESTINO, opera (1862)
AIDA, opera (1871)
Requiem (1874)
OTELLO, opera (1887)
FALSTAFF, opera (1893)

In November 1897 Verdi's adored Giuseppina died from pneumonia. He was desolate. His sight and hearing deteriorated and he suffered paralysis, but he nevertheless busied himself with setting up the Casa di Riposo per Musicisti in Milan, a retirement home for elderly musicians that survives to this day. In 1898 he composed his last work, *Quattro pezzi sacri* (Four Sacred Pieces). He spent Christmas 1900 in Milan with his adopted daughter, but he suffered a sudden stroke and died a few days later, at 3.00 in the morning on 27 January 1901. After a quiet funeral at his own request, his body and the remains of Giuseppina were transferred a month later to the crypt at Casa di Riposa in a state ceremony attended by the Italian royal family, diplomats, politicians and fellow composers. Tens of thousands of people lined the black-draped street as the chorus of La Scala sang 'Va, pensiero' conducted by the young Arturo Toscanini.

César
Franck

'Cathedrals in sound' Alfred Bruneau

1822–90

FRANCK IS UNUSUAL IN THAT ALMOST ALL HIS GREATEST WORKS WERE WRITTEN IN THE LAST FIVE YEARS OF HIS LIFE. His music was largely ignored for most of his career, his first taste of real success coming only months before his death. He did not appear to mind, for his character, reflected in much of his music, was one of serenity, peaceful acceptance and deep religious feeling. He was, arguably, the mildest and humblest man ever to become a great composer. His ambitions were simple: to serve music and God with equal reverence.

Franck was one of the great organists of the age, most famously at St Clothilde in Paris, where he presided from 1858 until his death. The influence of his organ playing is clearly apparent in much of his music, even in purely orchestral scores: one can visualize the hands transferring from one manual to another, subtly changing the registration by the fluent use of different stops, shifting the harmonies, modulating constantly. 'It is music for the cathedral and it has a kind of purifying effect on responsive listeners', as the American writer Milton Cross put it.

For some, Franck's music is too sentimental, too sickly sweet, his romantic idiom imbued with the gaudy sanctity of a Victorian stained-glass window. His critics find it too fragmentary, meandering and loosely constructed, a reflection, perhaps, of Franck's love of improvisation. His most adventurous innovation was the use of 'cyclical form' (similar to Liszt's experiments with thematic transformation in the 1840s and 1850s), where themes are developed out of short melodic phrases, then manipulated and expanded throughout the composition to bind the work together.

EARLY LIFE

Born on 10 December 1822 in Liège, Belgium, the young César (Auguste Jean Guillaume Hubert) Franck was a child prodigy. The early part of his career gave no indication of the path he would take, for his tyrannical music-loving father, a banker of German extraction, dreamed of his son becoming a brilliant, world-famous virtuoso. While studying at the Liège Conservatoire, he was only 12 when his father sent him on tour with his brother Joseph, a violinist. At 13 he won the Conservatoire's first prize for piano playing. In the autumn of 1835 the entire family moved to Paris to take advantage of the greater opportunities for musical study there. After lessons with Anton Reicha (who had been a pupil of Beethoven), Franck was enrolled in the Paris Conservatoire.

Already his ability to improvise and transpose on the piano and organ were legendary, and he might have walked off with all the important prizes had it not been for an unlikely mischievous streak. Part of his first-year examination was to sight-read Hummel's difficult A minor piano concerto. Just for the hell of it, Franck played it a minor third down in F sharp minor, an incredible feat. His impudence cost him first prize and he had to settle for second. For his fourth-year examination, he was given two themes. One was to be turned into a fugue, the other into a sonata. Franck, instead, was able to use both the themes within sonata form containing a fugue. Another second prize.

Franck's father continued to make strenuous efforts to turn his son into the star soloist he dreamed of, arranging private recitals to promote his career (there was even one for the king of

Belgium). But the young man was not interested. Composing music was what he wanted to do. Fame and worldly success were unimportant. In 1848 Franck married Mademoiselle Desmousseaux, who was – horror of horrors! – an actress. For his father, this was the last straw and he disowned him. Sadly, Franck soon discovered that he had exchanged an overbearing father for an oppressive wife, who disliked his music and, even more, his lack of ambition.

A DEDICATED LIFE

Very soon, Franck's life settled into a routine from which it deviated little thereafter. He would rise at 5.30 and compose for two hours. At 8.00 he left the house to teach all over Paris: at the Jesuit school of Vaugirard from 11.00 till 2.00, a bite of cheese and fruit for lunch, then on to somewhere like Auteuil, a fashionable institution for young ladies. And from 1858 there was the music for St Clothilde to supervise. 'There for thirty years, every Sunday, every festival day,' wrote one of his pupils, Vincent d'Indy, 'every Friday morning he came to stir up the fire of his genius on admirable improvisations frequently far loftier than hosts of pieces cleverly worked out.'

People remembered Franck rushing from one appointment to another through the streets of Paris, his coat too large, his trousers too short – the absent-minded professor to a T. From 1872 he was appointed professor of organ at the Paris Conservatoire. D'Indy again: 'It frequently happened that during lessons he would suddenly get up and retire into a corner of the room to jot down a few measures which he was anxious not to forget and then come back almost immediately to take up once more the demonstration or examination. Important works were composed in this manner, in bits, casually indicated and their connection never failed to be logical and consecutive.'

But whatever he wrote brought him no success or recognition. Imagine the tenacity needed to carry on in the face of years of cumulative disappointment: 'If you can trust yourself when all men doubt you . . .' His opera *Le Valet de ferme* was never performed; the oratorio *Rédemption* was given a terrible performance which it did not survive; another, *Les Béatitudes*, took ten years to write and, when Franck invited musical Paris to hear it, just two people turned up. Halfway through a rehearsal of Franck's symphonic poem *Les Djinns*, the conductor, Edouard Colonne, turned to the composer and

> *This music . . . is truly as much the sister of prayer as of poetry; it leads back to heaven and to the city of rest.'*
>
> GUSTAVE DEREPAS

SONATA BY MOONLIGHT

DESPITE PUBLIC ANTAGONISM AND INDIFFERENCE (INEXPLICABLE TO MODERN EARS), Franck's music could often have a rousing effect on its admirers. The Sonata for Violin and Piano, a work that stands alongside those of Beethoven, was written as a wedding present for the renowned Belgian violinist Eugène Ysaÿe and his bride. Its first performance was given in a room in Brussels in which valuable paintings were hung and where no artificial light was permitted. It was a winter's afternoon, and after the first movement it was so dark that neither Ysaÿe nor the pianist could see the music. They suggested abandoning the concert but the audience would have none of it and demanded to hear the whole sonata. So, with a cry of 'Allons! Allons!', Ysaÿe and his pianist plunged into the other three movements, playing in the dark from memory.

Essential works

PANIS ANGELICUS, song (1872)

PIÈCE HÉROÏQUE, organ (1878)

Piano Quintet in F minor (1879)

LE CHASSEUR MAUDIT, tone poem (1882)

Prelude, Chorale and Fugue, piano (1884)

Les Djinns, tone poem (1884)

SYMPHONIC VARIATIONS, piano and orchestra (1885)

Sonata for violin and piano (1886)

Prelude, Aria and Finale, piano (1887)

Symphony in D minor (1888)

String Quartet in D (1889)

Three Chorales, organ (1890)

asked tartly, 'Does it please you?' Franck replied yes, he was delighted. 'Well,' said Colonne turning to face the orchestra, 'it's all frightful music but we'll go on with it anyway.' It was only the persuasive powers of another conductor, Jules Garcin, that prevented the premiere of the now famous Symphony in D minor from being cancelled. Most of the orchestra of the Paris Conservatoire were opposed to playing it. After the performance, the composer Charles Gounod described it as 'the affirmation of incompetence pushed to dogmatic lengths'. What was Franck's reaction? 'He was radiant,' reported one of his pupils. 'He had heard his music played.' Small wonder he was known as '*Pater Seraphicus*' – 'Angel-like Father'.

It was his pupils that gave him some encouragement and recompense, for they all seem, universally, to have adored him. One in particular was the beautiful Franco-Irish composer and poetess Augusta Holmès, with whom it is said he had an affair. It was certainly she who provided the inspiration for the masterly Piano Quintet, a love letter of burning erotic intensity. At the work's first performance, Saint-Saëns was the pianist. For reasons of professional jealousy and his own feelings for Miss Holmès, he refused to return to the stage at its conclusion, leaving on the piano the music which Franck had publicly dedicated to him.

SUCCESS AT LAST

Franck's one public success came in April 1890 with the premiere of his String Quartet at a concert of the Société Nationale. When he mounted the stage to acknowledge the applause, it was the first time he had experienced a public ovation. He was 69. 'There,' he is said to have remarked after the concert, 'the public is beginning to understand me at last.' The quartet has been described as 'perhaps one of the most beautiful of all in the whole realm of chamber music'.

Shortly afterwards, while on his way to a pupil's house, Franck was struck in the side and knocked down by the pole of a horse-omnibus. He made it to his destination in great pain, fainted, recovered and then insisted on proceeding with the lesson. He made light of the accident, but it was after this mishap that his health began to deteriorate rapidly. He died only seven months later from pleurisy.

Bedřich
Smetana

The father of Czech music

1824–84

TO ALL INTENTS AND PURPOSES, SMETANA SINGLE-HANDEDLY CREATED CZECH MUSICAL NATIONALISM. He was the first composer to demonstrate how his country's folk and dance music could be used in the service of serious art, albeit within the mid-European tradition and much influenced by the orchestral devices of Liszt and Wagner.

In Smetana's day, of course, the Czech Republic did not exist. The lands of Bohemia merely constituted part of the Austro-Hungarian empire. Having been brought up to speak German exclusively, Smetana did not attempt to write a letter in Czech until he was over 30. Prague, though one of the great musical centres of the 18th century, was dominated by the taste of the Austrian regime. Meyerbeer and the Italian repertoire sung in Bohemian were its favoured works. It took many years for Smetana to realize his nationalist musical ambitions, but eventually his fresh, vivid music, welded to modern harmony and thematic construction, provided a voice for his countrymen. More than that, it created a new musical heritage, one which led to the works of Dvořák, Janáček, Martinů and others, and to Prague's great orchestras, opera houses and music schools.

EARLY LIFE

Smetana's father, a brewer by trade, was a talented amateur musician but appears to have done little to encourage his son's prodigious gifts. Though he was proficient enough to play first violin in a Haydn quartet at the age of five and to make his public debut as a pianist a year later (a transcription of an overture by Auber at an entertainment honouring Emperor Francis I of Austria), by the time he was 19 he had received little formal musical training. Born on 2 March 1824 in Leitomischl (Litomyšl), Bohemia, Smetana had begun composing when he was eight but was left to develop his skills by trial and error. He was never in doubt about his calling. 'With God's help and grace,' he wrote in his diary on 23 January 1843, 'I shall one day be a Mozart in composition and a Liszt in technique.'

'With me, the form of each composition is the outcome of the subject.'

SMETANA

His luck changed in 1843 when he met Kateřina Kolářová, the girl with whom he played piano duets and who would later become his wife. She encouraged him to concentrate on music and through her mother arranged for her own music teacher to give him lessons. Joseph Proksch (1794–1864) was one of the finest in Prague. For the first time, Smetana was given proper, systematic instruction. He began writing piano works while studying, supporting himself by teaching. Within a year he had been appointed music tutor to the family of Count Leopold Thun.

The year 1848 was an important one in Smetana's life. He received official permission to found a school of music in Prague – quite an achievement for someone who had enjoyed so little financial and career success thus far. At the same time he became involved in the unsuccessful movement to overthrow the oppressive Austrian regime. This was the 'Year of Revolution', and engagement in political activity awakened in him a national consciousness for the first time. The next year he

married Kateřina, and in 1850 he was rewarded with the profitable post of court pianist to Ferdinand I, the former Austrian emperor, then residing in Prague.

Smetana's marriage to his childhood sweetheart proved short and tragic. Of their four daughters, only one, Žofie, survived (his elegiac Piano Trio in G minor was inspired by the death of his first daughter), and in 1855 Kateřina showed signs of tuberculosis. Encouraged by Liszt, Smetana moved with his family for a five-year period to Gothenburg, Sweden. Here he made many important friends and connections, conducted the newly founded Gothenburg Philharmonic, gave piano recitals, taught extensively and composed. At last his musical vision was taking shape, and though the three symphonic poems he completed there – *Richard III*, *Wallenstein's Camp* and *Haakon Jarl* – were much influenced by Liszt's model, they attracted much attention. The Swedish climate, however, did not suit Kateřina's constitution. They set off for Prague in 1859, but Kateřina died before they reached their destination.

A NATIONAL VOICE

Smetana married for a second time the following year and resumed his profitable career in Sweden, but in 1861 he was back in Prague, this time for good. The following decade established him as his countrymen's foremost composer. He immediately immersed himself in the musical activities of the city, assuming direction of a choral society, taking charge of a new music school, becoming a music critic and promoting Bohemian music. He helped to found the Society of Artists, founded a drama school for Prague's Bohemian Theatre and was instrumental in instigating and directing the Philharmonic Society. In 1863 he completed his opera *The Brandenburgers in Bohemia*. It was the first national Bohemian opera ever written, though it is generally agreed that it is not a good work and suffers from a particularly poor libretto. It was, nevertheless, received enthusiastically.

Smetana's next venture was of a different order. *The Bartered Bride*, premiered in May 1866, is a comic folk opera that delightfully conjures up Czech rural life. The score is filled with dance rhythms and folk songs and includes an ebullient overture (often played separately), the popular Polka in Act 1, and the Furiant and Dance of the Comedians in Act 2. It was an unprecedented triumph for a native composer and is the only one of Smetana's operas to have remained in the international repertoire of every opera house the world

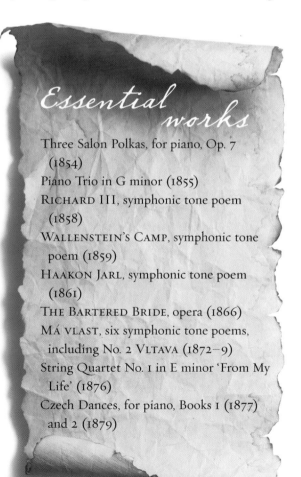

Essential works

Three Salon Polkas, for piano, Op. 7 (1854)

Piano Trio in G minor (1855)

RICHARD III, symphonic tone poem (1858)

WALLENSTEIN'S CAMP, symphonic tone poem (1859)

HAAKON JARL, symphonic tone poem (1861)

THE BARTERED BRIDE, opera (1866)

MÁ VLAST, six symphonic tone poems, including No. 2 VLTAVA (1872–9)

String Quartet No. 1 in E minor 'From My Life' (1876)

Czech Dances, for piano, Books 1 (1877) and 2 (1879)

DIGNITY IN AFFLICTION

SMETANA BORE THE UNIMAGINABLE LOSS (FOR A COMPOSER) OF HIS HEARING with dignity and courage. At first he heard a continual whistling in his ears, then a buzzing and roaring 'as though I was standing under a waterfall'. Finally, he explained, 'I hear nothing, not even my own voice . . . Concentration with me is impossible. I hear my own piano in fancy, not in reality. I cannot hear the playing of anybody else, nor even the performance of a full orchestra in opera or in concert . . . I have no pain in my ear, and my physicians agree that my disease is none of the familiar ear troubles, but something else, perhaps a paralysis of the nerves and the labyrinth. And so I am wholly determined to endure my sad fate in a calm and manly way as long as I live.'

over. Two other operas also based on Bohemian legends followed: *Dalibor* (1868) and *Libuše* (1871) and a further four, including *The Two Widows* (1874), a work that had a strong influence on the young Richard Strauss.

A SAD ENDING

During the 1870s, Smetana was at the height of his creative powers, but once again tragedy struck. In 1874 he began to suffer from severe headaches and quickly thereafter lost his hearing. On the very day he became profoundly deaf he conceived the main theme of the first of his six symphonic tone poems, masterpieces collectively known as *Má vlast* (My Homeland). The second of these is Smetana's most celebrated work, *Vltava*, a bustling portrait of the river that flows through Prague, its main theme derived, ironically, not from Czech but from Swedish folklore. From this period comes his autobiographical String Quartet in E minor subtitled 'From My Life' (1876). It portrays his youthful romance, his love of art and discovery of national music, and in the final movement, his deafness. Smetana explained that the long drawn-out high E in the coda 'is the fatal whistling in my ear in the highest registers that in 1874 announced my deafness. I permitted myself this little joke, such as it is, because it was so disastrous to me.'

Smetana's last years were spent suffering from the effects of syphilis. As well as deafness and headaches, he experienced hallucinations and frequently lost the power of speech. As he laboured on his second string quartet (1882), he gave in to violent depressions (on one page of the score he scribbled 'Composed in a state of disordered nerves'). Later, the composer Arnold Schoenberg judged the work to be years ahead of its time in its treatment of rhythm and harmonic language.

Having ceased to appear in public, in 1883 Smetana went to live in the country with his daughter Žofie and her husband. Soon afterwards, he was confined in an insane asylum in Prague, where he died on 12 May 1884. It was hardly a fitting or just end for 'the father of Czech music'.

ANTON
BRUCKNER

The idol of mystics

BRUCKNER'S REPUTATION
RESTS ALMOST ENTIRELY WITH HIS TEN SYMPHONIES. He wrote much church music, almost all of it forgotten with the exception of a magnificent *Te Deum*, and only a handful of chamber works and instrumental pieces. As one of the greatest organists of the day, one would have thought Bruckner would have produced dozens of works for his own instrument. But no – there are only six. The organ, though, is omnipresent in his symphonies – not the instrument itself but its character. There are long passages devoted to one combination of sound, similar to an organist dwelling on a particular choice of registration; sudden changes of texture, as when an organist changes manuals or activates a pre-set combination of stops; climactic sections of huge sonorities – all indicative of Bruckner the church organist.

Bruckner's symphonies have been described as the ones that Wagner never wrote. They are conceived on the same grand scale as Wagner's operas – sensuous, passionate, Olympian, grandiose, even sharing Wagner's propensity for overstatement and long-windedness. Bruckner's reverence for Wagner indeed bordered on infatuation (see box, page 107), but for all his faults, what sets Bruckner apart is the profound spirituality, the sheer magnificence of the orchestral sound, the epic scale of the conception and the unique rhetoric. His symphonies have never exercised popular appeal. You either love them or hate them. Brahms dismissed them as 'a swindle that will be forgotten in a few years' and 'greasy scraps from Wagner's table'. On the other hand, another contemporary, Hugo Wolf, thought that 'one cymbal clash by Bruckner is worth all four symphonies of Brahms with all the serenades thrown in'.

At one time Bruckner was frequently paired with Mahler, for (on the surface at least) they seem to have much in common. Both were Austrian, had complex personalities, wrote gigantic symphonies, and had to wait for decades after their deaths for their work to be accepted. But there all similarities end, for while Mahler was a sophisticated, articulate intellectual, and an egocentric, neurotic composer-conductor, Bruckner was a humble peasant, a church organist who was ill at ease in society, naïve, self-doubting and immensely pious (most of his works are inscribed 'omnia ad majorem Dei gloriam' – 'all to the greater glory of God'). Possessed of an almost childlike simplicity, dressed in ill-fitting suits, he was also an obsessive perfectionist, and hungry for honours and recognition.

EARLY LIFE
Josef Anton Bruckner was born in the small provincial town of Ansfelden, Upper Austria, on 4 September 1824, the son of the village schoolmaster whose duties included playing the organ and teaching music. When his father died in 1837, Bruckner enrolled as a chorister in the secluded monastery of St Florian near Linz (a few miles from Ansfelden) and learnt the organ, piano, violin and theory. Most of Bruckner's early life was one of continual study with an income derived from various meagre teaching and organ posts. He was 31 when he began lessons with the famous theoretician Simon Sechter in Vienna, remaining with him on and off until 1861. In 1855 he returned

to Linz to become cathedral organist, the result of his growing reputation as one of Europe's finest exponents of the instrument.

Bruckner was nearly 40 and studying Italian and German polyphony (especially Bach) with Otto Kitzler, a fine teacher ten years Bruckner's junior, when Kitzler introduced him to the music of Wagner. It was a Damascene moment: this was music that broke all the rules, this was the way forward. Bruckner realized that to create the symphonic music he had dreamed of he had to mirror Wagner's operatic achievements. All the conventions and theories he had so assiduously assimilated had to be abandoned. Up till then, Bruckner had composed little but proficient and worthy liturgical music. Now he set about producing a series of truly original works: his first three symphonies, Nos. 0, 1 and 2. (No. 0 was so designated because Bruckner felt his Symphony No. 1, written afterwards, was worthier of the title. He relegated his first-born to zero and the work remained unknown and unpublished until after his death.)

'Bruckner! He is my man!'

RICHARD WAGNER

In 1865 Bruckner came face to face with his idol when he attended the first performance of *Tristan und Isolde* in Munich. Somehow the shy, socially inept Bruckner summoned up the courage to introduce himself to the great man, but the meeting did nothing to dispel his lack of confidence in his abilities as a composer. In 1867 he suffered almost suicidal depression and a nervous breakdown that included a bout of numeromania (an obsession with counting). The following year, his life took a turn for the better when he succeeded his old teacher Sechter and joined the staff of the Vienna Conservatoire, teaching counterpoint and organ, and later becoming a professor there. And his music – at last – began to receive public performances.

CAUGHT IN THE CROSSFIRE

But if Wagner's music had opened the door to his creativity, it also put obstacles in the way of recognition. There was fierce opposition to Wagner's music in Vienna, orchestrated by the influential and venomous critic Eduard Hanslick, famously caricatured by Wagner as Beckmesser in *Die Meistersinger von Nürnberg*. Anyone who was so clearly in thrall to Wagner as Bruckner was also open to attack. In 1877, when the Vienna Philharmonic reluctantly agreed to perform Bruckner's Third Symphony, sections of the anti-Wagner pro-Brahms audience began filing out before the first movement was over; the remainder of the work was greeted with catcalls and boos until, by the end, only a smattering of Bruckner's friends remained. It was a scenario that would have constituted a shattering blow to the most confident of men; for Bruckner it was devastating. Courageously, he persevered.

The Third Symphony's reception makes all the more poignant Bruckner's reaction after the first performance of his Fourth Symphony, 'The Romantic', in 1881. The great conductor Hans Richter took charge of its premiere and later recalled the pathetic gesture of thanks that the tearful

WAGNER WORSHIP

WAGNER WAS BRUCKNER'S IDOL TO AN OBSEQUIOUS DEGREE, A VENERATION THAT VERGED ON THE NEUROTIC. The dedication of his Third Symphony to Wagner runs: 'To the eminent Excellency Richard Wagner, the Unattainable, World-Famous, and Exalted Master of Poetry and Music, in Deepest Reverence Dedicated by Anton Bruckner.' After hearing *Parsifal* for the first time, Bruckner fell on his knees in front of Wagner crying, 'Master – I worship you.' Only three things mattered to Bruckner: God, music and Wagner.

MISPLACED AFFECTIONS

BRUCKNER WAS A LONELY MAN. He never married or had a close relationship with a woman, and is said to have died a virgin. His emotional life was centred on adolescent girls. He was 43 when he fell in love with a 17-year-old whose parents terminated the relationship. In his mid-50s he fell for another 17-year-old. The parents, in this instance, gave the relationship their blessing, but the young girl tired of Bruckner and his passionate letters went unanswered. Later, he became infatuated with the 14-year-old daughter of his first love. Fortunately, this also came to nothing. At 70 he proposed to a chambermaid, but her refusal to convert to Catholicism ended that. Piety and pubescent girls: not an attractive combination.

composer made afterwards: 'Take it!' said Bruckner, squeezing a gulden into Richter's hand. 'Drink a pitcher of beer to my health.' Richter wore the coin on his watch chain for the rest of his life 'as a memento of the day on which I wept'.

Between 1871 and 1877 Bruckner composed four symphonies (Nos. 2 to 5) and then spent the following three years revising them. The subject of Bruckner's revisions and the reworkings of his music by others could fill a book. His lack of self-confidence and complete willingness to be advised by well-meaning friends led to a complicated maze of cuts, additions and substantially different versions of all the symphonies except Nos. 0, 5, 6 and 7. From 1879 to 1884, in a final burst of creative energy, he completed a further three symphonies (Nos. 6, 7 and 8) and the *Te Deum*. This last brief (20-minute) work for four soloists, choir organ and orchestra was regarded by the composer himself as his finest. 'When God calls me to Him and asks me: "What have you done with the talent I gave you?", then I shall hold out the rolled manuscript of my *Te Deum* and I know He will be a compassionate judge.'

LATE SUCCESS

The year 1884 saw the premiere of his Seventh Symphony under the baton of the charismatic Artur Nikisch. 'Since Beethoven,' the conductor affirmed, 'there had been nothing that could even approach it.' Bruckner, it seemed, had finally arrived. Certainly the Seventh Symphony gave Bruckner the biggest success in his lifetime and it remains the best loved of the cycle.

During the last few years of his life, Bruckner enjoyed some measure of the recognition he had yearned for. He was given an honorary doctorate (in philosophy) by the Vienna Conservatoire and invited by the emperor Franz Joseph to take up private rooms in the Belvedere Palace. Bruckner kept on working. He was working on his deathbed, struggling to complete his Ninth Symphony. Had he not been preoccupied with making needless revisions to his earlier symphonies, he might have finished it, but he died on 11 October 1896 after completing three of its four movements. He was buried, according to his wishes, under the organ at St Florian.

Essential works

Symphony No. 4 in E flat, 'The Romantic' (1874)
Symphony No. 6 in A (1881)
TE DEUM (1881)
Symphony No. 7 in E (1883)
Symphony No. 8 in C minor (1887)
Symphony No. 9 in D minor (1896)

Johann
Strauss II
The Waltz King

1825—99

PERHAPS THE MOST EXTRA-ORDINARY THING ABOUT THE MUSIC OF JOHANN STRAUSS THE YOUNGER – the king of the Viennese waltz – is that it managed to arouse as much admiration in disparate fellow composers as it did in ordinary music-loving members of the public. Verdi, Wagner, Offenbach and Gounod were united in their praise. It was *The Blue Danube*, one of the best-known pieces of music ever written, that prompted Brahms to sign the fan of Strauss's widow (his third wife) with the opening bars of the waltz and the words *'Leider nicht von Brahms'* ('Unfortunately not by Brahms'). Even the avant-garde Schoenberg was so enamoured of Strauss's waltzes that as well as making transcriptions of three of them, he set others as transcription exercises for his pupils.

The construction of *The Blue Danube* is typical of many of Strauss's works, based as they are on those of Josef Lanner and his own father, Johann the Elder: a tender prelude, a chain of five or so contrasting themes, and a rousing conclusion. With masterful orchestration and far more varied and sophis-ticated textures than earlier examples, Strauss's 'symphonies for dancing' defined an era, just as vividly as Gershwin's music characterized 1930s America and The Beatles' songs the 1960s. Any one of his roughly 400 waltzes, 300 polkas, quadrilles, gallops, marches and other dances transports you instantly back to Vienna in the second half of the 19th century – to the elegant, refined, confident capital of the Habsburg empire (or at least to Johann Strauss's fairytale, rose-tinted picture of it).

THE STRAUSS FAMILY

The Strauss family story has been told many times on film and television (it has even been the subject of an operetta), but it is Johann Strauss II (the Younger) who, as composer, conductor and shrewd businessman, stands head and shoulders above his father, Johann Strauss I (1804–49), and two brothers, Josef (1827–70) and Eduard (1835–1916). His grandfather, Franz, was a morose and humble innkeeper on the outskirts of Vienna who committed suicide by drowning in the Danube; his father developed a love of music from the itinerant musicians who played at Franz's inn. Having taught himself the violin and viola, Johann the Elder joined the orchestra of his friend Josef Lanner (1801–43). So successful was the venture that they formed a second band, Lanner conducting one, Strauss the other. Though they soon went their separate ways, the elder Strauss had managed to establish a reputation as conductor and composer with the Viennese, and before long he was touring all over Europe, his band had been appointed the official dance orchestra for Austrian court balls, and he was invited to play at Queen Victoria's coronation ball.

In 1824 Johann I had married Anna Streim, the

'Of all the God-given dispensers of joy, Johann Strauss is to me the most endearing.'

RICHARD STRAUSS

handsome and musical daughter of an innkeeper. Though rarely at home, he found the time to father six children (Johann Junior, the eldest, was born on 25 October 1825, followed by Josef, Nelli, Therese, Eduard and Ferdinand) as well as five illegitimate children by his mistress, an unintelligent and unmusical hatmaker named Emilie Trampusch. Johann I forbade his eldest son to have anything to do with music – he once gave him a severe whipping when he found him playing the violin – but eventually he left his family to live with his mistress, leaving Johann II free to pursue his musical ambitions, actively encouraged by his mother.

At the age of 19, the younger Johann founded his own orchestra and made his debut in October 1844. His success was immediate, leading to a headline in one Viennese newspaper that read: 'Good night, Lanner. Good evening, Father Strauss. Good morning, son Strauss.' Servicing Europe's insatiable demand for dance music, the two Strauss family orchestras ran side by side in open rivalry until 1849, when Johann I contracted scarlet fever from one of his illegitimate children. Within four days he was dead. His naked body was found in his apartment by his son Josef. Emilie, her children and all her possessions had disappeared, to vanish into obscurity.

Combining both orchestras, Johann II then took off on a career of fabulous success that he maintained for the rest of his industrious life, composing and conducting all over Europe with an apparently limitless supply of energy and memorable melodies. Running six orchestras simultaneously, with assistant conductors, copyists, librarians, publicists and booking agents, Strauss turned dance music into a goldmine. In 1863 he began to concentrate more on composition and most of his best-known works were written after this date: *Morning Papers* (1864), *Artist's Life* and *The Blue Danube* (1867), *Tales from the Vienna Woods* (1868), *Vienna Blood* (1873), *Roses from the South* (1878) . . . the list of Johann Strauss II's 'hits' is a long one.

A SECOND WIND

Strauss might have spent the remainder of his life composing dance tunes if it had not been for Jacques Offenbach. On a visit to Vienna for a production of his *Orpheus in the Underworld*, the French

THE BLUE DANUBE

The Blue Danube, the most famous waltz ever written, is Austria's second national anthem. *An der schönen, blauen Donau* (or the *Donauwalzer*, as it is also known) was commissioned by Strauss's friend Johann Herbeck, the director of the Wiener Männergesangverein (Vienna Men's Choral Society), who asked the composer to come up with a joyful carnival song to lift the spirits of the war-weary and economically depressed Viennese.

Strauss's inspiration came from a love poem by the Hungarian-born Karl Isidor Beck (1817–79). In Beck's poem each stanza ends with the same line: 'By the Danube, beautiful blue Danube' – though the river could never be described as blue and, at the time the waltz was written, did not even flow through Vienna (the city's present-day river bed is artificial, constructed between 1870 and 1875). To the finished waltz, the Choral Society's 'poet' Josef Weyl then added some humorous politically satirical lyrics.

The premiere of this original vocal version of *The Blue Danube* took place on 15 February 1867. Considering its enormous subsequent popularity, its reception was somewhat muted, a reaction that may have been due to the fact that the choir hated the words as much as the audience. Later that year, at the World Exhibition in Paris, Strauss introduced the waltz in its purely orchestral garb. It created a sensation. In 1872 he was invited to America to conduct *The Blue Danube* for the phenomenal fee of $100,000 for 14 performances.

composer suggested to Strauss that he try his hand at writing an operetta. His first attempts failed, partly as a result of poor libretti, but in 1874 he completed one of the most perfect examples of the genre, *Die Fledermaus* (The Bat), the only one of the 16 operettas Strauss composed that is actually set in Vienna, and the most popular of its kind. Apart from its enchanting waltz tunes, the comic intrigue of the plot and the gorgeous sets and frocks, there is the Overture (often heard separately) and highlights that include the famous Laughing Song and the Csardas (both from Act 2). *Eine Nacht in Venedig* (A Night in Venice) is still occasionally produced despite Strauss having composed the music without bothering to read the plot or dialogue beforehand. Otherwise the only Strauss operetta to survive in the regular repertory is *Der Zigeunerbaron* (The Gypsy Baron) of 1885.

Essential works

MORNING PAPERS, waltz (1864)
ARTIST'S LIFE, waltz (1867)
THE BLUE DANUBE, waltz (1867)
THUNDER AND LIGHTNING, polka (1868)
TALES FROM THE VIENNA WOODS, waltz (1868)
WINE, WOMAN AND SONG, waltz (1869)
VIENNA BLOOD, waltz (1873)
DIE FLEDERMAUS, operetta (1874)
ROSES FROM THE SOUTH, waltz (1880)
VOICES OF SPRING, voices (1883)
DER ZIGEUNERBARON, operetta (1885)
EMPEROR WALTZ (1889)

Strauss had inherited his father's roving eye, and his taste for actresses disrupted his first marriage (though he discovered to his surprise that his wife, Jetty, had children other than those he knew of from her previous marriage). After Jetty died in 1877, he married the actress Angelica Dietrich. That ended in divorce. Finally, aged 58, he married the devoted Adele Deutsch, a relationship which brought him the happiness he had been seeking. It was through her that he met Brahms, and the two composers enjoyed a close friendship. Brahms's death in 1897 cast him into a deep depression. He died in Vienna two years later on 3 June 1899 from double pneumonia.

Though the emperor Franz Joseph reigned until 1916, we can understand the sentiment of one court official who said that 'Emperor Franz Joseph reigned until the death of Johann Strauss'. The spirit of the old imperial Vienna died with him and, of course, was utterly destroyed only 15 years later with the outbreak of the First World War.

JOHANNES
BRAHMS

Romantic master of classical forms

1833–97

BRAHMS IS, UNARGUABLY, ONE OF THE GIANTS OF CLASSICAL MUSIC.

He wrote in every musical form except opera and ballet, and an extraordinary amount of his music is still in the active repertoire – a huge proportion compared to that of, say, Liszt or Schumann. Yet he was no innovator, writing in the traditional German idiom and using structures such as the symphony, variation form, the sonata and fugue, which many felt had outlived their purpose by the time he was writing. Brahms did not care in the least. 'I let the world go the way it pleases,' he wrote. 'I am only too often reminded that I am a difficult person to get along with. I am growing accustomed to bearing the consequences of this.'

Devoted to Bach, Handel, Haydn and Beethoven, Brahms's capacity for taking a melodic statement and expanding it into a convincing musical argument reveals a truly great craftsman. His other influences are the dark, introspective side of Schumann and the lyrical sweetness of Schubert, the folk songs and dances of his native land, and Gypsy music. Unlike most of his contemporaries, Brahms showed no interest in music that told stories or depicted events in literature or art, and he never used such relative newcomers to the orchestra as the cor anglais or tuba. Younger followers of the New German School, represented by Liszt and Wagner, sneered at Brahms's rock-like loyalty to classical thought and design. If there is little that is light-hearted or witty in his music, there is a confidence and ebullience, an irresistible melodic and lyrical appeal, and a noble body of meticulously worked masterpieces hewn from Olympian rock.

EARLY LIFE

Johannes Brahms was born in Hamburg on 7 May 1833, just six years after the death of Beethoven. The middle child of three, he had a sister Elisabeth and a brother Friedrich. His father was an impecunious double-bass player who played in the taverns of Hamburg (eventually he made it into the Hamburg Philharmonic). The family lived in St Pauli, a district near the famous Reeperbahn red-light district, where the local prostitutes were not only their neighbours but their friends. Johannes was a child prodigy on the piano, and as soon as he was proficient enough, he followed his father into the taverns to earn a living. He later recounted how 'these half-clad girls would try to drive the [visiting sailors] even wilder, so they used to take me on their laps between dances, kiss, caress and excite me. That was my first impression of the love of women.'

Perhaps these youthful experiences explain why Brahms, who loved women to excess, never married, preferring uncomplicated, uncommitted relationships, many of which he paid for. 'At least,' he said, 'it has saved me from opera and marriage.' Though he had many affairs with 'respectable' women, it was to the unrespectable ones (mainly prostitutes) to whom he constantly returned. After his death, one of Brahms's

'I believe in Bach the Father, Beethoven the Son and Brahms the Holy Ghost of music.' HANS VON BÜLOW

JOHANNES BRAHMS

biographers tried to find out more about the composer's private life and interviewed his housekeeper. All that she would say was: 'He was a very naughty old gentleman.'

Brahms had been trying his hand at composition since 1848, but it was not until 1853, after a series of propitious meetings, that his career took off. The Hungarian violinist Eduard Reményi invited Brahms to become his accompanist. In Hanover Reményi introduced him to the celebrated 22-year-old violinist Joseph Joachim, with whom Brahms formed an important and lasting friendship. Joachim in turn introduced him to Liszt.

AT THE HEIGHT OF HIS POWERS

Another meeting during the same year proved to be a decisive turning point. Brahms had always admired Schumann's music and called on him in Düsseldorf. The notoriously critical Schumann was immediately taken by the budding composer, predicting great things from him and introducing him to his publishers, Breitkopf & Härtel, who were to publish Brahms's early works. Clara Schumann found herself instantly attracted to the young man, 15 years her junior. The attraction was mutual. When Schumann was taken to the lunatic asylum where he was to end his days, Brahms moved into the Schumanns' house, supported Clara and her children, and was with her when her husband died in 1856. There is little doubt that Brahms and Clara Schumann were in love with each other. Whether the relationship ever went beyond a platonic friendship has never been proved (there were rumours that Clara's last child, Felix, was fathered by Brahms), but though they went their separate ways after Robert's death, their correspondence reveals a deep spiritual and artistic affinity. It was the most profound and enduring human relationship of Brahms's life.

Throughout the 1850s Brahms the composer was concerned with solo piano works, chamber music, songs and choral works. In 1855 he started what was to be his First Symphony (not completed until 1876), and in 1857 began work on *A German Requiem* (completed in 1868). The two Serenades for orchestra and the magnificent First Piano Concerto were the only large-scale compositions from this decade; the latter, inspired by Schumann's suicide attempt, was hissed at its premiere. Two string sextets, the *Paganini Variations* for solo piano and the *Liebeslieder* waltzes were among the fine music that Brahms produced in his 30s, but it was only from the late 1860s that he truly got into his stride. An invitation to

CRITICAL BUTT

OF THE BIG 'THREE BS', NONE HAS BEEN THE SUBJECT OF MORE CRITICAL ABUSE THAN BRAHMS. 'I have played over the music of that scoundrel Brahms,' Tchaikovsky confided in his diary. 'What a giftless bastard!' George Bernard Shaw described him as 'rather tiresomely addicted to dressing himself up as Handel or Beethoven and making a prolonged and intolerable noise'. 'His *Requiem*,' wrote Shaw, 'is patiently borne only by the corpse.'

conduct in Vienna, his mother's death in 1865 and his father's remarriage all served to loosen his ties with Hamburg, and in 1872 he decided to make the Austrian capital his base. The *German Requiem* and the *Alto Rhapsody* (1869) had made him famous, but the next two decades saw the full flowering of his genius. Within three years he had completed his First and Second Symphonies and the Violin Concerto (dedicated to Joachim), as well as the *Academic Festival* and *Tragic* Overtures.

From the rigours of conducting and playing his music all over Europe, Brahms escaped every summer to the country to stay either in Baden-Baden, where Clara Schumann had a house, or in Bad Ischl, where his good friend Johann Strauss II had a villa (Strauss was one of the few contemporary composers whom Brahms admired). Masterpiece followed masterpiece in the 1880s: the Second

Piano Concerto, the Third and Fourth Symphonies, and the Concerto for Violin and Cello, as well as a host of chamber music (the lovely Violin Sonata No. 3, for example) and songs.

FINAL YEARS

By this time, Brahms's appearance had been transformed from the striking, fair-haired, looks of his youth into the familiar image we have of him – long white beard, corpulent and unkempt (his scores, by contrast, were models of clarity and legibility). With an ever-present cigar in his mouth, he was always more sturdy Prussian than elegant Viennese. Even when financially secure, he lived modestly, eating at cheap restaurants and drinking a great deal of beer. His one indulgence was music manuscripts. At one time he owned the original score of Mozart's Symphony No. 40 in G minor and Wagner's *Tannhäuser*.

Despite his frugal lifestyle, Brahms was a wonderfully generous man, giving help and encouragement to young composers such as Dvořák and Grieg. He had a wide circle of friends, including the street women who knew him by name, sometimes calling out 'Guten Tag, Herr Doktor!' when he was walking around Vienna with friends – greetings which did not in the least embarrass him. Brahms could nevertheless be blunt to the point of rudeness on occasion. After one party in Vienna, he is said to have left with the words, 'If there's anybody here I haven't insulted, I apologize.'

From 1890 onwards, Brahms abandoned large-scale works to concentrate on chamber music and more intimate, personal works. His final three sets of piano music (Opp. 117, 118 and 119), the yearning melancholy of the Clarinet Quintet and the *Four Serious Songs* are imbued with a nostalgic autumnal glow. In May 1896 Clara Schumann died after suffering two strokes. Her death affected him deeply. His appearance deteriorated and his energy dissipated. Returning to Ischl after her funeral, he developed jaundice. Less than a year later he too had died (like his father) from cancer of the liver. He was 63.

Essential works

Hungarian Dances, piano duet, also orchestral (1852–69)
Piano Concerto No. 1 in D minor (1854–8)
Symphony No. 1 in C minor (1855–76)
A GERMAN REQUIEM (1868)
Variations on a Theme by Haydn ('St Anthony' Variations) (1873)
Violin Concerto in D (1878)
Piano Concerto No. 2 in B flat (1878–81)
Academic Festival Overture (1880)
Violin Sonata No. 3 in D minor (1886–8)
Clarinet Quintet in B minor (1891)

A VOICE FROM THE GRAVE

ALTHOUGH HIS HIGH-PITCHED VOICE ANNOYED HIM, you can hear Brahms speaking on a wax cylinder he made in November 1889 – the first major composer to make a recording of any kind. Intended as a kind of aural greeting card from Brahms to Thomas Edison, he shouts into the apparatus 'Grüsse an Herr Doktor Edison. I am Doctor Brahms . . . Johannes Brahms' and then launches wildly into a brief snatch of his own Hungarian Dance No. 1 on the piano. The sound may be execrable, but how extraordinary to hear the voice of Brahms over a century after his death!

CAMILLE
SAINT-SAËNS

The greatest musical mind of our times' HANS VON BÜLOW

1835—1921

TO AN EXTRAORDINARY

DEGREE, SAINT-SAËNS MASTERED EVERY FIELD OF ENDEAVOUR TO WHICH HE TURNED HIS ECLECTIC MIND. Outside his musical activities, he was a caricaturist, playwright, poet, philosopher and essayist, writing with authority on botany, science, mathematics, astronomy and archaeology. As well as composing more than 300 works touching every area of music, he was a critic, a scholarly editor of music, a conductor, and a world-class virtuoso pianist and organist. His compositions include ten concertos, five symphonies, 39 chamber works, 50 solo piano pieces, music for half a dozen stage plays, 12 operas, myriad secular and religious choral works, more than 90 songs and nearly 40 transcriptions. Saint-Saëns wrote the first significant score by a major composer for the fledgling art of the cinema (*L'Assassinat du duc de Guise*, 1908), and during the era of the silent screen his works accounted for 20 per cent of all music used to accompany films.

As a composer, Saint-Saëns was neither a revolutionary nor a mould-breaker. He was no Beethoven or Wagner scaling the Olympian heights, fuelled by lofty aims and philosophical musings. He composed with an ease and technical fluency that have rarely been matched in the history of music. That has marked him down in the eyes of many, for since the Romantic movement there has been a widespread belief that a composer needs to be tortured and depressed in order to write great music. 'The only great composer who wasn't a genius' – that's one famous swipe. 'Bad music well written' – that's another. Saint-Saëns has been sniffed at by critics and musicologists probably more than any other major composer. Yet for all the charges laid against him, no one, as one of his biographers observed, has ever been able to write a pastiche of Saint-Saëns.

EARLY LIFE

Charles-Camille Saint-Saëns was born on 9 October 1835 in Paris. His father died when he was a baby, leaving him to be brought up by his wife, Clémence, and her aunt, Charlotte Masson, who introduced the infant to music. Saint-Saëns began playing the piano at two, could read and write before he was three, and composed his first piece of music at three-and-a-half. At four years and seven months he gave his first public performance and, five months later, could be found analyzing the full score of Mozart's *Don Giovanni*. His official debut was made aged ten, when he could offer – as an encore – any one of Beethoven's 32 sonatas from memory. One of the most precocious of all musical prodigies, he was dubbed by the press 'the French Mozart'. 'I live in music like a fish in water,' he once remarked.

For such a prodigy, it took some time for Saint-Saëns's reputation as an important composer to be established – but not that long. After studying at the Paris Conservatoire, his first symphony was premiered in 1853. At 22 he was appointed to France's most prestigious organ post at the Madeleine in Paris. He remained there for nearly two decades, developing his legendary gift for improvisation.

THE CARNIVAL OF THE ANIMALS

IRONICALLY, THE MOST POPULAR WORK BY SAINT-SAËNS WAS NEVER INTENDED FOR PUBLICATION. The *Carnival of the Animals* (1886) was written as a *jeu d'esprit* and kept under lock and key until after his death. Fearing that his reputation as a serious composer might be harmed, he permitted only one section, 'The Swan', to be published during his lifetime. The first public performance of the complete work did not take place until April 1922.

PUBLIC TRIUMPH, PRIVATE DISASTER

By the end of the 1860s Saint-Saëns was acknowledged as one of the supreme living composers. His music is of its time and yet somewhat apart from it. As with other prodigies, such as Mendelssohn and Korngold, there is little distinctive change in style from his earliest years to his last, though of course the craftsmanship increases in assurance and polish. The harmonic vocabulary is typically elegant, tuneful and French. Fauré noted the pleasure of following 'the curve, the progression of the ample developments, where the lines keep such neatness, acquiring such "visibility" that one could believe one was reading them'.

By contrast, Saint-Saëns's private life was a disaster, utterly at odds with the orderly construction and harmonious colours of his music. It has been said that he 'longed to be a father without being a husband'. He remained a bachelor till he was 40, when he married (against his mother's wishes and after a whirlwind romance) Marie-Laure-Émille Truffot, the 19-year-old sister of one of his favourite pupils. There was no honeymoon, and after the wedding ceremony the couple returned to his house in the Rue du Faubourg St Honoré which he shared with his mother.

Despite Saint-Saëns's frequent absences, two sons were born in quick succession. In May 1878 the elder of the two, André, climbed out onto a fourth-floor window ledge, lost his balance and fell to his death. Barely six weeks later, his little brother, Jean-François, died suddenly from pneumonia. Saint-Saëns, influenced by his mother, blamed his wife for their deaths. While on holiday in the summer of 1881, he walked out of their hotel without warning, went back to his mother, and never saw or contacted his wife again. Marie Saint-Saëns died at the age of 95 in January 1950.

When his mother died at the age of 79 in 1888, Saint-Saëns contemplated suicide and thereafter led a nomadic life until his death. He travelled widely, not only to Russia and North America, but also to South America (he wrote a hymn for Uruguay's national holiday), Scandinavia, East Asia, the Canary Islands, and, most frequently, Algeria. Though his homosexuality was an open secret, he never divulged his destinations and often travelled under a false name so that he could combine sightseeing with encounters of an extra-musical kind.

A SULLIED LEGACY

After the death of his mother, Saint-Saëns's creative output diminished in productivity and scale. He became increasingly bitter and misanthropic –

'The artist who does not feel completely satisfied by elegant lines, by harmonious colours, and by a beautiful succession of chords does not understand the art of music.'
SAINT-SAËNS

and began to make enemies. Arrogant and opinionated, he had a fearsome reputation for rudeness and graceless behaviour. 'He was a most irritable man,' recalled the conductor Sir Thomas Beecham. His outspoken dislike of Brahms, Richard Strauss, Franck and d'Indy and his implacable opposition to the progressive music of Debussy and others won him no friends. In the final two decades of his life, the musical establishment turned its back on the irascible Saint-Saëns and his old-fashioned music. He had attended the premieres of works by Bellini, Mendelssohn and Schumann; not surprisingly, he found the first performances of works by Schoenberg and Prokofiev hard to comprehend. The premiere of *The Rite of Spring* left him speechless (though Stravinsky recalled that 'the sharp little man' remained bravely in his seat till the end).

Essential works

Fantaisie in E flat, organ (1857)
Introduction and Rondo Capriccioso, violin and orchestra (1863)
Piano Concerto No. 2 in G minor (1868)
Cello Concerto No. 1 in A minor (1872)
DANSE MACABRE, orchestra (1874)
SAMSON ET DALILA, opera (1877)
Violin Concerto No. 3 in B minor (1880)
Septet in E flat (1881)
Violin Sonata No. 1 in D minor (1885)
Symphony No. 3 in C minor (with organ) (1886)
THE CARNIVAL OF THE ANIMALS (1886)

This latter period of his life did much to damage Saint-Saëns's legacy, overshadowing the good work of his long career. He helped to found the Société Nationale de Musique in 1871. Its purpose was to give new French music a hearing, and this it did for many years, introducing works by Franck, d'Indy, Ravel and others. He promoted the music of Liszt, Berlioz and Wagner, and introduced Mussorgsky's *Boris Godunov* to French musicians (he brought the score back with him from Russia). In 1910, aged nearly 75, London heard him play 12 of Mozart's piano concertos in three concerts 'to draw the attention of the public to many valuable but at present almost unknown works'. He introduced to France the conception of the Lisztian symphonic poem and made many experiments with traditional structures, such as concertos in single or double movements with thematic sharing or transformation between sections.

When Saint-Saëns announced his retirement four months before his death, he had been performing in public for 75 years. His last appearance was in his father's home town of Dieppe. He died aged 85 on 16 December 1921 in the arms of his manservant under the winter sun and blue skies of Algiers. He was given a state funeral at the Madeleine in Paris.

EXOTIC INFLUENCES

SAINT-SAËNS DREW, TO A RARE DEGREE, ON THE MUSIC OF OTHER NATIONS FOR HIS INSPIRATION. Wherever he travelled, the sounds and themes he collected were used and transmuted into Westernized musical language: the Africa Fantasy for piano and orchestra (part of which the composer himself recorded in 1904); the 'Egyptian' Piano Concerto No. 5 (with a Nubian love song quoted in its second movement); the Arabian Caprice; the Algerian Suite; Persian Songs; and the charming one-act opera *La Princesse jaune* with its hints of Japonisme. He was also among the first composers to use folk-song – from Brittany, the Auvergne, Spain and Italy.

GEORGES
BIZET

Founder of French lyric opera

1838–75

THINK OF BIZET AND YOU THINK OF *CARMEN*,

the C in the ABC of the world's most popular operas, alongside *Aida* and *La Bohème*. But what else did he write to qualify him as a great composer? Most people would be hard pressed to name another work by Bizet. There are, in truth, few of his works that are regularly performed, but – exceptionally – we can admit him to the pantheon on the basis of a single masterpiece, for *Carmen* is indisputably such a work, one that has never ceased to entrance audiences ever since its first performance in 1875.

Carmen was, in a variety of ways, a revolutionary work. It was a precursor of the Italian *verismo* school of opera – the naturalistic approach adopted by composers such as Mascagni, Puccini, Giordano and Leoncavallo. Their subjects were drawn not from mythology or morality tales but from contemporary life, and typically they presented scenes of heightened violence in sordid surroundings. Since the 1830s the prevailing fashion in France had been for the grand operas of Meyerbeer and others, which generally involved huge choruses, elaborate scenic effects, ballets, ceremonials and processions. *Carmen* was the first French opera to depart from this model. Bizet's muse was altogether more restrained and refined. The characters in *Carmen* were believable, ordinary people invested with real human feelings (shocking as they were to Parisian audiences of the day). Bizet's rich orchestration conjured up a sensitive feeling for atmosphere, while the use of Wagner's leitmotif methods unified different elements of the score.

EARLY LIFE

Because his name is so inextricably linked with an opera, it comes as a surprise to learn that Bizet began his career as a child prodigy on the piano (in the course of his career he composed over 150 works for the instrument). Georges Alexandre César Léopold Bizet was born in Paris on 25 October 1838, the son of professional musicians. He entered the Paris Conservatoire at the age of only nine and remained there for a further nine years, studying piano, organ and composition, the latter with Jacques Halévy, himself remembered today for a single (once famous) opera, *La Juive*.

By the age of 17 Bizet had written his first symphony, quite the equal of anything that Mozart or Mendelssohn had composed at a comparable age. This Symphony in C, composed in just a month towards the end of 1855, remained completely unknown until 1935, when the composer Reynaldo Hahn presented the score with a pile of other manuscripts to the Paris Conservatoire. He had not found it particularly interesting. Bizet's English biographer, D.C. Parker, thought otherwise and handed the symphony to the great conductor Felix Weingartner, who gave the first performance of this youthful work 80 years after its composition.

While still at the Conservatoire, the precocious Bizet completed a one-act operetta, *Le Docteur Miracle*. It won a prize in a competition sponsored by Offenbach and was produced in Paris in April 1857. It was Bizet's first taste of operatic success. Though he had to wait a long time for another, in the same year he won the coveted Prix de Rome and went to Italy to study. He was joined there two years later by his lifelong friend Ernest Guiraud, the 1859 prize winner. All in all, it was a promising start. But then it all went wrong.

DISSIPATED ENERGY

Bizet's problem was his inability to decide on any one project, and those he chose generally turned out to be failures. Ideas that filled him with enthusiasm were soon abandoned in favour of something else. With an unerring ability to pick a weak libretto and then to set it to uneven music, throughout the 1860s he wrote a string of unsuccessful works, such as *Vasco da Gama* (a symphony with chorus) and the comic operas *Don Procopio* and *La Guzla de l'émir*. The latter was all set for production in Paris when Bizet changed his mind, withdrew the score and subsequently destroyed it. *Les Pêcheurs de*

perles (The Pearl Fishers) was premiered in Paris in 1863. It was a failure, though Berlioz much admired it and it is nowadays the only other opera of Bizet's in the repertoire. From Act 1 comes the celebrated duet for tenor and baritone, 'Au fond du temple saint' ('In the depths of the temple'), sung by the two fishermen Nadir and Zurga as they recall the love they both had for the same beautiful girl. Largely thanks to a famous recording of it

'Let us have fantasy, boldness, unexpectedness, enchantment – above all, tenderness, morbidezza!' BIZET

made in 1950 by Jussi Björling and Robert Merrill, radio listeners have on several occasions voted the duet their all-time favourite piece of classical music.

Finding it difficult to focus his creative energies, Bizet settled for an undemanding way of life. This included a relationship with the fantastic adventuress Céleste Mogador, his neighbour in Le Vésinet, the little village just outside Paris where Bizet lived in the cottage his father had built overlooking the banks of the Seine. He was a plump young man with a short temper and an addiction to chocolate, cakes and *petits fours*. He was invariably to be seen elegantly dressed and nibbling a bonbon. By the time he was 30, though, he had little to show for all his early promise.

In 1864 Bizet married Geneviève Halévy, the daughter of his old professor at the Conservatoire (she was later to become the model for Proust's Princess de Guermantes in *À la recherche du temps perdu*). His career slowly began to take shape, though not without further failures, including the operas *La jolie fille de Perth* (1867) and *Djamileh* (1872), the latter subsequently a great favourite of Mahler. Despite their unsuccessful productions, many began to discern an originality and lyrical gift that had not hitherto been recognized. A delightful suite of pieces for piano duet, *Jeux d'enfants*, appeared in 1871, while the incidental music he composed for Alphonse Daudet's play *L'Arlésienne* (1872) and the overture *Patrie* (1873) brought him some success – though not enough to lift him out of obscurity.

CARMENALIA

THE FIRST COMPLETE RECORDING OF *CARMEN* WAS MADE AS EARLY AS 1908 and covered 36 sides of 78-rpm discs. It was filmed the following year. Since then there have been 13 further screen versions and a stage adaptation (subsequently filmed) by Oscar Hammerstein II entitled *Carmen Jones* (1945). Apart from the two purely orchestral *Carmen* suites (the second arranged by Guiraud after Bizet's death), many composers have been inspired by the opera's themes, most notably Sarasate and Waxman (both for violin) and Moszkowski, Busoni and Horowitz (for piano).

THE RIGHT PATH — TOO LATE

A commission from the Opéra-Comique set him working on a new opera. He chose as his subject Prosper Mérimée's hot-blooded story *Carmen* and was introduced to two of Paris's leading librettists, both experienced men of the theatre, Henri Meilhac and Ludovic Halévy, a cousin of his wife. Bizet wrote to a friend of 'the absolute certainty of having found my path'. *Carmen* received its premiere on 25 March 1875. The low-life tale of passion and murder set against a background of gypsies, thieves and cigarette makers, the sight of women smoking on stage, to say nothing of the depraved character of *Carmen* herself — this was not quite what the puritanical, middle-class Parisian opera-goers were used to. Some found it shocking, others merely disappointing, though there was no doubting the generally enthusiastic response at the end of the first act. Bizet was heartbroken, pronouncing it 'a definite and hopeless flop'.

This was far from the truth. For a start his publisher had paid him the handsome sum of 25,000 francs for the score and, on the eve of the premiere, he had been made a Chevalier of the Légion d'honneur. Ticket sales picked up and Carmen received a thoroughly respectable run of 37 performances. But fate decreed that he should not live long enough to see his masterpiece acclaimed as such, for on 3 June 1875, the evening of the 31st performance of Carmen, Bizet died of a heart attack brought on by a throat infection (probably cancer). He was 36 years old. Had he lived another few months, he would have experienced the complete triumph of *Carmen*; another three years and he would have seen it, the first work of his maturity, produced in nearly every opera house in Europe.

Essential works

Symphony in C (1855)
THE PEARL FISHERS, opera (1863)
VARIATIONS CHROMATIQUES, piano (1868)
JEUX D'ENFANTS, piano duet (also orchestra) (1871)
L'ARLÉSIENNE (incidental music), orchestra (1872)
CARMEN, opera (1874)

UNCONSCIOUS BORROWING

ONE OF THE MOST FAMOUS TUNES IN *CARMEN* IS NOT BY BIZET AT ALL. 'L'amour est un oiseau rebelle' ('Love is a rebellious bird'), otherwise known as the 'Habanera', is written in the rhythm of a Cuban dance. Bizet thought it was a folk tune and inserted it into the opera without realizing that it was in fact a recently composed ditty called 'El Arreglito' by Sebastián de Yradier (1809–65).

Pyotr
Tchaikovsky

Tortured giant of Russian music

1840—93

ARGUABLY THE GREATEST –

AND CERTAINLY THE MOST POPULAR – OF ALL RUSSIAN COMPOSERS, Tchaikovsky had a melodic gift that few have equalled. To this he brought an exuberant orchestral imagination, piquant harmonies and the ability to strike at the heart of human emotion, so it is little wonder that so many love his music. The impact he had on succeeding generations was profound, from Rachmaninov (his musical heir) and Scriabin to Mahler, Elgar and Richard Strauss.

Tchaikovsky combined the nationalist elements of the 'Mighty Handful' (Balakirev, Mussorgsky, Rimsky-Korsakov, Cui and Borodin) with the European tradition. Every bar is unmistakably the work of a Russian, yet, as the critic Harold Schonberg so succinctly put it, 'where Rimsky-Korsakov spread out his arms to embrace Russian antiquity and folklore, where Mussorgsky spread out his arms to embrace the entire Russian people, Tchaikovsky spread out his arms to embrace – himself'. Has there ever been a more neurotic, troubled composer so willing to portray himself in music? Gloomy and passionate, childlike and ecstatic by turns, Tchaikovsky expressed himself with a heart-on-sleeve frankness, sometimes bordering on the hysterical, that some find embarrassing.

Self-doubt alternated with surging confidence. Throughout his life he was plagued with guilt over his homosexuality (in his letters he refers to it as 'Z'). It was this lifelong inner conflict that, with bitter irony, provided much of the well-spring of his genius. For Tchaikovsky was happiest when he was sad, viewing his sorrows with detachment and encapsulating them in music of the utmost beauty.

EARLY LIFE

The second of six surviving children, Pyotr Ilyich Tchaikovsky was born on 7 May 1840 in the Viatka district of Votkinsk. 'I grew up in a quiet place,' he recalled, 'and was drenched from my earliest childhood with the wonderful beauty of Russian popular songs.' He began improvising at the piano and composed his first song at the age of four. When he was eight, the family moved to St Petersburg, but the better position his father (an engineer) had hoped for there did not materialize. Pyotr and his elder brother Modeste were packed off to a brutal boarding school for two years. Highly strung and sensitive, he had to be torn away from his mother, even clinging to the wheels of her carriage to stop her leaving. His mother's death from cholera in 1854 was a blow from which, it can be argued, he never completely recovered.

After studying law in St Petersburg and working unhappily as a civil servant, in 1862 Tchaikovsky determined to follow his piano teacher Nikolai Zaremba to the newly-founded St Petersburg Conservatory. The following year he became a full-time musician. Only two years later, Nikolai Rubinstein invited Tchaikovsky to teach harmony at the Moscow Conservatory that he had recently founded.

The year 1868 was decisive in Tchaikovsky's career. His First Symphony, 'Winter Daydreams', was completed and well received at its first performance. He also became infatuated with the celebrated Belgian soprano Désirée Artôt and even considered marrying her, only to be deeply hurt when she deserted him to marry a Spaniard. The same year he was invited to meet the famous Five – 'the Mighty Handful' – in St Petersburg. Under their leader Balakirev's supervision, he began to compose some of

the most radiant love music ever written – the fantasy overture *Romeo and Juliet* – not as a reaction to the loss of Désirée but, it is now thought, inspired by his feelings for one Eduard Zak, one of the many young men for whom he developed a passion. Tchaikovsky later revised his fantasy into the masterwork we know today. For the next few years, his life proceeded on an untroubled course, composing, contributing to Moscow newspapers, teaching and making many trips abroad.

CRISIS AND CONSOLATION

The first of a series of crises was triggered late in 1875 when Tchaikovsky had completed his Piano Concerto No. 1. After he had played it through to Nikolai Rubinstein, to whom he had dedicated the work, Rubinstein denounced it as ugly and all but unplayable. Tchaikovsky was stunned and fell into a morbid depression, not helped by the initial failure of his ballet *Swan Lake*. Ironically, these two quickly became (and remain) two of his most popular works.

Then a guardian angel appeared in his life. An affluent and cultured widow, Nadezhda von Meck, commissioned Tchaikovsky to write some music, offering large fees for the work. She was a remarkable woman – 45 years old, the mother of 11 children and passionately fond of music. It was a relationship that developed into one of the most unlikely yet rewarding in music history. For the following 14 years, the two corresponded voluminously. In roughly 1100 intimate letters, Tchaikovsky poured out to her his innermost thoughts, aspirations and ideals. Nadezhda responded with understanding, sympathy, encouragement – and financial support to the tune of 6000 roubles a year. One of her conditions for this generous subsidy was that they should never meet. Once, when they did accidentally come face to face, both turned crimson with embarrassment and fled.

Early on in this curious friendship, the greatest crisis in the composer's life nearly ended in his death. A 28-year-old music student named Antonina Milyukova became obsessed with him. She was charming, pretty, neurotic and a nymphomaniac. Tchaikovsky found himself strangely drawn to her. She threatened to kill herself unless he married her. 'I am convinced,' Tchaikovsky confided to his brother Modeste, also homosexual, 'that my inclinations are the greatest and insuperable barrier to my well-being, and I must by all means struggle against my nature.' He married Antonina on 18 July 1877. Of course, it was an unmitigated disaster. After only five days he was beside himself and wrote to Modeste, 'Physically, she is totally repulsive to me.' On 7 August he fled to his sister Alexandra's estate at Kamenka. Shortly afterwards he attempted to kill himself in the freezing waters of the Moskva river. He failed even to catch a cold. The couple never met again and were finally divorced in 1881, but Antonina continued to pester him for many years, badgering him for

Essential works

ROMEO AND JULIET, fantasy overture
(1869, rev. 1870 and 1880)
Piano Concerto No. 1 in B flat minor
(1875, rev. 1879 and 1889)
Symphony No. 4 in F minor (1877)
SWAN LAKE, ballet (1877)
Violin Concerto in D (1878)
EUGENE ONEGIN, opera (1878)
Symphony No. 5 in E minor (1888)
THE SLEEPING BEAUTY, ballet (1890)
THE NUTCRACKER, ballet (1892)
Symphony No. 6 in B minor, 'Pathétique'
(1893)

'Oh, how difficult it is to make anyone see and feel in music what we see and feel ourselves.'

TCHAIKOVSKY

money and issuing veiled threats of blackmail.

Financially secure and with the marriage crisis over, Tchaikovsky poured forth a string of masterpieces all born out of personal despair, including the Fourth Symphony, the Violin Concerto and the opera *Eugene Onegin*. Other rather more uneven works followed: the G major Piano Sonata (1878), the four Suites for Orchestra (1878–87), the Second Piano Concerto (1880), the '1812' Overture (1880), then the dazzling *Capriccio italien*, the sublime Serenade for Strings and the emotionally wrought Piano Trio. Tchaikovsky was by now acknowledged universally as the foremost Russian composer.

FINAL YEARS

Between 1881 and 1888 the music dried up. Inspiration returned that year with the Fifth Symphony. The government settled an annual pension on Tchaikovsky and he toured Europe, conducting his works to enormous acclaim. *The Sleeping Beauty*, the richest of his ballet scores, appeared, as well as his great opera, *The Queen of Spades*. Then in 1890 came a letter from his patroness saying that, because of financial reverses, she could no longer subsidise him. In fact, as the composer discovered later, there were other unexplained reasons why Nadezhda von Meck had abruptly terminated the friendship – it certainly was not lack of money. In any case it was a devastating rejection.

A triumphant tour of the United States did little to raise his spirits and he returned to Russia in a profound gloom, fearing that he was going mad. Yet in 1892 he completed one of his most enchanting and brilliantly orchestrated scores, *The Nutcracker*, a perennially popular ballet based on the fairy-tale by E.T.A. Hoffmann. He then wrote in a fever of intensity what would be his last work and greatest symphony. The 'Pathétique', his sixth, is one of the most original, rewarding and personal in the repertoire. 'I can tell you in all sincerity,' he wrote to his nephew, 'that I consider this symphony the best thing I have ever done . . . I frequently wept as I worked it out in my mind.'

In October 1893 Tchaikovsky conducted the premiere (it was coolly received). On 2 November, after his evening meal, he drank a glass of unboiled tap water. Four days later he died, like his mother, from cholera.

CHOLERA OR SUICIDE OR . . . ?

THE QUESTION OF WHETHER TCHAIKOVSKY COMMITTED SUICIDE has fascinated scholars for over a century. One troubling aspect of the cholera theory is that though his body lay in state in his brother's bedroom and was then taken to Kazan Cathedral where hundreds of mourners filed past to pay their respects, not one person was reported as catching the highly contagious disease. Rumours persist that Tchaikovsky was having a relationship with the tsar's son and that Alexander III ordered Tchaikovsky's disappearance (to be poisoned by his doctor, claimed Tchaikovsky's sister-in-law). Yet another theory has him having an affair with the nephew of a Russian nobleman. There is no doubt that Tchaikovsky was fearful of posterity knowing about the sexuality he himself described as 'unnatural' and a 'vice'. Some suggest he killed himself in despair over his sexuality or from fear of its disclosure. We shall never know for certain.

ANTONÍN
DVOŘÁK

The greatest of all Czech composers

1841 — 1904

IF SMETANA WAS THE FATHER OF CZECH MUSIC, DVOŘÁK WAS THE COMPOSER WHO POPULARIZED IT. Like Schubert before him and his friend and contemporary Tchaikovsky, melodies simply flowed from him. Like Smetana, he did not use actual folk tunes but rather absorbed their essence, painting their character with his own more vivid colours.

Dvořák was a country boy, a rustic with a sunny, outgoing disposition. His music is pervaded by a love of the countryside and nature. Its supreme attractions are its directness and innocence, for – as one writer observed of Dvořák – 'life was a very wonderful, uncomplicated thing to him'. Instead of turmoil or neuroticism or dark brooding, we encounter a simple and sincere piety, such as only a deeply religious man is capable of.

EARLY LIFE

Antonín Dvořák was born on 8 September 1841 in the small Bohemian village of Nelahozeves on the banks of the Vltava some 50 miles north of Prague. His father was the local butcher and innkeeper. Until very recently it was believed not only that he wished his son to follow in his footsteps but that he actively discouraged him from pursuing a musical career. Both these 'facts' have now been proved to be myths. František Dvořák was a proficient zither player (he later turned professional) and was keen to nurture his son's obvious talents. Music seems to have been inborn, for Antonín taught himself the violin as a child, playing at village fairs, singing in church choirs and performing with local orchestras. When he was 12 years old, financed by an uncle, he was sent away to study music and learn German. By good fortune, the headmaster of the school was an excellent musician, one Antonín Liehmann, who taught Dvořák piano, viola and organ, as well as giving him a good grounding in musical theory. At 16, he entered the Prague Organ School, where, while studying and exploring the classical repertoire, he fell under the spell of Wagner.

'All the great musicians have borrowed from the songs of the people.'

DVOŘÁK

For most of the 1860s, Dvořák spent his time playing the violin and viola in cafés and theatres (one concert of Wagner excerpts in which he played was conducted by the composer himself). He composed prolifically, ruthlessly consigning many of the results to the flames. As a member of the Prague National Theatre Orchestra, he played under no less a figure than Smetana, and as a violist with the Opera Orchestra took part in a number of Smetana premieres, including *The Bartered Bride* and *Dalibor*.

But life was a struggle, with little money and recognition. Dvořák lived entirely for music – and trains, for like Hindemith half a century later, he was one of music's great trainspotters. He knew by heart all the timetables from the Franz-Josef Station in Prague and often said that he would have liked to have invented a steam locomotive, 'one of the highest achievements of the human spirit'.

In 1873 Dvořák's life changed. He abandoned the orchestra for the organ loft of St Adalbert's in Prague, a less demanding job that gave him more time to compose. In the same year he married one

of his former pupils, Anna Čermáková. This change in circumstances unleashed a burst of creative activity that produced two symphonies (No. 3 in E flat and No. 4 in D minor), a five-act opera called *Vanda*, three quartets (Opp. 9, 12 and 16), and a sequence of masterpieces including the Serenade for Strings, the G major Quintet and the Symphony No. 5 in F. This last work, as well as winning him the Austrian State Prize (he went on to win it three years in succession), also won the respect of Brahms, who was on the jury. The relationship between the two men developed into one of lifelong friendship. Brahms was instrumental in finding a publisher for the younger man's work and became a staunch champion. On one occasion, when some criticism of Dvořák's work had been voiced, Brahms is reported to have leapt to his defence, saying: 'I should be glad if something occurred to me as a main idea that occurs to Dvořák only by the way.'

A DISTINCTIVE VOICE

Dvořák was perceptive enough to recognize that his music up to 1873 had been a derivative copy of Wagner, Brahms and other German late Romantics. As soon as he began to use the musical character and rhythms of his native land, a personal, fresh, distinctive voice emerged. His first set of Slavonic Dances, published in 1878, made him famous. Within five years of his marriage, he was hailed throughout Europe as a major creative personality.

His works, notably the third Slavonic Rhapsody and the Symphony No. 6 in D, were played by the august Vienna Philharmonic Orchestra. He composed energetically – the Scherzo Capriccioso, the F minor Piano Trio, the opera *Dimitrij* – and by 1884 he had made sufficient money to buy a small farmhouse house in his beloved Czech countryside. The same year saw the first of many trips to England. Here he was greeted as a celebrity by enthusiastic audiences who warmed as much to his engaging personality as to his music. At London's Albert Hall and the Crystal Palace he conducted his oratorio *Stabat mater*, written in 1877 after the death of his child, and his Symphony No. 6. Thereafter, Dvořák made frequent visits to England. In 1891 he made two: one to conduct his Requiem at the Birmingham Festival, the other to receive an honorary doctorate from Cambridge University.

It was also in 1891 that Dvořák, shortly after being appointed professor of composition at the Prague Conservatory, was offered the directorship of the National Conservatory of Music in New York. At first he declined, but a combination of the persuasive and formidable Mrs Thurber, whose fortune had financed the Conservatory, and a salary of $15,000 proved too much to resist. In 1893 he and his wife moved to the United States after a string of farewell tours. Unsurprisingly, perhaps, Dvořák fell prey to acute homesickness, but this, coupled with his introduction to American indigenous music,

A HAPPY FIND

DESPITE THE INTERNATIONAL RECOGNITION HE HAD ACHIEVED, Dvořák lived in relative poverty as a result of unfavourable contracts with his music publishers. The great violinist Fritz Kreisler visited him at his home in 1903 and recalled that the scene looked like something out of *La Bohème*. The money from his tours and sojourn in America had gone. 'I had been playing some of Dvořák's Slavonic Dances,' wrote Kreisler, 'and visited the old man to pay my respects. I asked him if he had nothing further for me to play. "Look through that pile," said the sick composer, indicating a pile of unorganized papers. "Maybe you can find something." I did. It was the Humoresque [in G flat, Op. 101, No. 7 for piano].' Thanks largely to Kreisler's arrangement for violin and piano, which he recorded several times, the endearing little tune has become one of the most familiar in all classical music.

inspired his most popular works. Between January and May 1893 he composed the Symphony No. 9 in E minor, better known as the 'New World' Symphony. Despite its allusions to Negro spirituals and Native American music – the theme of its celebrated slow movement was turned into a song entitled 'Goin' Home' – the symphony has far more in common with the folk music of Bohemia than that of America.

In the summer of 1893, spent in the Czech-speaking community of Spillville, Iowa, he composed two of his best-known chamber works, the String Quartet in F (nicknamed the 'American') and the String Quintet in E flat. Also from his time in the States came the magnificent Cello Concerto, inspired by hearing that of his fellow teacher at the Conservatory, the operetta composer Victor Herbert. Completed in 1895, Dvořák 's work was premiered in 1896 in London, where it was an instant success. When Brahms heard it, he commented: 'Had I known that one could write a cello concerto like this, I would have written one long ago!'

Essential works

Serenade for Strings (1875)
STABAT MATER, oratorio (1877)
Slavonic Dances, Op. 46 (1878) and Op. 72 (1886)
Scherzo Capriccioso, orchestra (1883)
Symphony No. 8 in G (1889)
Piano Trio No. 4 in E minor, 'Dumky' (1891)
Symphony No. 9 in E minor, 'From the New World' (1893)
String Quartet No.12 in F, 'American' (1893)
Eight Humoresques, piano, Op. 101 (1894)
Cello Concerto (1895)
RUSALKA, opera (1901)

FINAL YEARS

Dvořák returned to Prague in 1895 and, restored to his familiar environment, produced a string of symphonic poems (among them *The Wood Dove, The Golden Spinning Wheel* and *The Noonday Witch*) based on old Czech legends. He resumed the professorship at the Prague Conservatory, and in 1901 was made its director. In the same year he was appointed a life member of the Austrian House of Lords, the first musician to be so honoured.

His last years were engaged largely in operatic activity, a period which produced the one opera that remains in today's repertoire, *Rusalka*, containing the ineffably beautiful soprano aria 'O silver moon'. His last months were clouded by a bitter dispute over his final opera *Armida*, and by its premiere in March 1904 Dvořák was too ill to sit through the performance. He died of heart failure on 1 May 1904. A national day of mourning was declared on the day of his funeral (5 May), and he was honoured with a burial in Vyšehrad Cemetery, where many other prominent Czechs are also buried.

DVOŘÁK DYNASTY

IN 1897 DVOŘÁK'S DAUGHTER OTYLKA MARRIED HIS PUPIL, THE CZECH VIOLINIST AND COMPOSER JOSEF SUK (1874–1935). Suk's grandson of the same name (b. 1929) is also an outstanding violinist. A more distant relation of Dvořák was August Dvorak (1894–1975), an American naval officer who invented an alternative arrangement of the typewriter keyboard in the 1930s.

EDVARD
GRIEG
The Chopin of the North

1843—1907

HANS VON BÜLOW, THE COMPOSER, CONDUCTOR AND (BRIEFLY) LISZT'S SON-IN-LAW, described Grieg as 'the Chopin of the North'. It is an apt description: not that Grieg's music is anything like Chopin's, but both composers were essentially miniaturists who used the piano as the basis for their musical expression and who fed off a proud nationalism. Neither relied on extant folk tunes for their material (at least, only rarely), yet in their different ways the music of Chopin and Grieg seems to define the character and landscape of their two nations.

Even though Grieg's best-known work is the masterly, evergreen Piano Concerto in A minor, it is not representative. The big canvas did not suit Grieg – his early symphony is not a success – and it is in his 140 songs and 66 short piano solos (*Lyric Pieces*) that we find his essentially intimate spirit. It is all the more remarkable, then, that this creator of tiny, perfectly fashioned jewels should have had such a far-reaching influence on those that followed. The impact on Manuel de Falla in Spain, for instance, and the creation of a nationalist school of music there was directly attributable to Grieg. His evocation of mood and atmosphere can be seen as a forerunner of 20th-century impressionism, and the works of Sibelius and Bartók.

EARLY LIFE

Grieg's great-grandfather was a Scot who emigrated to Bergen in Norway after the battle of Culloden, changed his name from Greig, and became British consul, a post subsequently held by his son and grandson. Edvard Hagerup Grieg was born in Bergen in the fjords of western Norway on 15 June 1843. His first lessons came from his mother, a talented amateur pianist. In 1858 the Norwegian violinist Ole Bull heard the young Grieg play the piano and persuaded his reluctant parents to send the boy to the Leipzig Conservatory. Grieg, who had considered becoming a priest, was no less unenthusiastic and hated his time there. Nevertheless, he studied with a distinguished trio of musicians – Ignaz Moscheles, Carl Reinecke and Moritz

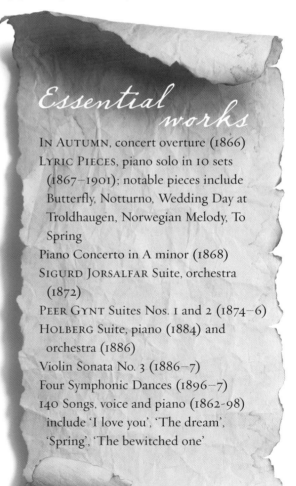

Essential works

IN AUTUMN, concert overture (1866)
LYRIC PIECES, piano solo in 10 sets (1867–1901); notable pieces include Butterfly, Notturno, Wedding Day at Troldhaugen, Norwegian Melody, To Spring
Piano Concerto in A minor (1868)
SIGURD JORSALFAR Suite, orchestra (1872)
PEER GYNT Suites Nos. 1 and 2 (1874–6)
HOLBERG Suite, piano (1884) and orchestra (1886)
Violin Sonata No. 3 (1886–7)
Four Symphonic Dances (1896–7)
140 Songs, voice and piano (1862-98) include 'I love you', 'The dream', 'Spring', 'The bewitched one'

AN INSPIRING MEETING

ON A VISIT TO ITALY IN 1869 GRIEG SHOWED THE BADLY WRITTEN MANUSCRIPT OF HIS PIANO CONCERTO TO LISZT, who read the entire work at sight ('it is significant,' wrote Grieg, 'that he played the cadenza, the most difficult part, best of all') and concluded this feat by handing back the manuscript to Grieg with the words: 'Keep steadily on. I tell you, you have the capability, and – do not let them intimidate you!' This was a moment of tremendous importance to Grieg. 'At times when disappointment and bitterness are in store for me, I shall recall his words, and the remembrance of that hour will have a wonderful power to uphold in days of adversity.'

Hauptmann (the young Arthur Sullivan was a fellow student); and it was here that he heard Clara Schumann play her late husband's piano concerto and heard Richard Wagner conduct his *Tannhäuser*. It was in Leipzig, too, that he developed pleurisy, leaving his left lung seriously impaired and bequeathing him precarious health for the rest of his life.

In the spring of 1862 Grieg's first composition was published (*Four Piano Pieces*) and the following year he settled, not in Oslo, but in Copenhagen, where he concluded his studies in 1865. Denmark's leading composer Niels Gade took the young Norwegian under his wing, inspiring him to form the Euterpe Society dedicated to promoting Scandinavian music. This Grieg did with the aid of another gifted young composer, Rikard Nordraak, a dedicated patriot and passionate advocate of Norwegian folk music. 'From Nordraak,' wrote Grieg, 'I learned for the first time to know the nature of Norwegian folk tunes and my own nature.' Rikaard died in 1866 at the age of 24 (not before having written what is now Norway's national anthem).

A NATIONALIST VISION

The following year Grieg married his cousin, the talented lyric soprano Nina Hagerup, who would become the chief inspiration for and interpreter of his songs. (The best known of these, 'I Love You', was written for her in 1865, with words by Hans Christian Andersen.) His marriage and a move back to his native country inspired a musical reawakening, and from this point on Grieg, having been thoroughly immersed in the Germanic musical tradition, began to produce the kind of music that made his name synonymous with his country. True, it is largely modelled on German-based Romanticism (Schumann in particular), but it derives its unique voice from being a synthesis of this and the idioms of Norwegian folk songs and dances.

No clearer example can be found than the Piano Concerto in A minor, written in 1868 and premiered in Copenhagen the following year with Norway's greatest pianist, Edmund Neupert, as soloist. The work's opening theme is built on intervals characteristic of Norwegian folk music, while the boisterous finale draws on the *halling*, a typical Norwegian folk dance. Grieg was an excellent pianist (he lived to make several recordings of his own music in 1903) and wrote it as a vehicle for his own talents. It has been in the repertoire of virtually every major pianist since it was written, though it is the slightly revised 1907 version that we hear nowadays.

Grieg's missionary zeal to form a nationalist school of music met with initial opposition. But by 1874 he was so famous and highly valued that the Norwegian government awarded him an annuity that allowed him to be financially independent for the rest of his life. The same year, the playwright Henryk Ibsen asked him to provide the incidental music for his play *Peer Gynt*, a task that occupied Grieg for two years. From 1880 to 1882 he was conductor of the Bergen Philharmonic Society, and in

1884 he composed the *Holberg Suite*, to mark the bicentenary of the birth of another great Norwegian playwright, Ludvig Holberg. Apart from this work, almost all Grieg's biggest successes were written by the time he was 33.

FINAL YEARS

In 1885 Grieg moved into the villa he had built overlooking the fjord at Troldhaugen (Troll Hill) a few miles south of Bergen. For the last 20 years of his life his routine rarely changed. He would spend the summer and spring composing at Troldhaugen, reserving the winter months for travelling and concerts. He was a frequent visitor to England. Indeed, he was a much-loved figure wherever he went – showered with decorations and honours, admired by both (unusually) Brahms *and* Tchaikovsky, and awarded honorary doctorates of music by both Cambridge and Oxford Universities. His 60th birthday in 1903 was designated a national holiday in Norway.

'His deliberate smallness is one of his greatest virtues.'

HUBERT FOSS

As he grew older, Grieg's health deteriorated. Tended by his devoted wife, he spent increasing amounts of time out of the public eye at Troldhaugen, composing little in his final years but keeping up an active performing schedule to the end. His last public appearances anywhere were in London in May 1906, where he conducted two concerts of his own compositions. After that, he became a recluse. On 4 September 1907 he died of a heart attack at Troldhaugen. Following a state funeral, his ashes were sealed in the cliff face below his house. When Nina died in 1935, her ashes were interred next to her husband's.

Only a year after Grieg's death, Schoenberg composed his first atonal works. If Grieg provides an undemanding experience (Debussy said of his music that it is 'as if one had in one's mouth the bizarre and charming taste of pink sweet stuffed with snow'), we can perhaps also agree with Louis Elson who, in his 1929 study of Grieg, wrote: 'In these days when much music suggests nervous maladies and the mad house . . . Grieg comes like a whiff of pure air.'

THE REWARDS OF FAME

GRIEG'S LIFE SEEMS NEVER TO HAVE BEEN TOUCHED BY SCANDAL OR IMPROPRIETY. He was a shy, retiring, modest man, a Republican not overly impressed by medals and orders bestowed by royalty – though he confessed that they made travelling easier. He would place them on the top layer of his luggage: 'The Customs officials are always so kind to me at the sight of them.'

EDWARD ELGAR

'Our Shakespeare of music'

ALICE STUART WORTLEY

1857—1934

'LAND OF HOPE AND GLORY',

'NIMROD', THE CELLO CONCERTO . . . In the popular imagination, Elgar's music epitomizes the very essence of Englishness: proud, confident and indomitable, with a nostalgic, even sentimental view of England's glorious past and its pastoral beauty. Photographs of Elgar convey the image of an upper-class Edwardian gent, secure in his beliefs and station in life. History has come to label him as the first significant English composer since Purcell, the man who single-handedly rescued England from its reputation as 'the land without music'.

Paradoxically, the tonal language Elgar used to achieve his effects was in the mid-European tradition of Mendelssohn, Wagner and Brahms, albeit with an English accent. It was the generation of English composers that followed Elgar, notably Vaughan Williams and Holst, whose use of English folk music and idioms makes their music more obviously nationalist. Moreover, though Elgar was the first British composer of his era to win international stature, Stanford and Parry before him had written a significant amount of fine music that showed that England was already, before Elgar's arrival, very much a land with music.

What singles Elgar out and makes him a great composer are his extraordinary orchestral and compositional technique (he was an orchestrator of unsurpassed brilliance), his melodic genius and his ability to mine the contradictory nature of his own make-up: music of 'stately sorrow and heroic melancholy', as it has been so aptly characterized. Perhaps 'extraordinary' is too bland a description, for, unlike the vast majority of great composers, Edward Elgar had no formal musical training. 'I am self-taught in the matter of harmony, counterpoint, form, and, in short, the whole of the "mystery" of music,' he wrote.

EARLY LIFE

Far from being the bluff, stiff-upper-lip country gentleman of his photographs – that was a role he grew into – Elgar was born into genteel poverty. His father was a piano tuner and ran a music shop in Worcester. He was also the organist of the cathedral city's Roman Catholic church, a post he held for nearly 40 years. Elgar's mother came from farming stock; she was more inclined to literary interests and remained a lasting influence on Elgar's development. Christened Edward William, he was born on 2 June 1857 at Broadheath, near Worcester. By the age of 12, Elgar had taught himself the violin, was joining in the music-making of local ensembles and deputizing for his father at the organ. He had won a reputation for his improvising abilities at the piano and, having decided that music must be his life, he began by giving piano and violin lessons locally. For five years from 1879 he was bandmaster at the County Lunatic Asylum, an experience that allowed him to experiment with every kind of instrumental combination at will.

There is music in the air, music all around us, the world is full of it and you simply take as much as you require.' ELGAR

EDWARD ELGAR

By the time of his marriage in 1889, Elgar was thoroughly versed in the ways of composing but had earned only limited success. His wife was one of his piano pupils, Caroline Alice Roberts, the daughter of a retired major-general. She introduced him to upper-class, moneyed society, gave him self-confidence and a creative impetus, and boosted his ambitions. All of Elgar's important music was written during his 30-year marriage to Alice. When she died, his inspiration dried up. They had one child, their daughter Carice, who was born in 1890 and died as recently as 1970.

RISE TO GREATNESS

After an unsuccessful year in London, the couple returned to Worcestershire in 1891 to settle in Malvern. Over the next 13 years Elgar transformed his life from that of a small-time provincial musician to a major composer of international standing with a knighthood. For most of the 1890s his preoccupation was with choral works, for which the country seemed to have an insatiable demand. Immersed in the Anglican and Catholic choral traditions and with his lifelong association with choral societies, Elgar produced a string of successful religious and secular cantatas: *The Black Knight* (1892), *King Olaf* (1895), *The Light of Life* (1896), *The Banner of St George* (1897) and *Caractacus* (1898), culminating in 1900 with his masterpiece in this field, *The Dream of Gerontius*. Using a text by Cardinal Newman on the soul of Gerontius as it passes from life into death, it is a powerful meditation on the soul's immortality.

By the time *Gerontius* appeared, Elgar had already produced an orchestral masterpiece, a work that finally made his reputation as a composer of individuality and depth: Variations on an Original Theme (very German), popularly known as the 'Enigma' Variations (very English), a series of musical portraits of himself, his wife and his friends. That was in 1899, the year before *Gerontius*, which itself was succeeded in March 1901 by the first performance of the tune that is now Britain's second national anthem. It was 'a tune,' Elgar rightly predicted, 'that will knock 'em – knock 'em flat.'

The tune in question appears in the Trio (central) section of his Pomp and Circumstance March No. 1, first heard with March No. 2 in Liverpool. A short time later, Henry Wood included them in a London Promenade Concert. After playing March No. 1, Wood recalled, 'The people simply rose and yelled. I had to play it again – with the same result; in fact they refused to let me go on with the programme . . . I played the march a third time.' It is the only time in the history of the Promenade Concerts that a work has been given a double encore. Queen Victoria had died in January that year and Elgar was asked to contribute something to the forthcoming coronation of Edward VII. Arthur Benson, a master at Eton and son of the archbishop of Canterbury, supplied

ENIGMA ENIGMAS

VARIATIONS ON AN ORIGINAL THEME, ELGAR'S OP. 36, WAS DEDICATED 'TO MY FRIENDS PICTURED WITHIN'. There is no mention of 'Enigma' in the title, though the word appears in pencil on the autograph score. Why 'Enigma'? It was the name that Elgar gave to the simple tune he had improvised at the piano one evening. Soon, simply for fun, he began adapting it to portray the varied personalities of his friends.

For over a century musicologists have speculated about a hidden, unplayed theme that supposedly fits over the 'Enigma' tune. 'Auld Lang Syne', 'Rule! Britannia' and the slow movement of Mozart's 'Prague' Symphony have all been contenders. Elgar loved riddles, puns and word play. For instance, the most famous variation, No. 9 – 'Nimrod' – is a portrait of his publisher and friend Alfred Jaeger, whose surname means 'hunter' in German: in the Book of Genesis we read of 'Nimrod, the mighty hunter before the Lord'. But if there is a hidden theme in the Variations, then Elgar was mischievously determined not to reveal its identity.

Elgar with some verses that fitted the big 'knock 'em flat' tune, beginning with the words 'Land of Hope and Glory'. Music and words made their first triumphant appearance together at the conclusion of Elgar's Coronation Ode in 1902.

Now living in London and with his religious faith receding, Elgar turned his attention to what he considered the pinnacle of the composer's art, the symphony. Fifty is an exceptionally late age for a first symphony, but Elgar's maturity and technical expertise shine though in every bar of his 1908 Symphony in A flat. As the great conductor Hans Richter prepared its premiere, he addressed the orchestra: 'Gentlemen, let us now rehearse the greatest symphony of modern times, written by the greatest modern composer, and not only in this country.'

The year 1910 saw the premiere of Elgar's next large-scale work, the immortal Violin Concerto (one of the longest and most taxing in the repertoire), played by its dedicatee, the legendary Fritz Kreisler. Elgar's Second Symphony was first heard the following year, dedicated to the memory of Edward VII. Soon afterwards, Elgar was awarded the Order of Merit, the highest British honour for an artist.

A QUIET END

Elgar's next major work was strangely prescient, for *The Music Makers* uses thematic ideas from his past work united in a single vision – prescient because after his symphonic study *Falstaff* (1913), he would write little of importance until the glorious Cello Concerto, the String Quartet and the Piano Quintet. And after that – virtually nothing. With his wife's death in 1920, he lost the urge to create. He toyed for some years with a third symphony but was unhappy with the sketches and, on his deathbed, asked for them to be burned. They were not and, controversially, they were assembled and orchestrated into a complete symphony in 1997.

Honours were heaped upon the ageing composer: he was made Master of the King's Musick in 1924 and given a baronetcy in 1931. He returned to his roots in Worcester and for the last 14 years of his life was all but silent, though during these years he was a frequent visitor to the recording studio. Elgar was the first great composer to leave a sizeable survey of his creative output in his own interpretations. The loss of his wife and the First World War's destruction of the world he knew left him bereft, while the dissonance and new fads of contemporary music meant little to him. He died from cancer on 23 February 1934 in Worcester.

Essential works

VARIATIONS ON AN ORIGINAL THEME, 'ENIGMA', orchestra (1899)
SEA PICTURES, five orchestral song settings (1899)
THE DREAM OF GERONTIUS, oratorio (1900)
COCKAIGNE (IN LONDON TOWN), concert overture (1901)
POMP AND CIRCUMSTANCE MARCHES NOS. 1–5, orchestra (1901–30)
INTRODUCTION AND ALLEGRO, for strings (1905)
Symphony No. 1 in A flat (1908)
Violin Concerto (1910)
Symphony No. 2 in E flat (1911)
Cello Concerto (1919)

GIACOMO
PUCCINI
Last giant of Italian opera

1858—1924

HOW IS IT THAT A SINGLE COMPOSER IS RESPONSIBLE FOR THREE OF THE MOST POPULAR OF ALL

OPERAS: *La Bohème, Tosca* and *Madama Butterfly* — to say nothing of 'Nessun dorma' (from *Turandot*), the most performed operatic aria of all? Puccini belonged to no school and led to no others. His obvious role model was Verdi, but he also absorbed elements of Wagner, Debussy and even (later on) Stravinsky and Schoenberg.

Puccini combined the essential lyricism of Italian opera with the colour of Russian orchestration, a sensuality comparable to that of the contemporary French novel, and a grasp of local atmosphere as masterly as his understanding of theatre. Few composers have written for the human voice with such haunting tenderness and melancholy. As a manipulator of audience emotions, Puccini was second to none. He has been much criticized for this, but moving the audience is a large part of what theatre is about. Many opera composers die without realizing this.

EARLY LIFE

Giacomo Antonio Domenico Michele Secondo Maria Puccini was the fifth of seven children in the fifth (and last) generation of a dynasty of Italian musicians. His ancestors had all held various posts as organists and church composers in Lucca in northern Italy, where he was born on 22 December 1858. At first he showed no interest in music, though a local teacher, Carlo Angeloni, eventually managed to inspire the boy and before long he was playing the piano and organ like a good little Puccini should. However, it was a visit to Pisa in 1876 to see a production of Verdi's *Aida* that had a revelatory effect on him. From that moment on, he was determined to follow in Verdi's footsteps.

Assisted by funds from a great-uncle and a stipend from Queen Margherita, Puccini studied at the conservatory in Milan with Bazzini and Ponchielli. In 1883 he decided to enter a competition for a one-act opera initiated by the publisher Eduardo Sonzongo. The result, *Le Villi*, was written in a matter of weeks and did not even get a mention when the prizes for the competition were announced in 1874. But soon afterwards Puccini was at a party with several influential people in the musical world and was asked to sing some extracts from *Le Villi*. Astonishingly, this led directly to the one-act opera being produced at the Teatro dal Verme in Milan in May 1874. It was an immediate success. The great Milanese publishing house Ricordi snapped up the rights and commissioned him to write another. This was the beginning of a lifelong association between Puccini and Giulio Ricordi, in whom he found a fatherly friend and wise guide.

The next opera, called *Edgar*, based on a drama by Alfred de Musset, took Puccini five years to complete. It was a subject wholly unsuited to his gifts. Its first performance at La Scala, Milan, in April 1889 was a dismal failure. Puccini rewrote its four acts into three (1892) and again made revisions in 1901 and 1905, all to no avail. In the composer's words, *Edgar* was 'a blunder'.

'God touched me with his little finger and said, "Write for the theatre, only for the theatre."' PUCCINI

During the gestation of *Edgar*, Puccini began an affair with Elvira Gemignani, the wife of one of his friends, a wealthy Lucca merchant. Divorce in Catholic Italy was not possible, but Elvira left her husband, followed Puccini to Milan with her small daughter, and in 1886 gave birth to Puccini's only son, Antonio. The couple had to wait until Gemignani's death in 1904 before they could marry.

HIT AFTER HIT

Puccini's next opera was based, somewhat riskily, on the same novel, *L'Histoire du Chevalier des Grieux et de Manon Lescaut* (1731) by Abbé Prévost, on which Massenet had based his opera *Manon*, an enormous success in 1884. Puccini's version was the work that made him internationally famous, assured his reputation and laid the foundation of his wealth. In fact, no first night of a Puccini opera ever again approached the rapturous welcome given to *Manon Lescaut* in Turin in 1893. It was a triumph that caused George Bernard Shaw, then a music critic, to remark prophetically, 'Puccini looks to me more like the heir of Verdi than any of his rivals.'

Manon was followed three years later in 1896 by *La Bohème*, which was more conversational in style, more grittily real in its subject matter and had a more impressionistic orchestral score. Its string of hit arias, which include 'Che gelida manina', 'Si, mi chiamano Mimì', Musetta's Waltz Song and the Act 3 quartet 'Addio, dolce svegliare', have helped contribute to the opera's enduring appeal. The conductor for the premiere was the young Arturo Toscanini (a broadcast performance of him conducting the work was recorded for posterity exactly 50 years later). Though initial reaction was cooler than for *Manon Lescaut*, within a very short time *La Bohème* had been produced all over the world. Today, it can claim to be the most popular opera ever written.

Puccini's next project is scarcely less admired. Based on Victorien Sardou's 1887 play *La Tosca*, *Tosca* (1900) was Puccini's second excursion into the world of operatic verismo, a style initiated by Bizet in *Carmen* and epitomized by Leoncavallo's *Pagliacci* and Mascagni's *Cavalleria rusticana*. The roles of Cavaradossi the painter, Tosca the opera singer, and the evil chief of police Scarpia provide three of the plum roles in the repertoire. Three outstanding arias, 'Recondita armonia', 'Vissi d'arte' and 'E lucevan le stelle', are among the best loved of all. Four years later in 1904 came the last of this remarkable trilogy, *Madama Butterfly*. Puccini went to great pains not to repeat himself musically, this time creating an exotic Japanese atmosphere and using authentic Japanese folk tunes in the score. The story was based on a real-life incident recounted in a magazine article and turned into a play by David Belasco. Puccini felt that the opera, concerning the tragic love of the young geisha Cio-Cio San for Lieutenant Pinkerton of the US Navy, was 'the most felt and most expressive opera that I have conceived'.

By now Puccini was a wealthy man. In 1900 he had built a villa in the village of Torre del Lago on the shores of Lake Massaciuccoli near Florence. Here he could indulge his passion for shooting wild ducks and other game birds (fast boats and fast cars were his other enthusiasms). He described

MASTER OF THE SOUND BITE

PUCCINI'S CANVASES MAY HAVE BEEN SMALLER THAN THOSE OF VERDI AND WAGNER, but this in large part explains his enduring popularity. He was the first major composer to benefit from the four-minute sound bite, for by a lucky coincidence many of his best-known arias fitted neatly onto one side of the newly invented 78-rpm disc and, later, the 45-rpm 'single'. Not many classical composers can claim to have had their music played on juke boxes and sung at football matches. 'The only music I can make is of small things,' he once said, but in the writing of small things he was a genius.

himself as 'a mighty hunter of wild fowl, opera librettos and attractive women'. Puccini had numerous affairs, but one relationship in particular might itself have furnished the plot of an opera. After their marriage, the relationship between Puccini and Elvira descended from a passionate love match to a series of frequent and violent quarrels. Elvira became convinced that her husband was having an affair with their servant Doria Manfredi. Mad with jealousy, Elvira made public accusations against her, carrying out such a vicious campaign of harassment against the girl that she killed herself by taking poison. The autopsy revealed that she had died a virgin. Puccini fled to Rome where, it is said, he wept for three days. Elvira was sentenced to five months in prison.

Essential works

MANON LESCAUT, opera (1893)
LA BOHÈME, opera (1896)
TOSCA, opera (1900)
MADAMA BUTTERFLY, opera (1904)
IL TRITTICO, opera (1918); comprises IL
 TABARRO, SUOR ANGELICA and GIANNI
 SCHICCHI
TURANDOT, opera (1926)

Puccini turned to another play by Belasco for his next venture, *La fanciulla del West* (*The Golden Girl of the West*), set in the 1849 Californian gold rush. Despite Toscanini on the rostrum for the premiere in 1910 and the presence of Enrico Caruso in the leading role of Dick Johnson, the opera never caught on, partly as a result of the absence of any hit arias. *La rondine* (1917), an unhappy mix of opera and operetta, was only the second failure of Puccini's career. His fortunes were restored by *Il trittico* (*The Tryptych*) (1918), which consisted of three one-act operas: *Il tabarro* (The Cloak), *Suor Angelica* (Sister Angelica) and the comedy *Gianni Schicchi* (the opera's eponymous hero), from which comes the much loved 'O mio babbino caro' ('O my beloved father').

PIONEER TO THE END

For his last opera, *Turandot*, left incomplete at his death, Puccini presented himself with more self-imposed challenges. Its sadistic plot, lack of dramatic cohesion and subtle use of contemporary musical trends (there are many dissonant and polytonal vocal and orchestral passages) make its most famous aria, 'Nessun dorma', distinctly unrepresentative of the work. Still, it remains a testament to Puccini's unflagging adventurousness as a composer – an inspired craftsman who was adroit enough to take the public with him whatever novelties he introduced. Writing in 1922, Puccini observed that 'By now the public for new music has lost its palate. It loves or puts up with illogical music devoid of all sense. Melody is no longer practised – or, if it is, it is vulgar. People believe the symphonic element must rule, and I, instead, believe this is the end of opera.' *Turandot* was, arguably, the last opera written in the 20th century to have entered the standard repertoire and also remain popular with the general public (as opposed to opera lovers).

Puccini died on 29 November 1924 in Brussels. He had a heart attack while undergoing treatment for cancer of the larynx – ironically, for it was his exalted writing for the voice and the string of roles that have attracted the greatest singers that will ensure his immortality.

GUSTAV
MAHLER
Mighty symphonist and neurotic

1860 — 1911

THE 50 YEARS OF MAHLER'S LIFE COINCIDED WITH SOME OF THE MOST RADICAL CHANGES in musical history, a period that encompassed the final flowering of the grand Romantic tradition in Bruckner and Brahms and the revolutionary language of Schoenberg. Mahler's music is the link between the two. But it stands out in one other respect: arguably, no other composer has drawn so exclusively on his response to the world around him and his own (troubled) psyche. Mahler's music is obsessed with his literary tastes, his neuroses, his reaction to nature, the inseparable mingling of pain and joy, of sensual gratification and human suffering, and above all the cycle of life and death.

Mahler's four great song collections are all concerned with these themes and, indeed, provided a melodic repository for his nine mighty symphonies (he left a tenth unfinished). At the end of his life, Mahler fused song and symphony together into what many consider to be his most beautiful and personal work, *Das Lied von der Erde* (The Song of the Earth). 'A symphony must be like the world,' he wrote. 'It must contain everything.' He practised what he preached, for these mammoth works make huge demands on the performers, some single movements lasting longer than an entire symphony by Mozart or Haydn. The last great cycle of Romantic symphonies, conveying 'lofty concepts of universal art', they take music to the very brink of atonality (that is, music without a fixed key). 'My symphonies represent the contents of my entire life; I have written into them all my experience and all my suffering,' he wrote. 'There too will be found my *angst*.'

EARLY LIFE

Mahler revelled in these fears and anxieties, the product of a singularly traumatic childhood. He was a manic depressive, an egomaniac, a musical despot, a neurotic with a mother fixation (according to Freud, who analyzed him) and an undoubted genius. Mahler's ambitious father, Bernhard, had transcended his humble origins by becoming the owner of a small, ramshackle brandy distillery and marrying the daughter of a wealthy soap manufacturer. Bernhard was a brute, regularly thrashing his children and their mother, Marie, who had been born with a limp and a heart condition. Of Gustav's 13 siblings, five died in infancy of diphtheria; his beloved younger brother Ernst died of hydrocardia aged 12; his oldest sister died of a brain tumour after a brief, unhappy marriage; another sister was

ESCAPE TO THE MOUNTAINS

IN ORDER TO MAKE TIME FOR HIS CREATIVE WORK IN BETWEEN HIS PROFESSIONAL DUTIES, Mahler's established routine was to take a long summer vacation in the Austrian mountains and lakes. From 1893 to 1896, to avoid being disturbed by holiday makers, he worked in a purpose-built lakeside shack at Steinbach on the Attersee. In 1900 he built a permanent summer residence overlooking the lake at Maiernigg on the Wörthersee, with another little 'composing hut' put up in the woods nearby. Here, as in Steinbach, he demanded absolute silence. Cows were ordered to be stripped of their bells, poultry was cooped up, cats and dogs banned. Even harvesters were forbidden to sharpen their scythes. In such calm he composed his Fourth to Eighth Symphonies.

subject to fantasies that she was dying; another brother was a simpleton in his youth who became a forger in adult life; while yet another brother, Otto, a humble musician, committed suicide.

Mahler was born on 7 July 1860 and began to learn the piano at the age of six. He was already marked out as a keyboard prodigy by the age of ten, when he gave a sensational debut. As a student at the Vienna Conservatory, he played the ferociously difficult first movement of Scharwenka's Piano Concerto No. 1. But the path of a virtuoso soloist was not for the diligent, single-minded Mahler. Within a short space of time, conducting and composition had taken over his life to the exclusion of everything else.

> 'Whoever listens to my music intelligently will see my life transparently revealed.' MAHLER

MAHLER THE CONDUCTOR

Realizing that he would not be able to survive by composing the kind of music he dreamed of, Mahler dedicated himself to building up a career as a conductor. For the next 15 years, he moved from one opera house to another, each of increasing importance, steadily building a reputation and composing in his spare time. In one season alone in Leipzig, he conducted over 200 performances, edited a Weber opera, fell in love with the wife of Weber's grandson, and completed his First Symphony. By the time he took over at the Royal Opera House in Budapest in 1886, he was recognized as a conductor of visionary brilliance whose meticulous preparations for concert programmes and opera productions set new standards. Here, he won the praise of Brahms; in Hamburg, Tchaikovsky allowed him to conduct *Eugene Onegin* in his stead. 'The conductor here,' he wrote to a friend, 'is not of the usual kind, but a man of genius who would give his life to conduct the first performance.'

In 1897 Mahler tactfully converted to Catholicism. As a Jew he would never have gained the one position he yearned for: artistic director of the Vienna Court Opera. During the following decade when he ran this, the world's most prestigious opera house, and the Vienna Philharmonic, he raised the city's musical fortunes to a height not seen since Beethoven's day and, some say, not equalled subsequently. Though his musicians respected him as an artist, they loathed him as a man. He was an uncompromising martinet who could reduce individual players to tears. His lack of social niceties and small talk coupled with his open contempt for those who opposed him or failed to match his standards made him many enemies.

Essential works

Symphony No. 1 (1884–8)
Symphony No. 2, 'Resurrection' (1888–94)
Symphony No. 3 (1896)
Symphony No. 4 (1900)
Symphony No. 5 (1902)
Symphony No. 6 (1905)
Symphony No. 8, 'Symphony of a Thousand' (1907)
DAS LIED VON DER ERDE, song symphony (1909)
DES KNABEN WUNDERHORN, song cycle (1888–99)

147

MAHLER THE COMPOSER

If Mahler excited adulation as a conductor, his music was received with a mixture of bewilderment and indifference. After his First Symphony, full of the sounds of nature and ingratiating dance melodies and rhythms, the four movements of the gargantuan Second Symphony, known as the 'Resurrection', are an allegory on the life of man (the finale is one of the most thrilling climaxes to any symphony). The equally extraordinary Third Symphony, composed between 1893 and 1896, Mahler described as 'a gigantic hymn to the glory of every aspect of creation'. The Fourth Symphony (1900) is the shortest and most joyous, 'a child's conception of heaven,' he said, 'and the colour of blue sky.'

Mahler's creative life moved into another phase when he fell in love with the beautiful and accomplished Alma Schindler, step-daughter of the avant-garde Viennese artist Carl Moll. Alma, a talented composer in her own right and one of the most eligible girls in Vienna, was 19 years Mahler's junior. It was a remarkable relationship, not without its ups and downs, one in which Mahler demanded complete subservience from Alma, who gave up her composing to devote herself to him as wife, mother and amanuensis.

The next five years saw Mahler at his happiest and at the height of his powers. His two daughters, Maria ('Putzi') and Anna ('Gucki'), were born and he created three more symphonies. The best known of these is No. 5 with its heartachingly beautiful fourth movement (Adagietto), a love song to Alma and famous from its use in Visconti's film *Death in Venice*. Then, in 1907, disaster struck. 'Putzi' contracted scarlet fever and died, leaving her parents distraught with grief. The same year, Mahler's doctor diagnosed the heart condition, inherited from his mother, that would bring his life to a premature end. He decided to leave Vienna, accepting a lucrative offer from a New York impresario.

FINALE IN AMERICA

Initially, Mahler was overwhelmed by America ('Fortissimo at last!' he is said to have exclaimed when he first saw the Niagara Falls). The engagement meant that he could provide a secure financial future for his family, but two seasons at the Metropolitan Opera led to friction and more unhappiness. Worse came when he took over the conductorship of the New York Philharmonic in 1909. Ruthless in his administration of the orchestra, he was cordially loathed by the players as much as the audience, yet few could argue with the exalted music-making he produced. In September 1910, Mahler returned briefly to Munich for the premiere of his gigantic Eighth Symphony, its electrifying first half a setting of the Latin hymn 'Veni Creator Spiritus', its second a setting of the final scene of Goethe's *Faust* in which Faust's redeemed body is drawn heavenwards. It met with overwhelming acclaim, one of the few triumphs Mahler ever enjoyed as a composer during his lifetime.

Back in New York in late 1910, Mahler collapsed under the strain of giving 65 rigorous concerts. He travelled back to Europe in the spring of 1911, seriously debilitated by the time he reached Paris. An infection set in, and he died of pneumonia in a nursing home in Vienna on 18 May aged 50. As requested, he was buried in Heitzing cemetery next to his daughter. At his request, his tombstone reads simply 'Mahler'. As he said, 'Any who come to look for me will know who I was, and the rest do not need to know.'

MAHLER'S WIDOW

IN JULY 1910 MAHLER DISCOVERED THAT ALMA WAS HAVING A PASSIONATE AFFAIR with the architect Walter Gropius. Despite their marriage breakdown, Alma stayed with her husband. She went on to marry Gropius in 1915. Although she enjoyed the role of 'Mahler's widow', Alma cared little for his music. She died in 1964 aged 85. The music for her funeral, which she chose herself, contained not one note of Mahler.

Claude
Debussy

'The poet of mists and fountains'

1862–19·18

ACHILLE-CLAUDE DEBUSSY.

HIS EUPHONIOUS NAME SOUNDS LIKE HIS

MUSIC, for Debussy was 'the poet of mists and fountains, clouds and rain; of dusk and glints of sunlight through the leaves; he was moonstruck and seastruck and a lost soul under a sky strewn with stars . . . In transmuting Nature into harmony, he has made sonorous his own emotions; never with any beating of the breast or invoking the high heavens to look down upon his agony or his transport of joy. Always here is reticence; always sobriety.' This poetic sketch by Oscar Thompson is balanced by the more prosaic Christopher Headington, who considered Debussy to be 'perhaps the most subtly and profoundly influential of all the twentieth century's composers', an influence that extended even into popular music.

From his earliest days Debussy was a rebel. Had he not been, he would never have been able to create the entirely new sounds that he did. He distrusted 'lifeless rules invented by pedants'. Beethoven bored him. He had no interest in Brahms or Tchaikovsky. Asked by the registrar of the Paris Conservatoire why he imagined that dissonant chords did not have to be resolved and what rule he followed, Debussy replied curtly, 'Mon plaisir'. Technically, the Debussyian sound world so familiar from works like *Prélude à l'après-midi d'un faune* and 'Clair de lune' (his two most popular compositions) was achieved by the use of such devices as the oriental pentatonic scale (strike all

> *'As there are no precedents, I must create anew.'*
> DEBUSSY

the black notes on a piano in sequence from C sharp upwards and you have a pentatonic scale – five notes to the octave), the whole-tone scale (C–D–E–F#–G#–A# on the piano), unresolved discords in succession, and consecutive fifths and fourths. Traditional construction and formal development of themes – principles on which classical music had securely rested – were thrown out of the window.

EARLY LIFE

It was some time before Debussy achieved his objectives. He was past 30 before he wrote anything significant. He was born on 22 August 1862 above his parents' china shop in St Germain-en-Laye on the outskirts of Paris. His aunt, rather than his parents, was the first to recognize and nurture his musical gifts. He had his first piano lessons with her in Cannes at the age of nine. Back in Paris he had further lessons from Antoinette Mauté de Fleurville, a pupil of Chopin and the mother-in-law of the poet Verlaine. Just three years later he was good enough to play the Chopin F minor Concerto, having entered the Paris Conservatoire aged 11. His earliest compositions date from this time.

Though a brilliant student, the rebellious streak began to assert itself during his seven years of study at the Conservatoire with such distinguished figures as César Franck and Léo Delibes. Not quite 18, Debussy accepted the unlikely role of household pianist and teacher to the children of Madame Nadezhda von Meck, Tchaikovsky's patroness. He travelled throughout Europe with the

family and stayed on the von Meck estate in the summers of 1881 and 1882, but he was asked to leave when he fell in love with Madame von Meck's eldest daughter. His immediate aim, though, was to win the coveted Prix de Rome. This he did at his second attempt in 1884 with a cantata, *L'enfant prodigue*, a work that had all the academic niceties guaranteed to please the judges.

Instead of completing the four years of study in Italy to which the Prix entitled him, Debussy left dissatisfied after two. Here, though, he met Liszt, who introduced him to the music of Lassus and Palestrina, the austere spirituality of which made a deep impression on him. Back in Paris, there was a brief infatuation with Wagner's music (though *Parsifal* was one work in which he delighted for the rest of his life) before he fell under the spell of the eccentric *enfant terrible* of French music, Erik Satie. Here was someone who encouraged him to go his own way: 'Break the rules, defy convention' might have been his credo.

BREAKING RULES IN LIFE AND MUSIC

Influenced by Satie, the impressionist paintings of Monet, Cézanne, Renoir, Pissarro and others, as well as the symbolist poetry of Mallarmé, Verlaine and Rimbaud, Debussy's unique style began to crystallize. The stories of Edgar Allan Poe, too, fascinated him (for a while he worked on an orchestral piece based on *The Fall of the House of Usher*). An even greater influence on his development was Javanese gamelan music. This he heard for the first time in 1889 at the Grande Exposition Universelle, where he fell in love with the gamelan orchestra's exotic textures and counterpoint.

In his early masterpieces, the String Quartet in G minor and *Prélude à l'après-midi d'un faune*, we hear for the first time the musical equivalent of the impressionists' paintings. Here, the musical colours, the half-lit delicate tonal mezzotints, are far removed from the sounds of the then fashionable German, French and Russian schools. People began to sit up and take notice of Debussy.

If his music was unconventional for the time, so was his private life. For the ten years prior to his first successes, he lived with Gabrielle Dupont – 'green-eyed Gaby' – in a shabby apartment in Montmartre. She took care of him, supported him (somehow – no one seems to know how) and kept creditors at bay. In 1899 Debussy left her to set up with the sweet but provincial Rosalie Texier ('Lily-Lilo' as he called her). They, too, separated, but then Debussy suddenly changed his mind and wished to marry her, threatening suicide if she refused. On hearing of Debussy's marriage, Gaby shot herself. She survived but thereafter simply disappeared into oblivion.

Five years later, Debussy had had enough of Rosalie ('the sound of her voice makes my blood run cold,' he once said) and left her for the singer Emma Bardac, the witty, sophisticated wife of the

STRANGE CHARISMA

DEBUSSY HAD ENORMOUS PERSONAL MAGNETISM. The writer Colette referred to 'his unrelenting gaze [in which] the pupils of his eyes seemed momentarily to dart from one sport to another like those animals of prey hypnotised by their own searching intensity'. Yet he was a strange-looking man with a bulging forehead (the French call it 'un double front') which he hated and tried unsuccessfully to cover with his hair or one of the many wide-brimmed hats he sported. Short, plump, pale and bearded, his resemblance to some medieval paintings of Christ earned him the hideous nickname 'Le Christ hydrocéphalique'. A chain-smoking, sensual sybarite who surrounded himself with fine books and pictures; a gourmet with a fondness for caviar; exquisitely turned out in finely cut clothes: he was an egoist who cared little for others. Xenophobic (he hated Mahler and Schoenberg), jealous, fickle, unscrupulous and with a caustic tongue, Debussy was not a pleasant man.

wealthy banker Raoul Bardac and former mistress of Fauré. It was a move that lost Debussy many friends. Rosalie, too, reacted by trying to commit suicide by shooting herself. She, too, survived. Having divorced her, Debussy married Emma in December 1908. She already had grown-up children from her first marriage. Her only child with Debussy was born in 1905 before her divorce. This was his adored Claude-Emma, nicknamed 'Chouchou', to whom he dedicated his *Children's Corner* piano suite (1908). Tragically, she died aged 14, just a year after her father.

SUNLIGHT AND SHADOW

During the emotional turmoil with Gaby and Rosalie, Debussy worked on the score of his opera *Pelléas et Mélisande*, based on the play by Maeterlinck. It is a variation on the *Tristan und Isolde* story, though, as Debussy stated, 'my procedure, which consists above all in dispensing with Wagner, owes nothing to him'. It is a misty, dreamy work of shadows and imagery in which the orchestra, far from linking, commenting or accompanying, provides a tonal backdrop; the sung word becomes almost as natural as speech (there are no big tunes or hit arias). *Pelléas*, premiered in April 1902, has been defined by critics and musicians as 'a landmark in operatic history' that 'let in not only sunlight but modern music'. Paradoxically, it has never caught the public imagination.

After *Pelléas* came the three symphonic sketches *La Mer*, and between 1905 and 1913 the two volumes of *Images* and the two books of *Préludes*, all for piano. Book 1 of *Images* has one of the finest musical evocations of water, 'Reflets dans l'eau'; book 1 of the *Préludes* has 'La fille aux cheveux de lin', 'La cathédrale engloutie' and 'Minstrels'. 'Clair de lune' comes from the earlier *Suite bergamasque*, while 'Gollywog's Cakewalk', another of Debussy's best-known short pieces, is No. 6 of the 1908 suite dedicated to Chouchou.

Internationally famous now, awarded the Légion d'honneur and on the advisory board of the Paris Conservatoire, Debussy was in demand all over Europe, travelling as far afield as Moscow and St Petersburg. But from 1909 his health began to deteriorate. In 1915 he underwent an operation for rectal cancer which left him with a colostomy bag. He had a second operation. Radium and morphine were administered. Towards the end of 1917 he wrote: 'Music has quite left me, and I could never force anyone's love.' By the beginning of the following year in Paris he could not leave his room and he died there on 25 March. Only a handful of friends were present at his funeral.

Essential works

SUITE BERGAMASQUE, piano (1890)
String Quartet in G minor (1893)
PRÉLUDE À L'APRÈS-MIDI D'UN FAUNE, orchestra (1894)
NOCTURNES, orchestra (1899)
PELLÉAS ET MÉLISANDE, opera (1893–1902)
LA MER, orchestra (1905)
IMAGES, piano, books 1 (1905) and 2 (1907)
CHILDREN'S CORNER suite, piano (1908)
PRÉLUDES, piano, books 1 (1910) and 2 (1913)
JEUX, ballet (1912)

RICHARD
STRAUSS

Creator of monumental tone
poems and operas

1864—1949

WRITING IN 1909, THE CONTEMPORARY CRITIC ARTHUR ELSON OFFERS AN INTERESTING ASSESSMENT OF RICHARD STRAUSS. Elson sees no valid reason why other composers should not rise to a greatness comparable to that of Richard Wagner, 'yet for more than a dozen years after his death, no one seemed worthy to wear the mantle of the departed . . . At last, however, a new star has risen in the firmament. In Richard Strauss, not inaptly called Richard the Second, the world has again found a man who dares to say what he wants in his own way, and who utters his orchestral convictions in no uncertain tone. Richard Strauss,' asserts Elson, '[is] today reckoned as the world's leading composer.' Such enthusiasm was matched, it has to be said, by equally ardent opprobrium from other quarters.

The music that Strauss presented to the world was startling in its boldness and originality. On display were naked passion and sensuality couched within a virtuosic treatment of the orchestra, creating sounds that had never been heard before. Bold excursions from (though never abandonment of) tonality and wild passages of dissonance shocked audiences and fellow composers alike. Yet even as Elson's words were being written, Strauss was working on his operatic masterpiece, *Der Rosenkavalier*, and with its completion his burning originality disappeared. For the remaining 40 years, Strauss, while certainly not resting on his laurels, fell back on his extreme technical accomplishment, professional adroitness and sophistication.

EARLY LIFE

Music was in his blood. His father, Franz, was the brilliant first horn of the Bavarian Court Opera to whom Wagner had entrusted the important solos for the premieres of *Tristan und Isolde*, *Die Meistersinger* and *Parsifal*. (Ironically, Franz Strauss, an arch conservative, detested Wagner's music but lived long enough to see his son become one of Wagner's most passionate advocates and finest interpreters.) Richard Georg Strauss was born in Munich on 11 June 1864. He was a musical *wunderkind*, beginning piano lessons at the age of four, completing his first composition (a Polka in C major) aged six, and seeing his Op. 1, *Festmarsch* for orchestra – composed when he was just 12 – published in 1880.

Strauss never required any formal musical training. His technical know-how, if not his style, seemed to be pre-formed. By the age of 20, he had had premieres of his first symphony, a violin concerto and a second symphony (played by the New York Philharmonic, no less). Not many composers have matched that kind of early success, but these were merely formative works. Strauss had not yet got into his stride.

The powerful conductor, composer and pianist Hans von Bülow took the young Strauss under his wing,

'Melody . . . is the greatest of divine gifts, not to be compared with any other.'
RICHARD STRAUSS

and when von Bülow left his orchestra at Meiningen in 1885 for a year, he handed over the reins to the 21-year-old. Influenced by von Bülow (an ardent Wagnerite despite having been cuckolded by the great man) and by the poet and musician Alexander Ritter, who was married to Wagner's niece, Strauss was won over to the musical aesthetics of Liszt and Wagner. Abandoning traditional, restrictive classical forms and adopting the concept of 'music as expression', Strauss struck out on a new path. From 1886 onwards, his music would have a literary or philosophic outline.

FROM TONE POEM TO OPERA

Over the next 12 years Strauss produced a series of tone poems that made his name throughout the musical world. *Aus Italien* (1886), *Macbeth* (1888) and, especially, *Don Juan* (1888) created a furore. These were followed by *Tod und Verklärung* (1889), the boisterous *Till Eulenspiegel* (1895), the magnificent, rambling *Also Sprach Zarathustra* (1896, inspired by Nietzsche's philosophy and famous now for the use of its opening pages in Stanley Kubrick's film *2001: A Space Odyssey*) and *Don Quixote* (1897), inspired by Cervantes' novel. In 1898, at the age of only 34, Strauss had the self-confidence to compose a tone poem entitled *Ein Heldenleben* (A Hero's Life) in which the last section makes liberal use of quotes from the works of the hero, who was, of course, the composer himself.

When these pieces appeared, critics competed with one another to find novel ways and ever juicier adjectives with which to condemn them. Now they are as much part of the orchestral repertoire as Beethoven's symphonies. Not only was Strauss considered one of the most provocative and important composers, but by the end of the 19th century he was also one of the world's leading conductors. In 1898 he landed one of the most prestigious posts in the musical world, conductor of the Berlin Philharmonic. He remained in the position for 12 years. With his immense influence, he introduced a system whereby German composers would for the first time be entitled to receive a royalty from every performance of their work given by a major orchestra or opera house.

Then, at the age of 40, after the completion of another autobiographical piece, his *Symphonia Domestica* (1903), Strauss changed direction. There were exceptions – notably the superb Alpine Symphony (1915) and the late *Metamorphosen* (1945) for 23 solo instruments – but thereafter Strauss devoted himself to opera. His first efforts, *Guntram* (1894) and *Feuersnot* (1901), had been failures, but when he met the poet and librettist Hugo von Hofmannsthal in 1900, he embarked on one of the great collaborations in opera history.

Salome (1905), based on the play by Oscar Wilde, was followed in 1909 by *Elektra*. Audiences

SKAT KING

STRAUSS MARRIED THE SOPRANO PAULINE DE AHNA IN 1894. She had sung the lead role in *Guntram* and the two remained together, in spite of a stormy relationship, until the end of Strauss's life (she died only a few months after him). Music lovers would make pilgrimages to their beautiful villa at Garmisch in the Bavarian Alps. Strauss became immensely wealthy, but he was notoriously, even pathologically, mean. Pauline ruled Strauss with a rod of iron, held the purse strings and gave him a small allowance to live on. This he supplemented by insisting that members of the orchestra played Skat with him, a card game at which he was uniquely skilled. The musicians could hardly refuse and invariably lost to him. Though most could ill afford the amounts of money involved, Strauss always insisted on being paid. Their discomfort seemed to be a source of delight to him. Some lost so much money to him in Bayreuth one year that they refused to continue to play. Only when Winifred Wagner reimbursed them did they rejoin the orchestra.

were shocked by the moral corruption of the stories and baffled by their unfamiliar, dissonant musical language. The critics descended on Strauss with the same fury that had been reserved for the tone poems. As if by way of concession, Strauss and von Hofmannstahl's next venture could not have been more different. *Der Rosenkavalier* (1911) is a delightful Mozartian comedy, with graceful waltzes derived from the world of Lanner and Johann Strauss the Younger. In the famous final Trio of Act 3 we have one of the most beautiful passages of music composed in the 20th century.

NAZI LINKS

Throughout the 1920s and 1930s, Strauss wrote prolifically and was amply rewarded for his work. A further ten operas flowed from his pen, among them *Intermezzo* (1923), *Arabella* (1932) and *Capriccio* (1941), which show Strauss as an ingenious orchestrator and an unrivalled master in his understanding of the soprano voice. However, his life entered a problematic phase in 1933 when he accepted the position of president of the Third Reich Music Chamber. Some of his subsequent conduct is hard to excuse: he supported the boycott of Jewish music in Germany, and when Bruno Walter was removed from his post as head of the Leipzig Gewandhaus Orchestra, Strauss promptly substituted for him; Toscanini refused to conduct at Bayreuth, Strauss accepted. True, in 1935 he was sacked when he insisted on working with the Jewish librettist Stefan Zweig. Thereafter he was merely tolerated by the Nazi regime, but when he was asked later why he had not left the country, Strauss is reported to have replied: 'Germany had 56 opera houses; the United States had two. It would have reduced my income.'

Strauss was investigated as a Nazi collaborator after the war and acquitted. Despite all this, he was still revered by the musical world, and in 1947, taking his first flight in an aeroplane, he travelled to London where he was fêted as the greatest living German composer. His final autumnal flourish of inspiration includes one of his most widely loved works, the ineffably touching *Four Last Songs*. Each of the first three of these ends with a solo passage for horn, an instrument as close to Strauss's heart as the soprano voice for which they were written. His 85th birthday was celebrated worldwide, just a few months before he died at his villa on 8 September 1949.

Essential works

Horn Concerto No. 1 in E flat (1883)
DON JUAN, tone poem (1888)
TILL EULENSPIEGELS LUSTIGE STREICHE, tone poem (1895)
DON QUIXOTE, tone poem (1897)
EIN HELDENLEBEN, tone poem (1898)
DER ROSENKAVALIER, opera (1911)
Alpine Symphony (1915)
CAPRICCIO, one-act opera (1942)
METAMORPHOSEN for 23 solo strings (1945)
FOUR LAST SONGS (1948)
Songs, including 'Morgen', 'Wiegenlied', 'Ständchen', 'Cäcilie' and 'Traum durch die Dämmerung' (Strauss's own favourite)

Jean
Sibelius

Finland in music

1865—1957

THAT HUGE, BALD, CRAGGY HEAD MUST MAKE SIBELIUS ONE OF THE MOST INSTANTLY RECOGNIZABLE of all great composers. His face is somehow in keeping with the character of his music – massive, unsmiling, intense, unforgettable. There is very little merriment in Sibelius's music: the light touch was not part of his make-up. An austere grandeur of icy brooding impels admiration and inspires awe, for here is the bleak Finnish landscape in sound. Its vast forested interior with some 60,000 lakes, its bird life – especially the cranes, geese and curlews – inspired some of the greatest symphonic music of the late 19th and early 20th centuries. Sibelius is Finland in music; he is Finnish music.

To his countrymen he was and remains a national hero. While he was still alive, the Finnish government issued stamps with his portrait and would have erected a statue in his honour had Sibelius himself not discouraged the idea. Rarely has a composer meant so much to his native country. His career coincided with a pan-European movement of nationalist music, but Sibelius's compositions, infused with Finnish mythology, came to symbolize the plight, the aspirations and the pride of his small nation. Finland was under the despotic rule of tsarist Russia, a grand duchy ruled by a Swedish-speaking minority. Patriots were imprisoned, newspapers suppressed, and Finnish culture and history subsumed into the Russian empire. The voice of independent Finland was further underlined by one of Sibelius's greatest achievements – becoming one of the few Scandinavian composers to have completely emancipated himself from the academic traditions of Germany.

EARLY LIFE

Born on 8 December 1865 in Hämeenlinna, a small town in southern Finland, he was christened Johan Julius Christian Sibelius. Grieg was 22, Dvořák 24, Brahms 32 and Wagner 52; when he died, Shostakovich was at the height of his powers and young composers like Harrison Birtwistle and Peter Maxwell Davies were beginning to make names for themselves. Sibelius was the son of a heavy-drinking Swedish-speaking regimental doctor who died during the cholera epidemic of 1867–8. With his sister Linda and younger brother Christian, he was brought up by his mother (an attractive preacher's daughter 'straight out of Ibsen') and grandmother. In his teens, he changed his name to Jean after inheriting a set of visiting cards used by his seafaring uncle, who had Gallicized his name from Johan to Jean.

Sibelius had begun composing at the age of ten and saw his future as a violinist, but like many other composers in this volume, he was initially drawn to the law (at Helsinki University). The young Italian composer and virtuoso Ferruccio Busoni was on the university staff and the two became lifelong friends. Law was abandoned after a year and he took himself off to study in Berlin (as a student of the contrapuntist Albert Becker) and Vienna (with Karl Goldmark), where he won a reputation as a high-living womanizer. He returned to Finland in 1891. The following year he produced his first major composition, the Kullervo Symphony, based like many of his subsequent works on the great Finnish epic poem *Kalevala*.

The success of this work led in the same year to the commissioning of *En Saga*, a tone poem rather in the style of Rimsky-Korsakov. It allowed him to marry his fiancée Aino Järnefelt, 'the prettiest girl in Finland' and the sister of his friend and fellow student Armas Järnefelt. Still nurturing dreams of becoming a violinist, he even auditioned for the strings of the Vienna Philharmonic while on his honeymoon. The long-suffering Aino would bear her husband five daughters, one of whom, Kirsti, died of typhus at the age of 15 months in 1900.

En Saga was followed by two of his most popular works. The three-movement *Karelia Suite* (1893) finds Sibelius at his most extrovert in this portrait of the inhabitants of Karelia, in the eastern part of Finland, a work conceived for a student theatre production. *The Swan of Tuonela*, composed in the same year, draws again on *Kalevala*, depicting a swan gliding along the black river encircling Tuonela, the Finnish equivalent of Hades.

FAME AT HOME AND ABROAD

The First Symphony (1899) consolidated Sibelius's reputation in his home country, but it was his tone poem *Finlandia* of the same year that made him internationally famous. One of the most requested of all classical works, its hymn-like central section, often sung to the words 'Be Still my Soul', is the Finns' second national anthem. So powerfully did it evoke nationalist sentiments that the Russians banned it. His popular Second Symphony (1902) illustrates Sibelius's predilection for using short themes that gradually build into a larger whole.

Despite a grant from the enlightened Finnish senate that enabled Sibelius to give up all other work and concentrate on composing, he and his wife found themselves constantly in debt. The couple were not free of financial worries until the end of the First World War. Ironically, one of his most popular compositions, the salon trifle *Valse triste*, was sold outright for 300 marks. It made the publishers a small fortune. Sibelius was a heavy drinker and his addiction to beer and cognac as well as fine cigars posed its own problems. In 1901 a disease of the ear threatened to make him deaf. It was successfully treated, but seven years later he had to undergo a series of no less than 13 operations on his throat to remove a malignant growth that had been initially diagnosed as cancer. He gave up alcohol and tobacco for a time but gradually took them up again from 1915. On many occasions during Sibelius's long marriage, drink brought the relationship to the verge of destruction.

Sibelius's uncertain health may well account for the increased bleakness and austerity of his music at this time, the Fourth Symphony (1911) in particular, but the change also coincided with a

A WILD MAN OF MUSIC

THE BOISTEROUS SIDE OF SIBELIUS'S CHARACTER is nicely captured by the conductor Sir Henry Wood in his memoir *My Life of Music*: 'I could generally manage Busoni when I had him to myself, but my heart was always in my mouth if he met Sibelius. I never knew where they would get to. They would forget the time of the concert at which they were to appear; they hardly knew the day of the week ... They were like a couple of irresponsible schoolboys.' But there was a darker side, as Sibelius himself admits in a letter to his brother Christian in 1903: 'There is much in my make-up that is weak ... When I am standing in front of a grand orchestra and have drunk half a bottle of champagne, then I conduct like a young god. Otherwise I am nervous and tremble, feel unsure of myself, and everything is lost. The same is true of my visits to the bank manager ... You can see from this that my drinking has genuine roots that are both dangerous and deep. I promise you to try and cope with it with all my strength.'

'Give me the loneliness either of the Finnish forest or of a big city.' SIBELIUS

move away from the bright lights of Helsinki to the Villa Ainola, the home he built in Järvenpää in 1904, 20 miles north of the capital. By then his development had entered a new phase. After the superlative Violin Concerto of 1903 – not an initial success but now one of the central works of the violinist's repertoire – his art assumed a deeper, more individual character which finally relinquished the influence of Tchaikovsky, Grieg and Brahms. Increasingly he turned away from the complex, rich language of contemporaries such as Richard Strauss, Scriabin and Mahler.

During the first decade of the 20th century, Sibelius travelled extensively through Europe conducting his own works to huge acclaim. The second decade saw him conquer America, but the Great War deprived him of contact with the major musical centres and also cut off his royalties. Only one significant work was completed during the conflict, the heroic and much-loved Fifth Symphony, completed in time for his 50th birthday celebrations on 8 December 1915. Finland proclaimed its independence after the October Revolution and was plunged into a civil war after a coup d'état by the Red Guards. Sibelius's brother was murdered and the composer was forced to flee his home.

THE REST IS SILENCE

After the war, Sibelius composed the Sixth (1923) and Seventh (1924) Symphonies, the symphonic poem *Tapiola* (1926) and, in 1925, the incidental music for a production of Shakespeare's *The Tempest*. His last known work was completed in 1929. After that, silence. He would potter down to the local tavern, walk in the forests or work in his garden, but he discouraged visitors and disliked discussing music. After the Second World War he became a virtual recluse. For years there was the promise of an Eighth Symphony (part of it was sent for copying in 1930), but the work, if it was ever completed, was withheld and the manuscript finally consigned to the flames.

Revered and much honoured by his countrymen and throughout the world, for the last 28 years of his life Sibelius published nothing. He died from a cerebral haemorrhage on 20 September 1957 at the grand age of 91. He was given a state funeral ten days later and buried in the grounds of Ainola. Aino survived her husband by nearly 12 years, dying shortly before her 98th birthday on 8 June 1969. She lies next to him.

Essential works

EN SAGA, tone poem (1892)
KARELIA SUITE, orchestra (1893)
THE SWAN OF TUONELA (from Lemminkäinen Legends), tone poem (1897)
FINLANDIA, tone poem (1899)
Symphony No. 2 in D (1902)
Violin Concerto in D minor (1903)
Symphony No. 4 in A minor (1911)
Symphony No. 5 in E flat (1915)
Symphony No. 7 in C (1924)
TAPIOLA, tone poem (1926)

RALPH
VAUGHAN
WILLIAMS

The reflowering of British music

1872—1958

WHILE ELGAR'S MUSICAL LANGUAGE IS DEEPLY ROOTED IN THE GERMANIC TRADITION, just as Stanford's and Parry's were before him, it was Vaughan Williams and his lifelong friend Gustav Holst who broke the mould and created the first truly original English musical voices since Purcell 250 years earlier. *The Lark Ascending*, the *Fantasia on a Theme by Thomas Tallis* and the *Fantasia on 'Greensleeves'* are among the most frequently played pieces by any English composer. His best work transcends the folk-music idiom, as all great nationalist music does, and is infused with the mysticism and poetry that were so important to him.

Vaughan Williams was related to an eminent family of lawyers on his father's side and to both Charles Darwin and Josiah Wedgwood on his mother's. He was one of those rare souls – a composer with a private income. Ralph (pronounced Rayf) was born on 12 October 1872 in the village of Down Ampney, Gloucestershire, where his father was the vicar. After his father's early death at the age of 40, VW (as he is often affectionately referred to) was brought up in the grand home of his maternal grandmother in Leith Hill, Surrey. There was a strong musical tradition in the Wedgwood house and Ralph was taught the piano by his aunt Sophy. It was for this instrument that he wrote his first composition, at the age of six – a little four-bar fragment entitled *The Robin's Nest.*

FIRST STEPS

But Vaughan Williams was no musical prodigy. Indeed, his development as a composer was arguably the slowest of any major composer. After Charterhouse, in 1890 he went to the Royal College of Music where he studied under Parry. Two years later he left to take a music degree at Trinity College, Cambridge, before returning to the RCM in 1895 for lessons with Stanford. It was here that he met Gustav von Holst (as he was then known), who VW admitted later was 'the greatest influence on my music'. Three days before his 25th birthday he married Adeline Fisher, whom he had met at Cambridge. The two spent an extended six-month working honeymoon in Berlin, where VW arranged to take lessons from Max Bruch. As late as 1908, even though he had begun to make a name for himself, he went to Ravel in Paris for (as he put it) 'a little French polish'.

AN ENGLISH VOICE

Vaughan Williams's first success had come in 1901 with a setting of a poem by William Barnes called 'Linden Lea' ('Within the woodlands, flow'ry gladed . . .'). It brought his name to public attention and he followed it with settings of poems by Dante Gabriel Rossetti, one of which is 'Silent Noon'. This and 'Linden Lea' remain two of his most popular works. If both sound like English folk songs, it was not a coincidence, for in the early 1900s, through the

'What we want in England is real music [that] possesses real feeling and real life.'

VAUGHAN WILLIAMS

influence of the recently formed English Folk Music Society, VW had begun to refine his style. He and Holst went out to collect the indigenous music of England. It was said that Vaughan Williams used to dress for these expeditions 'as though stalking the folk song to its lair'. The material had never been collected or notated before and the cataloguing and research undertaken by the two composers, contemporaneous with the work of the folk-song collector Cecil Sharp, was of considerable cultural significance.

Vaughan Williams's earliest orchestral and choral works, such as the impressive 1907 cantata *Towards the Unknown Region*, sound like any one of a dozen accomplished composers writing at the beginning of the 20th century. But with his deep knowledge of Tudor music and English folk music, his English conservatoire training and his absorption of modern French orchestral technique, Vaughan Williams emerged as an adventurous, unmistakably English composer with a distinctive voice of his own.

Word settings inspired much of his work prior to the First World War, notably *Songs of Travel* (verses by Robert Louis Stevenson) and *On Wenlock Edge*, which uses some of Housman's *A Shropshire Lad* poems. There was his work on the *English Hymnal* (see box) and then his mighty Sea Symphony – six years in the making – a setting of words by Walt Whitman. This was premiered in 1910, just weeks after the first performance of his *Fantasia on a Theme by Thomas Tallis*. His second symphony was composed between 1912 and 1913 – A London Symphony, a tribute to his favourite city. The exquisite *The Lark Ascending* for solo violin and orchestra, which took its title from a poem by George Meredith, was written in August 1914 but not performed until after the First World War.

At the age of nearly 42, Vaughan Williams volunteered for active service and became a private in the Royal Army Medical Corp, serving in France and Salonica. In 1917 he returned to England for officer training and the following March left for France again as a Second Lieutenant (aged 45) with the Royal Artillery in charge of 200 horses. His war experiences were reflected in his Third Symphony (A Pastoral Symphony), justly regarded as his war requiem.

The war over, Vaughan Williams was able to resume his composing, conducting and teaching, untroubled by material worries. The only cloud in his life was the health of his wife, a victim of crippling arthritis. In 1928 the couple decided to move from Cheyne Walk, Chelsea, their home for 25 years, to a bungalow on the outskirts of Dorking which they rechristened 'The White Gates'. The fifth, sixth and seventh decades of Vaughan Williams's life were his most prolific, with works for every genre, including: opera (*Sir John in Love*), concerto (Piano Concerto), choral (*Dona nobis pacem* and *Serenade to Music*), orchestral (*Job*, *Fantasia on 'Greensleeves'*, *Dives and Lazarus*) and symphony (Nos. 4, 5 and 6).

THE ENGLISH HYMNAL

IN 1904 THE REVEREND PERCY DEARMER INVITED VAUGHAN WILLIAMS to be the musical editor of a new hymn book to be used as a rival to *Hymns Ancient and Modern*. Despite being a 'Christian agnostic' and with only a handful of compositions to his credit, VW got the job. The work took him two years. The new book appeared in 1906 under the title *The English Hymnal*. By 1956 it had sold over 5 million copies. Over 30 folk-song tunes were adapted by VW into hymns, the best-known being 'O little town of Bethlehem', 'Teach me, my God and King' and 'Who would true valour see'. VW's own contributions are the tunes for 'God be with you till we meet again' (Randolph), 'Come down, O Love divine' (Down Ampney), and 'For all the Saints' (Sine nomine); the last two are probably the most frequently performed of all Vaughan Williams's music. 'Two years of close association with some of the best (as well as some of the worst) tunes in the world,' wrote Vaughan Williams later, 'was a better musical education than any amount of sonatas and fugues.'

THE PRIVATE VW

WHAT WAS VAUGHAN WILLIAMS REALLY LIKE? James Lees-Milne of the National Trust found the composer 'handsome and distinguished, not at all practical . . . a very sweet man, with a most impressive appearance. He is big and broad and has a large head with sharply defined features, and eyes that look far into the distance.' VW's young friend and definitive biographer, Michael Kennedy, discovered that the composer had a sense of humour that could be 'Rabelaisian' and that when he laughed 'his whole body shook in abandoned enjoyment'.

A PRODUCTIVE OLD AGE

After the mid-1930s, VW and Adeline led increasingly separate lives. At the end of the decade a young poet and writer, Mrs Ursula Wood, introduced herself to Vaughan Williams, almost 40 years her senior. As well as collaborating on various projects, she helped the composer with his work and soon became his regular companion. Her young soldier husband subsequently died (of a heart attack), so when, in 1951, the frail Adeline Vaughan Williams also died, the 78-year-old composer lost no time in proposing. After his death Ursula Vaughan Williams kept her husband's flame burning brightly.

Vaughan Williams worked on into old age with undiminished creative powers, the Grand Old Man of English music. He had declined the offer of a knighthood in the early 1930s and he turned down the post of Master of the King's Musick twice – in succession to Elgar and again when the next

incumbent, Sir Walford Davies, died in 1941. But when, in 1935, King George V invited him to join the Order of Merit, he accepted this rare honour (only 24 members are admitted at any one time).

Vaughan Williams's Eighth Symphony appeared in 1955 (the score includes parts for vibraphone and xylophone), while his Ninth, composed at the age of 85, uses a trio of saxophones. The latter was heard at the Proms in early August 1958, conducted by Sir Malcolm Sargent. On 25 August Vaughan Williams retired to bed in the house to which he had moved in Regent's Park, London. He was looking forward to attending the recording session of his Ninth Symphony the following day under the baton of his old friend Sir Adrian Boult. Sadly, he passed away in his sleep just before dawn on 26 August 1958.

Essential works

'Linden Lea', song (1901)
Symphony No. 1 (A Sea Symphony) (1903–9)
Fantasia on a Theme by Thomas Tallis (1910)
THE LARK ASCENDING (1914)
Symphony No. 3 (A Pastoral Symphony) (1921)
JOB, a masque for dancing (1931)
Symphony No. 4 in F minor (1931–4)
Fantasia on 'Greensleeves' (1934)

164

SERGEI
RACHMANINOV

The last of the great Romantics

1873—1943

A RENOWNED CONCERT

PIANIST SAID RECENTLY THAT THE ONLY TIME SHE EVER SAW HER MUSIC-LOVING FATHER CRY was when he heard of the death of Rachmaninov. The Russian composer could have that sort of affect on people; they worshipped the ground he walked on. On the other hand, some of his more snobbish critics have dismissed his music as artificial, gushing and likely to quickly lose its appeal. So far, there is no sign of that happening – quite the reverse, in fact. As the composer of some of the world's most popular works for the piano; as one of the greatest pianists in history; and, before the First World War, as an internationally acclaimed conductor – Rachmaninov was one of the few musicians ever to combine three musical disciplines with equal success.

A Romantic writing after the Romantic era had passed, a composer who defied the progressive critics and was unmoved by the onslaught of modernism, Rachmaninov clung tenaciously to tonality, structure, harmonic beauty and melodies of overpowering expressiveness. 'I try to make my music speak simply and directly that which is in my heart at the time I am composing,' he wrote. 'If there is love there, or bitterness, or sadness, or religion, these moods become part of my music, and it becomes either beautiful, or bitter, or sad, or religious. For composing music is as much a part of my living as breathing and eating. I compose music because I must give expression to my feelings, just as I talk because I must give utterance to my thoughts.'

'I compose music because I must give expression to my feelings.'

RACHMANINOV

EARLY LIFE

Sergei Vasilyevich Rachmaninov was born on the family's Oneg estate near Novgorod in Russia on 1 April 1873. His aristocratic grandfather had been a good amateur pianist and a pupil of the Irish-born composer and pianist John Field. Sergei's extravagant and amorous father, Vassili, was also a pianist. Though born into wealth, by the time he was nine his father's profligacy had left the family with nothing. The estate had to be sold and his parents separated. Having clearly inherited the family's pianistic gifts, in 1883 he moved with his mother and five siblings to live in St Petersburg, where he won a scholarship to the conservatory.

Two years later, on the advice of his cousin Alexander Siloti, he entered the Moscow Conservatory and lived in the household of the strict (and probably paedophile) professor of piano Nikolai Zverev. He studied composition with Taneiev and Arensky; Tchaikovsky took a keen interest in his music; by the age of 19 he had written his First Piano Concerto and a one-act opera (*Aleko*) that made a considerable impression; and when he graduated in 1893, he won the Great Gold Medal for piano. Altogether, it was an impressive start to a career.

Rachmaninov had also written the short piano piece that would make him internationally famous. The second of his Five Pieces, Op. 3 (1892), dedicated to Arensky, is the Prelude in C sharp minor, nicknamed by Rachmaninov 'It' because at every recital he was forced to play 'It'. It contains

in microcosm many of the hallmarks of his mature works: nostalgia, Slavic melancholy, a minor key, chanting, bells, keyboard virtuosity, a memorable melody and a precisely judged emotional climax. Because Russia was not a signatory to any international copyright agreement, Rachmaninov made precisely 40 roubles from the Prelude – the fee the publishers paid him.

DISASTER AND TRIUMPH

Then came a profound setback. The 1897 premiere of his First Symphony, a work that had taken him two years to complete, was an unmitigated disaster. Glazunov, who conducted the performance, was drunk and the critics tore the music to shreds. The 23-year-old Rachmaninov's self-confidence evaporated. He destroyed the score (the orchestral parts were preserved but not found until 1945, when the work was heard again). Self-doubt and depression prevented him from writing music of any significance until 1900.

In an attempt to overcome this creative block, Rachmaninov consulted a Dr Nikolai Dahl, who recommended a course of 'positive suggestion therapy'. Unlikely as it might seem, the hypnosis worked and Rachmaninov was able to set about composing a second piano concerto. The finished work was dedicated to Dahl and has since become the most popular of its kind written in the 20th century. With its soaring themes, drama, emotional climaxes and taxing solo part, it is not hard to see why. The year after its premiere in 1901, conducted by Siloti, another cousin made an important impact on Rachmaninov's life when he married Natalie Satina. The music started to flow again, including the *Variations on a Theme of Chopin* (his first extended piano work), the great set of Ten Preludes, Op. 23, and the magnificent Second Symphony (1908), its lush Adagio movement one of the most heartfelt and moving in all Russian music.

Having been briefly (1904–5) chief conductor of the Bolshoi Opera in Moscow, the 1905 revolution prompted Rachmaninov to leave Russia for Dresden. For all his well-known love of his country, the composer spent little of the rest of his life there. He was back in Russia in 1910, where he completed a second set of piano preludes (Op. 32), and then moved to Rome and Berlin in 1913. He returned to Russia for the duration of the war, until the Bolshevik revolution forced him into permanent exile in December 1917. After that, he vacillated between America and Europe, and never saw Russia again.

Rachmaninov's first visit to America had been in 1909, a tour for which he wrote his Third Piano Concerto (Mahler conducted its second performance in New York), arguably the finest of the

BRIEF ENCOUNTER

IT WAS ONLY RECENTLY MADE KNOWN BY THE COMPOSER'S GRANDSON that, according to his grandmother, the real reason for Rachmaninov's visits to Dr Dahl was not so much for hypnosis as to court the doctor's daughter. In a story kept secret for 50 years, Rachmaninov had fallen in love with her, and it was she who was the true inspiration behind the famous concerto and who remained a shadowy figure throughout his married life. Whatever the truth, the C minor Concerto is a work that commands an undiminished affection in the concert hall, made even more familiar by its unforgettable use in David Lean's film *Brief Encounter* – so effective that many people believed that Rachmaninov had written the music specially for the film (though he had been dead two years when it appeared). The second and third movements were composed first and, interestingly, the famous opening bars of the first movement are almost the same as the closing bars of the C sharp minor Prelude played in reverse. Dr Dahl, a good amateur violist, occasionally played in performances of the concerto, eliciting applause whenever his identity was revealed.

four he wrote and one of the most taxing in the repertoire to play. His success led to him being offered the conductorship of the Boston Symphony Orchestra. He turned it down – and again in 1918 when the offer was repeated. From 1911 he was conductor of the Moscow Philharmonic, and by this time he had become one of the most respected musicians of his generation, though he was left with little time to compose. During this period came the two sets of *Études-Tableaux* for piano, the magical wordless *Vocalise*, the choral symphony *The Bells*, the first version of the Piano Sonata No. 2, and his haunting setting of the Vespers, *All-Night Vigil*.

LIFE OUTSIDE RUSSIA

When Rachmaninov and his family left Russia in 1917, it changed his life for ever. He arrived in America with very little money. Within a very short space of time, he built an entirely new career by becoming a concert pianist. This involved an extraordinary amount of work, for compared with most other pianists he had a small repertoire. By specializing in the music the public wanted to hear – Beethoven, Schumann, Chopin, Liszt and, of course, his own compositions – he made a spectacular success.

His hectic schedule allowed little time for creative work and, in truth, he composed few major pieces after his departure from Russia. ('How can I compose without Melody?' he replied to an interviewer in 1924 when asked why he was not composing.) The first of these – the Fourth Piano Concerto of 1927 – was completed a full ten years after he left Russia. This was followed by the *Variations on a Theme of Corelli* (1931) for solo piano and the immensely popular *Rhapsody on a Theme of Paganini* (1934) for piano and orchestra, based on the last of Paganini's 24 Caprices for solo violin. His last major works were the Symphony No. 3 (1936) and the Symphonic Dances, written in 1940 in both orchestral and two-piano versions, originally intended as a ballet for the choreographer Fokine.

During the 1930s, Rachmaninov divided his time between Senar, his lakeside villa in Lucerne, Switzerland, and his apartment in New York's exclusive Riverside Drive, but the last years of his life were spent in Los Angeles. Here his home was an exact replica of the one he had left in Moscow, right down to the food and drink. When he was aged 70, cancer was diagnosed too late to be operable. He continued playing in public until a month before his death on 28 March 1943, just a few weeks after becoming an American citizen. He was buried in the Kensico Cemetery, New York, far away from the horrors of Leningrad and Kharkov.

Essential works

Piano Concerto No. 1 in F sharp minor (1891, rev. 1917)

Five Pieces, piano, Op. 3 (1892) (includes Prelude in C sharp minor)

Piano Concerto No. 2 in C minor (1901)

Ten Preludes, piano, Op. 23 (1901–3)

Symphony No. 2 in E minor (1908)

Piano Concerto No. 3 in D minor (1909)

VOCALISE, Op. 34, No. 14 (1912)

Piano Sonata No. 2 in B flat minor (1913, rev. 1931)

Vespers (1915)

Piano Concerto No. 4 in G minor (1927, rev. 1941)

Rhapsody on a Theme of Paganini, piano and orchestra (1934)

Arnold
SCHOENBERG

A new starting point for aesthetic truth

1874 – 1951

TO SOME HE IS THE BOGEYMAN
OF CLASSICAL MUSIC, TO OTHERS HE IS ITS
SAVIOUR. Musicians and those au fait with the subject
find it hard to comprehend that the average person has not
only never heard a note of Schoenberg's music but has
hardly heard his name. If ordinary people did hear any of
his music, they would listen to it in complete
bewilderment, for nearly a century after his first revolutionary works were
composed, Schoenberg's music remains simply baffling, a series of unpleasant
disjointed sounds that bear no relation to what most people think of as music.
No longer is it a 'sweet and healing balm of troubles' (Horace) but 'the organi-
sation of sound' (John Cage). After Schoenberg, the easy pleasure of music
could no longer be taken for granted.

While many struggle to come to terms with Schoenberg's ideas, others acclaim his invention of a
revolutionary new musical language. What form did this take? For the first time, music was written
without a key. Schoenberg did not merely do away with the traditional concepts of consonance and
dissonance; he actually wrote atonally (though Schoenberg himself disliked the term 'atonality',
preferring to describe it as 'pan-
tonality'). His Piano Piece Op. 11, No.1,
completed on 19 February 1909, was the
first musical composition to dispense
with tonality. No one had dared do this
before. The work might sound chaotic
and random, but in fact it is highly
organized and structured. Later,

> *'I am a conservative who
> was forced to become a
> revolutionary.'*
>
> SCHOENBERG

Schoenberg ventured further into what has become known as serial music, 12-tone technique or
dodecaphony. The first formal published example of this was his Five Piano Pieces of 1923. The
Canadian pianist Glenn Gould could think of 'no composition for solo piano from the first quarter
of the [20th] century which can stand as its equal'.

Like any great revolutionary creative artist, Schoenberg's genius was founded on traditional
skills. Before venturing boldly into uncharted territory, Schoenberg had acquired a sound
composition technique. It is, therefore, surprising to learn that the man who was to become the most
revered musical theoretician of the age had remarkably little formal training.

EARLY LIFE
Arnold Franz Walter Schoenberg was born on 13 September 1874 in Vienna. His father Samuel ran
a shoe shop and sang with local choral societies but died when Arnold was 16, forcing him to take a job in
a bank to support his mother and sister. He learned the cello and violin and taught himself theory until
1894, when Alexander Zemlinsky began giving him lessons in counterpoint (he married Zemlinsky's sister
Mathilde in 1901). By the age of 25, Schoenberg claimed to have seen each of Wagner's major operas
more than 20 times. Wagner is the omnipresent influence in his two early masterpieces, the opulent

string sextet *Verklärte Nacht* (Transfigured Night), first heard in 1902, and *Gurrelieder* (Songs of Gurre), a colossal, romantic, opulently scored choral work begun in 1900 but not premiered until 1913.

In 1901, with the help of Richard Strauss who obtained the Liszt Scholarship for him, the newly married composer moved to Berlin as a conductor and teacher. After three years, during which he composed his Straussian tone poem *Pelleas und Melisande*, he moved back to Vienna. There he devoted himself to composition and teaching, gradually gaining a formidable reputation as a musical thinker and attracting devoted disciples who shared his experimental compositional aims. Among them were Alban Berg and Anton von Webern, with whom he formed a group now referred to as the Second Viennese School (the first having been the school of Haydn and Mozart). His First String Quartet (1905) and First Chamber Symphony (1906) stretched tonality to the limits. With little money and even less public recognition for her single-minded husband, Mathilde embarked on an affair with a young painter, Richard Gerstl, who lived in the same house as the Schoenbergs. Mathilde was persuaded by mutual friends to return to the marriage (which she did), but during her month-long absence Schoenberg wrote a quartet movement around a theme from a Viennese street song which bore the words 'alles ist hin' – 'all is lost'. Part of the work had no formal key signature. On 27 September 1908 Schoenberg then composed the first piece in which tonality is completely suspended, the song 'Du lehnest wider eine Silberweide' from the song cycle *The Book of the Hanging Gardens*. Gerstl could not bear Mathilde's return to her husband and committed suicide in November 1908 at the age of 25.

MOVE FROM TONALITY

Schoenberg followed these excursions with the string of completely atonal works by which he is chiefly known, among them the piano pieces that make up his Op. 11 and Op. 19, and the Five Orchestral Pieces, Op. 16. Critical reaction to his music extended to anti-Semitic smears and violent abuse, while the premiere of his expressionistic song cycle *Pierrot Lunaire* in 1912 met with outright hostility. So complex was the latter that it required 40 rehearsals, with the soprano soloist employing the technique of *Sprechgesang*, a form of declamation halfway between singing and speaking.

During the First World War, Schoenberg served in the ranks of the Austrian army. After the war he founded, with Berg and Webern, the Society for Private Performances, where his music and that of his followers could be heard by a subscription audience without critics and where expressions of approval or disapproval were discouraged. In 1923, having composed little since the war, he published his next completed works: the five Piano Pieces, Op. 23, Serenade Op. 24 and his 1921 Suite for piano, Op. 25 (the last of these was the first work composed wholly

TWELVE-TONE MUSIC

WITH 12-TONE MUSIC, SCHOENBERG BELIEVED HE HAD FOUND 'a method of composition that will assure the supremacy of German music for 1000 years'. In Western music there are 12 different notes in an octave. These notes are C, C#, D, Eb, E, F, F#, G, Ab, A, Bb, B; played in sequence, you have what is called a chromatic scale. In contrast to atonalism, where the composer is free to choose any note from the chromatic scale at will, in 12-tone music the composer makes a tone row or series (hence 'serialism') from the 12 notes and arranges them in a certain order. The tone row can be played note by note, backwards, or inverted, but no note can be repeated until the whole series has been played, giving all 12 notes of the chromatic scale equal value. No longer are there any major or minor chords or scales, no key or tonic to hang on to, as in almost all Western music written before Schoenberg.

in the 12-note method; see box). The same year saw the death of his wife.

In 1925 Schoenberg was appointed professor at the Prussian Academy of Arts in Berlin in succession to Busoni. The following year he married Gertrud, the sister of the violinist Rudolf Kolisch, who bore him three children to join the two from his first marriage. Overall, this was probably the happiest and most financially secure decade of his life and one in which he produced a number of important works, including the Variations for orchestra (1928) and the first two acts of the opera *Moses and Aron* (1930–2), left incomplete at his death. ('Aron' is spelt thus, incidentally, because of Schoenberg's superstition about the number 13; the conventional spelling of Aaron would have totalled an unlucky 13 letters in the title.)

The advent of the Nazis ensured Schoenberg's dismissal from Berlin. Though born a Jew, he had converted to Protestantism in 1898. Having moved to Paris in 1933 and witnessed the German persecution of Jews, he reconverted to Judaism and left Europe for America, at the same time changing the spelling of his name from 'Schönberg' to 'Schoenberg'. After a year in Boston, he moved to Los Angeles, where he taught at the University of California. On 11 April 1941 he became an American citizen. The principal works from this period are the Violin Concerto (1936), the Piano Concerto (1942), the cantata *A Survivor from Warsaw* (1947) and the String Trio (1946), which describes his experience of almost dying from a heart attack.

Schoenberg's health, not robust since the early 1930s, began to decline and he died in Los Angeles in July 1951 – on the 13th and aged 76 (7 + 6 = 13).

Essential works

VERKLÄRTE NACHT, string sextet (1899) (arr. for string orch. 1917)
Three Piano Pieces, Op. 11 (1909)
Five Orchestral Pieces (1909)
GURRELIEDER, voice and orchestra (1900–11)
PIERROT LUNAIRE, cycle of 21 short melodramas (1912)
Five Piano Pieces, Op. 23 (1920–3)
Suite for piano (1921)
Variations for orchestra (1928)
MOSES AND ARON, opera (1932)
Piano Concerto (1942)

SEISMIC IMPACT

THOUGH CONTROVERSIAL AND UNLOVED BY MOST PEOPLE, 12-tone music has been used in every field of music from symphonies and operas to areas where its use would scarcely be recognized, such as cartoons and film scores. Schoenberg's innovations have influenced every generation of composers since the 1920s. In his writings and teaching, and through many of his pupils and disciples, he is undoubtedly among the most influential musicians in history.

MAURICE
RAVEL

'The finest ear that ever existed' DEBUSSY

1875—1937

'I AM NOT ONE OF THE GREAT COMPOSERS,' WROTE RAVEL TOWARDS THE END OF HIS LIFE. 'All the great have produced enormously. There is everything in their work, the best and the worst, but there is always quantity. But I have written relatively very little . . . and at that, I did it with a great deal of difficulty. I did my work slowly drop by drop. I have torn all of it out of me in pieces.' It is true that in terms of quantity Ravel does not qualify as a great composer (it has been calculated that you could listen to his entire output in less than 14 hours), but what he did produce is pure gold, all of it in distinctive nuggets stamped 'Made by Ravel'.

Ravel's significance was to establish, with Debussy, a distinct school of French music loosely defined as Impressionism. The German tradition had dominated the previous generation of composers such as Gounod and Massenet. Ravel and Debussy distanced themselves from that tradition, sharing many of the same techniques to create an altogether new sound world. They used medieval church scales, the pentatonic scale, rich chords and vibrant dissonances. Both were master orchestrators. But where Debussy, 13 years Ravel's senior, is sensuous and emotional, employing adventurous harmonies and vague forms, Ravel is crystalline, clear-cut, precise and piquant. Comparing photographs of the two composers, the difference in their physical appearance reveals as much: Debussy – foppish, saturnine, cheroot in hand, with a mischievous twinkle in his eye; Ravel – urbane, formal, conservative and ever so slightly chilly. Stravinsky described Ravel and his music succinctly: 'The perfect Swiss clockmaker.' A solitary, aloof figure, then, but one whose striking individuality surreptitiously infiltrated any number of film scores and the consciousness of composers that include Vaughan Williams, Gershwin, Messiaen and Boulez.

EARLY LIFE

Joseph Maurice Ravel was born on 7 March 1875 in Ciboure in the Basses-Pyrénées but was only three months old when the family moved to Paris. Many composers have an inherited musical gene, but there was nothing in Ravel's family history to suggest he would become one of France's greatest composers (though his brother Edouard was also musical). His father, of Swiss descent, was a railway engineer. His mother came from a family of Basque fishermen and sailors. Yet, by the time he was seven, Maurice was taking his first music lessons, and by 14 he was studying at the Paris Conservatoire. Fauré was among his teachers at the Conservatoire, where he stayed for the unusually long time of 16 years. One reason was his determined efforts to win the coveted Prix de Rome, which Berlioz, Bizet and Debussy had been awarded before him. He was placed second in 1901, tried again and failed in 1902 and 1903, and then was eliminated, humiliatingly, before the final stage of the 1905 competition. With charges of favouritism flying about, the jury's decision on this occasion became something of a cause célèbre – 'l'affaire Ravel' – and led to the resignation of the conservative director of the Conservatoire, Théodore Dubois, to be replaced by Fauré.

If anything, the scandal enhanced Ravel's reputation, for by that time he was already an established and well-respected composer. His serene *Pavane pour une infante défunte*

The only love affair I have ever had was with music.' RAVEL

IGOR
STRAVINSKY

Seminal figure of 20th-century music

1882–1971

FOR THE FIRST HALF OF THE 20TH CENTURY, NO COMPOSER HAD A STRONGER INFLUENCE ON CONTEMPORARY MUSIC THAN STRAVINSKY. Indeed, he can claim to be one of the dominant figures in the formation of the aesthetic of modernism. Like Picasso, his work was rooted in tradition but, by inventing his own landscape, he established a tradition of his own.

His long creative career went through three distinct stages, yet the average music lover knows little of his second (neoclassical) period and even less of the third (serial) period of the 1950s and 1960s. It is principally on his three early ballet scores that Stravinsky's fame and popularity rest.

EARLY LIFE

Stravinsky came from an affluent family of the lesser Russian nobility. His mother was a fair amateur pianist, while his father Feodor, at the time of Stravinsky's birth, was the leading bass-baritone of the Russian Imperial Opera (he created the role of Varlaam in Mussorgsky's *Boris Godunov*). Igor Fyodorovich Stravinsky was born on 17 June 1882 in Oranienbaum, a resort town on the Baltic not far from St Petersburg. One of four brothers, he was educated at home until he was 11; thereafter he attended a private school, taking piano lessons and reading voraciously – both books and his father's scores. But it was a performance of Tchaikovsky's 'Pathétique' Symphony, played in memory of the composer who had just died, that provided him with 'the beginning of my conscious life as an artist and musician'.

Discouraged by his father from following a career in music, Stravinsky enrolled in 1901 at St Petersburg University to study criminal law and legal philosophy. His friendship with the two sons of the composer Rimsky-Korsakov led to him becoming a family friend. With Feodor Stravinsky's death the following year, Igor began taking lessons in orchestration from the great man. These lessons (which were given free of charge) and his own examination of counterpoint were the only musical studies Stravinsky undertook. He never attended a conservatory or took a music degree.

In 1905 Stravinsky married his cousin Catherine Nossenko. His progress as a composer was slow. He absorbed the colourful idiom of some of his mentor's later works, though his early Symphony in E flat (1908), a weak, technically deficient affair, was modelled on those of Tchaikovsky and Glazunov. Two shorter works for orchestra followed: *Scherzo fantastique* and *Feu d'artifice*; the latter, written to celebrate the wedding of Rimsky-Korsakov's daughter (his adored teacher died a few days later), shows the influence of Scriabin's daring concepts of harmony.

> *'I know that the twelve notes in each octave and the variety of rhythm offer me opportunities that all of human genius will never exhaust.'*
>
> STRAVINSKY

IGOR STRAVINSKY

THREE GREAT BALLET SCORES

These works attracted the attention of the impresario Serge Diaghilev, who engaged Stravinsky to orchestrate a couple of numbers for *Les Sylphides* (based on the music of Chopin) for his 1909 Paris season of the Ballets Russes. This in turn led to Diaghilev's commission of a full ballet score. The result was *The Firebird*. When it was presented at the Paris Opéra in 1910, it made Stravinsky instantly famous.

Immediately, Diaghilev persuaded him to write a second ballet. *Petrushka,* with its electrifying rhythms, novel instrumentation and daring polytonality (passages written in two different keys sounding simultaneously), provided the young composer with a second triumph. This was how far and fast Stravinsky had come in the space of four years since his Symphony in E flat. Now he was hailed as among the most significant of living composers.

These successes were as nothing compared with the third masterpiece commissioned by Diaghilev. *The Rite of Spring* was the Big Bang of modern music and its premiere in Paris on 29 May 1913 created one of the most notorious scandals in musical history. So violent was the reaction to the music (as well as, it must be emphasized, to the costumes and the choreography by Nijinsky), stoked up by a certain amount of well-orchestrated Parisian Russophobia, that a riot ensued. Everything in Stravinsky's score was such a violent wrench from every tradition that had gone before that it seemed to many people like the work of a madman. Nearly a century on, though, it has long been an established part of the concert repertoire.

Nothing that Stravinsky wrote subsequently had a similar impact on the musical world, yet it would be misleading to think that he composed nothing else of significance. Two more ballets followed (*Le Rossignol* and *Les Noces*). Then the Russian Revolution of 1917 took place and Stravinsky's life changed irrevocably. When it became clear that his estate in Volhynia would be confiscated and his royalties would dry up, he opted for voluntary exile in Paris. In 1934 he became a French citizen.

NEOCLASSICISM AND SERIALISM

The second stage of Stravinsky's musical development was marked in 1920 by yet another Diaghilev ballet commission. In *Pulcinella*, Stravinsky used themes by the 18th-century composer Pergolesi and other Italian contemporaries. The classical form for this and future works, such as the Piano Concerto, Violin Concerto and the Octet for Wind Instruments, relied on structures that had fallen out of fashion and gave birth to the musical movement we now called 'neoclassicism'. The opera *Oedipus Rex* (1927), the Symphony of Psalms (1930), the melodrama *Perséphone* (1934) and his 'Dumbarton Oaks' Concerto (1938), loosely modelled on Bach's Brandenburg Concertos, are other notable works from the interwar decades.

In 1938 Stravinsky's daughter Ludmilla died of consumption. The following year his wife died of the same illness. A few months later, his elderly mother passed away. Presented with these changes to his personal circumstances and sensing the onset of a second war, Stravinsky accepted an invitation from Harvard University to take up the chair of professor of poetry. Shortly afterwards, he was joined by his long-time mistress Vera Sudeikina (the two had lived together openly since 1922).

> ## IGOR'S ARCHIVE
>
> WHEN THE MANUSCRIPT OF *THE RITE OF SPRING* CAME UP FOR AUCTION IN 1982, it fetched $548,000, at that time the highest price paid for a manuscript by any composer. It was bought by the Swiss conductor and philanthropist Paul Sacher, whose foundation in Basle now houses the entire Stravinsky archive of 166 boxes of letters and 225 drawers of manuscripts. It cost Sacher $5,250,000.

CRITICAL VERSE

THE RITE OF SPRING WAS SAVAGED BY ITS EARLY CRITICS. 'It has no relation to music at all as most of us understand the word,' wrote one London critic in 1913 after the work's London premiere. The 1924 American premiere of the ballet's orchestral suite inspired the following verse in the *Boston Herald*:

Who wrote this fiendish Rite of Spring?
What right had he to write this thing?
Against our hapless ears to fling
Its crash, clash, cling, clang, bing, bang, bing!

They married in 1940 and became American citizens shortly after the Second World War. Some of the works produced during this period have the distinct whiff of 'needs must' about them (*Circus Polka*, Ode, Ebony Concerto), though music of higher aims and quality appeared in 1940 (Symphony in C) and 1945 (Symphony in Three Movements). The next major achievement and the high watermark of Stravinsky's neoclassical period was the opera *The Rake's Progress* (1951), which was based on Hogarth's series of engravings and had a libretto by W.H. Auden and Chester Kallman.

While working on the opera, Stravinsky was introduced to a young American musician and conductor, Robert Craft, who not only became his musical factotum but inspired his latent interest in the music of Schoenberg and the Second Viennese School. Stravinsky had hitherto studiously avoided serialism. (Though he and Schoenberg, its leading exponent, were neighbours in Hollywood, they never met and it was only after Schoenberg died in 1951 that Stravinsky began experimenting.) Not only was Craft a persuasive advocate but Stravinsky realized that he needed a new stimulus for his flagging inventiveness. Thus began, when he was 75 years old, the third period of his creative life. Its first fruit was the Septet (1953); perhaps its greatest, the ballet *Agon*, written for George Balanchine (1957). Many other works manifest a preoccupation with biblical figures. Though remaining distinctly Stravinskian in its rhythmic animation, none of the music from this last period (*Abraham and Isaac*, for example, *Threni* or *Requiem Canticles*) has found favour with the public.

The last decade of Stravinsky's life was marked by ill health, which, while slowing him down, did not prevent him from touring worldwide as he had done in the 1930s, including a triumphant return to Russia just before his 80th birthday. Fêted as the greatest living composer, he recorded a great many of his works during this time. In 1966 he moved to New York, where he died on 6 June 1971. His body was flown to Venice to be buried on the island of San Michele near the resting place of Serge Diaghilev.

Essential works

THE FIREBIRD, ballet (1910)
PETRUSHKA, ballet (1911)
THE RITE OF SPRING, ballet (1913)
PULCINELLA, ballet (1920)
LES NOCES, ballet (1923)
OEDIPUS REX, opera (1927)
Symphony of Psalms, choir and orchestra (1930)
Symphony in Three Movements (1945)
THE RAKE'S PROGRESS, opera (1951)

SERGEI
PROKOFIEV

Revolutionary traditionalist
of Russian music

1891—1953

FOR MANY PEOPLE, PROKOFIEV IS THE ACCEPTABLE – AND ACCESSIBLE – FACE OF 20TH-CENTURY CLASSICAL MUSIC.
Challenging and disquieting though some of his music may be, his voice speaks directly to the heart, mind and emotions. The composer, he felt, should be 'where he is needed most, where his words, music, his chisel can help the people live a better, finer life'.

Prokofiev's novel harmonic and melodic ideas are so idiosyncratic that, after only a few bars, their author is unmistakable. He may begin with a banal little tune and then suddenly have it leap up an unexpected interval; he uses orthodox chords in unorthodox relations; his weapons are irony and sardonic humour; and, though some of his music is intentionally dissonant and aggressive, he never abandons tonality completely. Despite the shock tactics and the self-conscious mockery of tradition in his early works, Prokofiev belongs to the same great tradition as Tchaikovsky.

EARLY LIFE
An only child, Sergei Prokofiev was born on 27 April 1891 in the farming village of Sontsovka in the south-eastern part of what is now the Ukraine (then part of the Russian Empire). His father was a relatively wealthy agricultural engineer. The musical genes came through his mother, an accomplished amateur pianist. The piano remained at the very heart of Prokofiev's musical thinking throughout his life. A child prodigy, he wrote his first music aged five.

By the age of nine he had become an outstanding pianist and produced an opera, an overture and other works. He was only 13 when he entered the St Petersburg Conservatory, the youngest student ever to be admitted. Within no time, he had become known as an *enfant terrible*, blazing with self-confidence – a trait that did not always endear him to his teachers. These included Glazunov, Liadov and Rimsky-Korsakov for composition, and Anna Essipova for piano (a former pupil and later wife of Theodor Leschetizky, who, with Liszt, was the most influential piano teacher of the 19th century).

Blessed with such an original, natural talent, Prokofiev felt stifled by the Conservatory's conservative teaching – and rebelled. His First Piano Concerto (1912), written for his graduation, caused a sensation with its belligerent keyboard acrobatics, angular rhythms, and unexpected harmonic and melodic twists. By the time he left the Conservatory shortly before the outbreak of war in 1914, he had become one of the most famous (for some, notorious) avant-garde composers in Russia, with a reputation for pugnacious, percussive music.

'I abhor imitation and I abhor the familiar.'

PROKOFIEV

A commission from Diaghilev produced his most violent work to date, the ballet *Ala and Lolly* (1915), rejected by the impresario but later reworked as the composer's *Scythian Suite*. A second ballet suite for Diaghilev, *Chout* (eventually staged in 1921), was followed by his popular 'Classical' Symphony (1917), a witty pastiche of the symphonies of Mozart and Haydn. The First Violin Concerto, the piano suite *Visions fugitives* and the first four of his nine piano sonatas were completed by the end of the war.

In 1918 Prokofiev embarked on a tour of America by way of Japan, travelling on the last trans-

GRAND MAESTRO

PROKOFIEV WAS AN OUTSTANDING CHESS PLAYER. In 1909 he drew with Emanuel Lasker – world chess champion for an astonishing 27 years – in an exhibition in which Lasker was playing against several opponents simultaneously. Later, in 1914, Prokofiev played in three simultaneous exhibitions given in St Petersburg by the future world champion, the Cuban player José Raúl Capablanca. After losing in his first two attempts, in his third try Prokofiev beat Capablanca.

Siberian express to leave Russia that year. Though only intending to stay for a few months, it was to be nine years before he saw Russia again and a further 15 years before he returned to live there again permanently. While America fêted him as a pianist, it took less kindly to his music, notably his dotty and whimsical opera *The Love for Three Oranges* (1919) and, less understandably, the great Third Piano Concerto. Today, this is by far the best known of the five he wrote and one of the most frequently played of all 20th-century concertos.

RETURN TO RUSSIA

After flitting between his homeland and various European cities, Prokofiev decided in 1932 to settle in the new Soviet Union for good. Wishing to write more simply and directly, Prokofiev's artistic vision had matured in a way that chimed with the socialist realism of the 1930s. Perhaps he was, as Stravinsky asserted, politically naïve or perhaps he was so confident of his reputation that he expected to be treated differently. If so, he was quickly disabused. He must surely have known the pressures to which artists were subjected under Stalin's regime. Easier by far to live and work abroad like Stravinsky and Rachmaninov.

For a short time, all went well for Prokofiev, but in mid-1936 he moved to Moscow with his Spanish-born wife, the singer Lina Llubera, and their two sons. He could not have chosen a worse time. In January of that year, in one of a series of Stalinist attacks on cultural life, Shostakovich was accused of 'anti-people formalism' and his opera *Lady Macbeth* denounced in *Pravda*. Prokofiev ventured a sensible definition of formalism as 'music which one does not understand at first hearing'. Such aesthetic niceties were wasted on Stalin's cohorts (who included the ghastly opportunist and Communist apologist, the composer Tikhon Khrennikov). Prokofiev began to find work hard to come by and performances of his work suddenly cancelled.

As relations between the authorities and Prokofiev disintegrated, so did his marriage. In 1939 he began an affair with an intelligent young student named Mira Mendelson, and in 1941 he left his family to live with her. After his marriage to Lina had been annulled by a decree forbidding matrimony between Soviet citizens and foreign nationals, Prokofiev was 'advised' to wed Mira, an order with which he complied in January 1948. Lina's fate was terrible. She was arrested by the authorities, sentenced to ten years for 'espionage' and deported to the Arctic colony of Vorkuta. She never saw her husband again.

Ironically, during this period Prokofiev produced some of his finest music. This includes three great film scores: *Lieutenant Kijé*

CRITICALLY UNLOVED

'IN HIS NEW OPERA, *THE STORY OF A REAL MAN*, Prokofiev goes back to all the negative and repulsive usages present in his music of the period of reckless infatuation with modernistic trickery. Chaos, coarse naturalism, complete absence of melody, harmonic muddiness and bad taste, characterize this thoroughly vicious work.'
SOVIETSKAYA MUSICA, MOSCOW, DECEMBER 1948

(1934), *Alexander Nevsky* (1939), later adapted into a cantata, and *Ivan the Terrible* (1945); two ballet masterpieces, *Romeo and Juliet* (1936) and *Cinderella* (1944); the Second Violin Concerto (1935), the Fifth Symphony (1944), the Sixth Symphony (1947), the three 'War' Sonatas for piano (Nos. 7–9) and the opera War and Peace (1943). Much performed as these works are, however, none comes close to the enduring popularity of *Peter and the Wolf* (1936). Subtitled 'symphonic fairy tale for narrator and orchestra', it was written to teach children the different sounds of the orchestra. Now a vehicle for celebrity narrators of varying abilities, its over-familiarity tends to mask the work's skill and originality.

A SORRY END

In 1948 the Central Committee of the Communist Party denounced Prokofiev, Shostakovich and others for formalism, which it defined as music that had no immediate function and did not extol the virtues of the Stalinist regime. A humiliating public apology was issued jointly by the accused composers: 'We are tremendously grateful to the Central Committee of the All-Union Communist Party and personally to you, dear Comrade Stalin, for the severe but profoundly just criticism of the present state of Soviet music . . . We shall bend every effort to apply our knowledge and our artistic mastery to produce vivid, realistic music reflecting the life and struggles of the Soviet people.'

His health undermined, impecunious and his artistic vision fatally compromised, Prokofiev's final years are a sorry tale, their one bright spot being his friendship with the young cellist Mstislav Rostropovich. Prokofiev died from a massive brain haemorrhage aged 61 on 5 March 1953, exactly 55 minutes before Stalin. Because of official state mourning, only 44 people were able to attend Prokofiev's funeral service. David Oistrakh played two movements of the composer's First Violin Sonata. Prokofiev's body was later buried at the Novodevichy Cemetery in Moscow.

Mira Mendelson devoted the rest of her life to administering the composer's archive and effects. She died in 1968. Lina Prokofiev was released from prison camp in 1956 following the general amnesty after Stalin's death. She was not allowed to leave the Soviet Union until 1974, when she made her home in Paris. During her last years, she too devoted her considerable energy to promoting her husband's work. Lina survived until 1989.

Essential *works*

VISIONS FUGITIVES, piano (1915–18)
'Classical' Symphony (1917)
Piano Concerto No. 3 (1921)
LIEUTENANT KIJÉ, orchestral suite (1934)
ROMEO AND JULIET, ballet (1936)
Violin Concerto No. 2 (1935)
PETER AND THE WOLF, narrator and
 orchestra (1936)
Piano Sonatas Nos. 6–8 (1939–44)
Symphony No. 5 (1944)

George
GERSHWIN

Classical meets Broadway and the Jazz Age

1898—1937

THINK OF GERSHWIN AND YOU

THINK OF *RHAPSODY IN BLUE*, the string of popular songs and the ground-breaking opera *Porgy and Bess*. His music defined his era for America; the man himself lived the American dream – the son of poor immigrants who owed his phenomenal success to a melodic gift that was on a par with Schubert and Tchaikovsky. Whether he was, like them, a 'great composer' is a moot point. He was certainly a great composer of popular songs; he wrote pioneering music that sought to combine the best elements of the European Romantic tradition with the newly minted forms of ragtime, jazz and the blues. Later he drew on Latin-American influences, and the music of the African Americans of the southern States.

Until comparatively recently the classical music world looked down its nose at Gershwin. Leonard Bernstein, for instance, writing about *Rhapsody in Blue* in the 1950s, felt that 'It's not a composition at all. It's a string of separate paragraphs stuck together – with a thin paste of flour and water.' Such musicological considerations as awkward modulations, lack of thematic development and strained transitions pale into insignificance besides Gershwin's originality and melodic gifts.

EARLY LIFE

Gershwin's father, Moishe Gershovitz, was a Russian Jew from St Petersburg who had arrived in the United States in 1891. A restless, ambitious man, he changed his name to Morris Gershvin, married a fellow immigrant, Rose Bruskin, in 1895, and made a decent living in a factory making women's shoes. The second of four children, George (originally Jacob) was born in Brooklyn, New York, on 26 September 1898, two years after his brother Ira (originally named Israel). When he was six years old, George heard a pianola in the street playing Anton Rubinstein's once popular Melody in F. It entranced him, and when in 1910 Morris bought a piano for Ira, it was George who immediately took to it. Within four years he was good enough to get a job as a song plugger with Remick's, a leading music publisher and seller.

George had lessons from various highly qualified teachers, among them the pianist Charles Hambitzer, whom he described as 'the first great musical influence of my life'. Hambitzer wrote to his sister: 'The boy is a genius without a doubt . . . He wants to go in for this modern stuff, jazz, and what not. But I'm not going to let him for a while. I'll see that he gets a firm foundation in the standard music first.' That meant Chopin, Liszt and Debussy among others. He had theory lessons from Edward Kilenyi, another fine pianist, but for the rest Gershwin picked up his musical knowledge from printed tutors, attending concerts and his fellow musicians.

Jerome Kern and Irving Berlin became his role models. He wrote his first song, 'Since I found you', in 1913; the first to be published followed three years later. By the age of 21 he had written his first full-scale musical, *La La Lucille*. It was not the hit Gershwin had hoped for, but the score contained one song, 'Swanee', so successful that if he had written nothing else, he could have lived comfortably off its royalties for the rest of his life. Throughout his career, Gershwin wrote the music for about 860 songs, the vast majority of them to lyrics by brother Ira. They include some of the best loved of

RHAPSODY IN BLUE

ON 3 JANUARY 1924 GERSHWIN WAS PLAYING BILLIARDS WITH HIS BROTHER at 52nd Street and Broadway when Ira noticed a newspaper story that announced a Paul Whiteman concert on 12 February. For this event, the article read, 'George Gershwin is at work on a jazz concerto . . .' It was the first the composer knew about it. His musical *Sweet Little Devil* was due to open in three weeks' time in Boston. Somehow, on the train to and from rehearsals, Gershwin produced a two-piano score of a work originally entitled *American Rhapsody*. Ira came up with the eventual title after seeing an exhibition of Whistler's work that included his painting of the Thames at Chelsea, *Nocturne in Blue and Green*. *Rhapsody in Blue* was orchestrated (first for jazz band, later for full orchestra) by Whiteman's brilliant in-house arranger, Ferde Grofé.

all time, from 'The man I love', 'Someone to watch over me', and 'I got rhythm' to 'A foggy day', 'S'Wonderful' and 'Let's call the whole thing off'.

MOVING BEYOND SONG

Gershwin's extraordinary energy and ambition inevitably meant he would want to prove himself by writing more demanding music. Early in 1924, the bandleader and self-styled 'King of Jazz', Paul Whiteman, asked Gershwin for a concert piece. The result was a 16-minute work for piano and jazz band, *Rhapsody in Blue*, one of the first examples of the fusion of jazz and classical idioms. Premiered in New York in February 1924, it was an instant hit and became the first American composition to enter the standard classical repertoire.

The following year, Gershwin produced his Piano Concerto in F, effectively orchestrating it himself. Some critics thought it a work of genius (and today it is the most performed of any American concerto), while others, despite its jazz inflected score, thought it relied too heavily on impressionistic harmonies and earlier European Romantic concerto models. His next major success in the concert hall was the inspired tone poem *An American in Paris*, sketched in the French capital, orchestrated in Vienna and premiered by the New York Philharmonic in 1928. His *Second Rhapsody* (salvaged from the music dropped from his score for the film *Delicious*) was less successful, but in the 1932 *Cuban Overture* Gershwin successfully amalgamated the salsa rhythms of Latin America into an exuberant showpiece that presaged a decade of American fascination with Latin rhythms.

Gershwin was a warm, gregarious personality – and, inevitably, a trifle vain and egotistical. His friend, the pianist and actor Oscar Levant, once asked him, 'George, if you had to do it all over again, would you still fall in love with yourself?' Gershwin never married or had children, despite numerous relationships with various women, including the actress Paulette Goddard, then married to Charlie Chaplin. Most notable was the ten-year affair he had with the sophisticated and witty song composer Kay Swift, whom he frequently consulted about his music. His musical *Oh Kay!* was named for her.

UNFULFILLED PLANS

Towards the end of his life, Gershwin spoke of plans for a symphony, a string quartet, a ballet and a cantata

'He is the prince who has taken Cinderella by the hand and openly proclaimed her a princess to an astonished world.'

WALTER DAMROSCH

Essential works

RHAPSODY IN BLUE, piano and jazz band (1924)

Concerto in F, piano and orchestra (1925)

Three Preludes, piano (1926)

AN AMERICAN IN PARIS, tone poem (1928)

SECOND RHAPSODY, piano and orchestra (1932)

CUBAN OVERTURE (1932)

Variations on 'I got rhythm', piano and orchestra (1934)

PORGY AND BESS, folk opera (1935)

... and those 860 songs (1913–37)

based on Lincoln's Gettysburg address. None of these was realized, but after the success of his musical comedy *Of Thee I Sing* (1931) – the first of its kind to be awarded a Pulitzer Prize – he turned his attention to writing an opera. *Porgy and Bess* was based on the novel *Porgy* by DuBose and Dorothy Heyward and proved to be the first (and still foremost) American opera, a firm departure from European tradition. The score, which includes parts for banjo and an array of percussion, contains reminiscences of indigenous folk songs and speech patterns, popular music idioms, jazz and spirituals. In it, the white characters only speak, the black characters only sing. The 560-page score includes the imperishable 'Summertime', 'I got plenty o' nuttin'', 'Bess, you is my woman now', and 'It ain't necessarily so'.

While in Hollywood in 1937 to work with Ira on music for the films *Shall We Dance* and *Damsels in Distress*, Gershwin began to suffer from headaches and spells of dizziness and complained of a constant smell of burning rubber. A brain tumour was diagnosed too late and he died shortly after an unsuccessful operation to remove it on 11 July 1937. He was just 38 years old. His grief-stricken brother was left to complete the lyrics that he and George had begun for the follow-up film, *Goldwyn Follies*, among them the touchingly apposite 'Love is here to stay'. The novelist John O'Hara summed up the nation's shock at Gershwin's sudden passing: 'George Gershwin died last week. I don't have to believe it if I don't want to.'

IF IT AIN'T BROKE . . .

GERSHWIN WAS ALWAYS PAINFULLY AWARE OF HIS TECHNICAL SHORTCOMINGS and throughout his career sought the advice of established classical composers to compensate for his lack of formal musical training. Three of them, all of whom merit a chapter in this book, turned him down: Ravel, Stravinsky and Schoenberg. An apocryphal story has Gershwin asking the composer of *The Rite of Spring* how much he charged for lessons. Stravinsky, by way of reply, asked Gershwin how much money he earned a year. 'About 250,000 dollars,' came the answer, whereupon Stravinsky asked Gershwin for lessons. Late in his short life, after he had moved from Broadway to Hollywood, Gershwin sought out lessons from Arnold Schoenberg, then living in Los Angeles. Schoenberg refused. 'I would only make you a bad Schoenberg,' he said, 'and you're such a good Gershwin already.' They settled instead for playing tennis and painting portraits of each other.

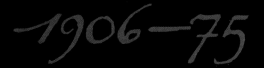

DMITRI
SHOSTAKOVICH
Greatest master of the Soviet era

1906–75

SHOSTAKOVICH WAS THE
FIRST – SOME MIGHT SAY THE ONLY – GREAT COMPOSER TO EMERGE FROM THE USSR. Unlike Prokofiev, who grew up and was educated in tsarist Russia, Shostakovich's entire career was conducted under the Communist regime. Dying in 1975, only four years after Stravinsky, he was the last composer who could claim the admiration of both traditionalists and modernists throughout the Western world. Many rate him as the finest composer of the 20th century; few would argue that he is among the most vital, original and unmistakable voices of that period.

Equally, it must be admitted that his output is horribly uneven – a composer who could, after an overpowering passage, become (in the words of one commentator) 'as naïve as a schoolboy, almost as if he cannot discriminate between the good and the bad'. He is certainly not without his critics: 'Derivative, trashy, empty and second-hand' (Gerald McBurney); 'the second, or even third pressing of Mahler' (Pierre Boulez); 'a hack in a trance' (Filip Gershkovich).

EARLY LIFE
Shostakovich came from an intellectual, comfortably-off family. His father was a chemical engineer employed in the weights and measures office, blessed with a good singing voice and a great love of music; his mother was a conservatoire-trained pianist. Dmitri was born on 25 September 1906 in St Petersburg (which became Petrograd in 1914 and Leningrad in 1924). He was nine before he had his first piano lessons (from his mother). Aged 13, he auditioned for Glazunov at the Petrograd Conservatory, playing repertoire pieces and compositions of his own. For his graduation composition in 1926 he produced his First Symphony, a work of great technical assurance that made him internationally famous at the age of 20. Here, ready-formed, was Shostakovich's voice, one from which he never deviated far.

His Second Symphony, with its choral finale and revolutionary sentiments, is subtitled 'To October'; his Third Symphony is called 'The First of May', its finale saluting May Day (International Workers' Day) – an important Soviet holiday. Shostakovich, child of the Revolution, believed it was the duty of an artist to serve the state, to produce music that was accessible without being regressive. He never abandoned tonality. True, he used dissonant harmonies and the avant-garde techniques of his day, but at its heart the chief characteristics of Shostakovich's music are melody, folk song and a rapid exchange of emotional extremes (very Russian) from the sublime to the banal, from sarcastic wit to brooding melancholy.

STRUGGLES WITH THE SOVIET STATE
Yet as early as 1929, with his satirical opera *The Nose*, Shostakovich began to attract the critical attention of the Soviet authorities. *The Nose* was attacked as 'bourgeois decadence', the Third Symphony as a mere 'formal gesture of proletarian solidarity'. But far worse was to come. Two years after the successful premiere of his opera *Lady Macbeth of the Mtzensk District* in 1934 – a work generally welcomed by Soviet musicians as being as good as anything currently being produced in the West – the official Communist Party newspaper *Pravda* published an article headed 'Chaos instead of Music'.

The opera's scenes of adultery, murder and suicide had shocked puritan officialdom, and in a series of attacks instigated by Stalin the paper accused Shostakovich of creating 'a bedlam of noise', 'a confused stream of sounds', and 'petty bourgeois sensationalism'. 'Soviet art,' he was told, 'can have no other aim than the interest of the people and the state.'

This was 1936, the year which marked the beginning of Stalin's terrifying orchestration of political repression and purges. Many of Shostakovich's relatives and friends were imprisoned or killed. He derived some consolation from the birth of his daughter Galina in 1936 and his son Maxim two years later.

'By studying my music you will find the whole truth about me as a man and as an artist.'

SHOSTAKOVICH

In response to *Pravda's* condemnation, Shostakovich withdrew his Fourth Symphony (already being rehearsed in Leningrad but not heard again until 1961) and composed a tepid ballet, *The Limpid Brook*. This too was condemned by *Pravda* as 'being insufficiently dignified on the subject of Soviet life'. He followed this with the magnificent Fifth Symphony, subtitled 'A Soviet artist's practical creative reply to just criticism'. It was a triumphant success with critics and audiences alike. Even the Soviet regime agreed, calling it 'a model of true Soviet art'. It has remained the most popular and frequently heard of all Shostakovich's symphonies, a majestic and powerful conception that ends in a blaze of brass and timpani.

Shostakovich now concentrated on writing symphonies and string quartets, composing little further for the stage until 1955. During the war, he volunteered for active service but was turned down because of his poor eyesight. Despite this, he served for two months in 1941 as a fire-fighter during the siege of Leningrad before being evacuated further east to the temporary Soviet capital, Kuybyshev (now Samara). Critical they may have been, but the ever-mindful authorities were careful to look after a valuable People's Artist. In Kuybyshev Shostakovich completed his Seventh Symphony, 'The Leningrad', the score of which was smuggled out of the USSR on microfilm and given performances in every Allied country, making its composer something of an artistic war hero.

After the war, Shostakovich settled in Moscow, where he was appointed professor of composition at the Conservatory. Despite his celebrity status, he quickly found that he was still not immune from state bullying. He, along with Prokofiev and many other prominent Soviet composers, was denounced in the famous edict of 1948 which accused them of 'formalism' and 'anti-people art'. Shostakovich was dismissed from his professorship, most of his works banned, and his family's privileges withdrawn; until after Stalin's death in 1953, he wrote little more than film scores and patriotic music. His Symphonies

A BAG OF TICS

FOR A CREATIVE LIFE LIVED IN THE SHADOW OF STATE TERROR, it is hardly surprising to learn that Shostakovich was of a nervous disposition. So certain was he that he was about to be arrested in 1948 that he would wait outside on the landing in order that the family, at least, would not be disturbed. His face in later life was described by a friend as 'a bag of tics and grimaces'. According to his daughter Galina, he was 'obsessed with cleanliness'. He insisted on all the clocks in his apartment being synchronized and regularly sent cards to himself to test the efficiency of the postal service. Shostakovich was a dedicated sports fan. Uniquely among the great composers he was also a qualified football referee.

Nos. 10 (1953) and 11 (1957) were passed without comment, though for many people the Tenth is Shostakovich's finest achievement. Completed after the death of Stalin, it seems to reflect the dark ages that had passed and optimism for the future. No. 11 ('The Year 1905') is a more public work and won a Lenin Prize. Symphony No. 12 ('1917'), dedicated to the memory of Lenin, was well received, but with No. 13 Shostakovich once more came up against official criticism, this time from the chairman of the Communist party, Nikita Khrushchev. The choral part of the work, it was claimed, referring to the massacre of the Jews in Kiev during the Second World War, did not pay sufficient attention to the others who were slaughtered; the text was amended to meet official requirements.

LIFE AFTER STALIN

Shostakovich's first wife, Nina Varazar, died in 1954. Two years later he married a young teacher, Margarita Kainova, but the pair proved ill-matched and divorced after three years. Meanwhile, Maxim Shostakovich was progressing with his musical studies (today, he is one of his father's most distinguished interpreters). For him Shostakovich wrote his sparkling Piano Concerto No. 2 (1957), full of private family musical jokes in the solo part and with a meltingly beautiful slow movement. One of Shostakovich's great pleasures in his later years, when restrictions on the arts had slackened, was the friendship of fellow musicians. Among these were the pianist Tatyana Nicolayeva, for whom he wrote the 24 Preludes and Fugues (1951); the violinist David Oistrakh, dedicatee of the Violin Concerto No. 1 (1948); and the cellist Mstislav Rostropovich, the inspiration for the Cello Concertos Nos. 1 and 2.

In 1960 Shostakovich joined the Communist Party, an event which has been variously attributed to expediency, moral cowardice, firm commitment and political pressure. His third wife, Irina Supinskaya, stated that Shostakovich had been blackmailed into taking party membership. It was during the early 1960s that his health began to decline, though he maintained a steady consumption of cigarettes and vodka. For his last years, Shostakovich was left alone to write in a wholly personal way, music that is preoccupied with musings on his own mortality. He completed the last of his 15 string quartets the year before he died and produced two more symphonies, Nos. 14 and 15, the latter famous for its quotes from Rossini's *William Tell*, Wagner's *The Ring* and his own Fourth Symphony.

Shostakovich died of lung cancer in Moscow on 9 August 1975. *The Times* stated that he was beyond doubt 'the last great symphonist'. Would he have been a greater composer without the denunciations and state interference? Many commentators believe so. Shostakovich himself admitted that 'without "Party guidance" . . . I would have displayed more brilliance, used more sarcasm, I could have revealed my ideas openly instead of having to resort to camouflage.'

Essential works

Symphony No. 1 in F minor (1925)
LADY MACBETH OF THE MTZENSK DISTRICT, opera (1934)
Symphony No. 5 in D minor (1937)
15 String Quartets (1938–74)
Symphony No. 7 in C, 'The Leningrad' (1941)
Violin Concerto No. 1 in A minor (1948)
24 Preludes and Fugues, piano (1951)
Symphony No. 10 in E minor (1953)
Piano Concerto No. 2 (1957)
Symphony No. 15 in A (1971)

BENJAMIN
BRITTEN

Towering figure of British music

19-13—76

BRITTEN IS ROUTINELY

DESCRIBED AS 'THE GREATEST BRITISH COMPOSER SINCE PURCELL'. He is more accurately characterized as 'one of the most significant English-born composers of the 20th century', for apart from the implied inferiority of Elgar, Parry and Vaughan Williams (the latter's music despised by Britten), the unmistakable voice in which he wrote was decidedly un-British, its musical language indebted to Berg, Stravinsky, Schoenberg and, especially, Mahler. Yet there is no doubt that when Britten came of age in 1934 – the year in which Elgar, Holst and Delius died – he rapidly attained a position of dominance in British music that he held for the rest of his life and, for many, continues to hold to this day.

The British establishment never quite came to terms with this pacifist, socialist homosexual. He was an outsider, prey to bouts of paranoia, tetchy in his dealings with people and, as revealed in his music, pessimistic in his view of humanity. There is little room for larks and high jinks in Britten's public utterances. Intense, cerebral – 'too clever by half', according to *Grove* – and emotionally buttoned up, Britten was a musicians' musician and greatly admired as such. The only work of his with which the general public (as opposed to the classical devotee) is at all familiar is *The Young Person's Guide to the Orchestra*, though the opera *Peter Grimes*, *A Ceremony of Carols*, the War Requiem and the masterly *Serenade for tenor, horn and strings* have a wide appeal.

EARLY LIFE

Edward Benjamin Britten was born, appropriately enough, on St Cecilia's Day, 22 November 1913. The patron saint of music blessed him with an abundance of precocious gifts. He began playing the piano at two and was reading symphony and opera scores in bed at the age of seven. By his tenth birthday he had completed an oratorio and a string quartet; by the age of 16 he had produced a symphony, six quartets, ten piano sonatas and other smaller works.

The Britten family home in Lowestoft, Suffolk, directly faced the sea. 'My childhood,' he wrote, 'was coloured by the fierce storms that sometimes drove ships into our coast and ate away whole stretches of the neighbouring cliffs.' East Anglia and the sea were to prove central to his life and music. Ben, as he was universally known, was the fourth and youngest child of a dental surgeon and his strong-willed wife, an accomplished amateur pianist who believed her son to be the fourth B in the constellation of great composers whose names begin with B. Britten's first important teacher happened to be a fifth B – Frank Bridge, one of the most forward-looking of English composers, who introduced him to Berg, Bartók and Schoenberg, and instilled in him his lifelong pacifist sentiments.

Soon after he had completed his studies at the Royal College of Music, Britten's youthful cantata, *A Boy was Born*, received its first broadcast by the BBC. It happened to take place on the very day – 23 February 1934 – that

'If wind and water could write music, it would sound like Ben's.'

YEHUDI MENUHIN

Elgar died, a coincidence which many found symbolic. To earn some much-needed money, he accepted a commission from the GPO (General Post Office) film unit to write the music for a number of innovative documentaries, most notably *Night Mail*, in which he collaborated with the second influential figure in his life, the poet W.H. Auden. Auden, seven years his senior, and Christopher Isherwood 'overwhelmed him with their lust and sophistication' (Norman Lebrecht). Auden, apart from helping Britten to acknowledge his homosexuality and reinforcing his political and pacifist convictions, awakened in him an awareness of the beauties of poetry and of the potential of setting words and music, providing the text for Britten's early song cycles *On This Island* and *Our Hunting Fathers*.

FINDING HIS ROOTS

The year 1937 proved to be a significant one in Britten's life. His mother died and soon afterwards he met the man who would be his partner for the rest of his life, the tenor Peter Pears. He was commissioned to write a piece for string orchestra. Dashed off in four weeks, *Variations on a Theme of Frank Bridge* was premiered at the Salzburg Festival that year. The composer Aaron Copland penned a review: 'The piece is what we would call a knock-out,' he wrote. The same year, Britten came across a mill in the Suffolk village of Snape and moved there in 1938.

East Anglia, however, was put on hold when, in his own words, 'muddled, fed-up and looking for work, longing to be used', he and Pears left England for America in 1939, a few months after Auden. It was to be a three-year exile in which he produced a string of mature works that included *Les Illuminations* (1939), settings of poems by Rimbaud; the Violin Concerto (1939); the *Sinfonia da Requiem* (1940); and the operetta *Paul Bunyan* (1941) with a text by Auden, a piece which was – as Britten put it – 'politely spat at'. While in Los Angeles in 1941, Britten read an article by E.M. Forster on the 18th-century Suffolk poet George Crabbe. 'I suddenly realised where I belonged and what I lacked,' he wrote.

Britten and Pears returned home to Snape in 1942. Appearing before the Tribunal of Conscientious Objectors, the composer was exempted from military duty and allowed to continue composing on condition that he took part in concerts as part of the war effort. Before the end of the conflict, he had produced two of his most frequently heard works, *A Ceremony of Carols* (1942) and the *Serenade for tenor, horn and strings* (1943), written for Pears and the brilliant horn player Dennis Brain. But it was to Crabbe's poem 'The Borough' that he turned for the basis of his next project, one that would make him internationally famous – the opera *Peter Grimes* (1945).

The first night at the newly reopened Sadler's Wells theatre is said to have marked the rebirth of British opera (though Britain has never had an operatic tradition in the same way as France, Italy or Germany). That said, *Peter Grimes* is a milestone in modern opera. Set in an East Anglian fishing village, it tells the story of the eponymous solitary fisherman who is treated with distrust by the villagers after the death of an apprentice at sea. After a second boy dies, Grimes takes his boat out to sea and scuttles it. The theme of the outsider, of man's struggle against intolerance and prejudice was a subject to which Britten returned frequently. *Billy Budd*, which followed in 1951, was adapted from Hermann Melville's

CHILDREN'S COMPOSER

BRITTEN WAS PARTICULARLY ADEPT at writing music for children that was accessible without being condescending. Works such as *Let's Make an Opera* and *Noye's Fludde* have dated quickly, but *The Young Person's Guide to the Orchestra* has been a striking and stimulating first visit to a concert hall for generations of schoolchildren. It is a set of variations based on a theme by Purcell (always close to Britten's heart), the Rondeau from the incidental music for the play *Abdelazer*.

FOREVER YOUNG

'Britten remained essentially a young man in his physical appearance, manner and dress, until he was sixty. He was wiry and athletic – walking with him, I found it difficult to keep pace with his stride. On the tennis court he made me feel like a rabbit; on the beach, I used to shiver watching him while he took his daily dip . . . His manner was always relaxed except when he was composing, when his whole facial expression changed and he appeared stern with concentration, taut and utterly ruthless . . . He never gesticulated, seldom lost his temper. With orchestral players and singers he was patient and tactful, though he had no time for journalists and hangers-on. He was essentially shy except with his closest friends... Children loved him and he loved children. Indeed, he always remained a child.'

Ronald Duncan, *Working with Britten*

novel of naval mutiny – the sea again – and deals with many of the same themes as *Peter Grimes*.

None of Britten's subsequent operas achieved the same impact as these two studies of man confronting his fellow men and his own conscience, though each one shows the composer to be a master of inventiveness: *The Rape of Lucretia* (1946), *Albert Herring* (1947), *The Turn of the Screw* (1954), *A Midsummer Night's Dream* (1960), *Owen Wingrave* (written for television in 1971). Britten's War Requiem was written in 1961 to celebrate the consecration of the newly built Coventry Cathedral, replacing the building destroyed in the war. It is a powerful and profound work that uses the words of the Latin Mass and the poems of the First World War poet Wilfred Owen.

FINAL YEARS

In 1948, with Eric Crozier and Peter Pears, Britten had inaugurated the Aldeburgh Festival, which became (and remains) a beacon of musical excellence. In the mid-1960s the festival moved to the nearby Maltings at Snape, allowing for larger-scale productions. It was here that Britten's last major composition, the opera *Death in Venice*, was premiered in 1973. As with so much of Britten's work, Peter Pears was the inspiration behind this confessional, autobiographical piece.

It became clear while he was working on *Death in Venice* that the heart disease that had weakened Britten for years was likely to be fatal, and in the last few years of his life he was reduced to doing very little. Having been awarded the coveted Order of Merit in 1965, in 1976 he accepted a life peerage, the first musician in history to be so honoured. Less than six months later, on 4 December, he died in his beloved Aldeburgh.

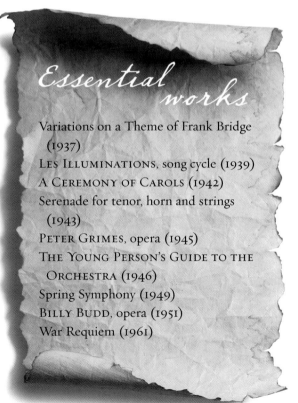

Essential works

Variations on a Theme of Frank Bridge (1937)
LES ILLUMINATIONS, song cycle (1939)
A CEREMONY OF CAROLS (1942)
Serenade for tenor, horn and strings (1943)
PETER GRIMES, opera (1945)
THE YOUNG PERSON'S GUIDE TO THE ORCHESTRA (1946)
Spring Symphony (1949)
BILLY BUDD, opera (1951)
War Requiem (1961)

INDEX

First published in Great Britain in 2007 by

Quercus
21 Bloomsbury Square
London
WC1A 2NS

Copyright © Jeremy Nicholas 2007

A CIP catalogue record for this book is available from the British Library

Cloth case edition   ISBN-10: 1 84724 182 4
                        ISBN-13: 978 1 84724 182 5

Printed case edition ISBN-10: 1 84724 013 5
                        ISBN-13: 978 1 84724 013 2

Paperback edition   ISBN-10: 1 84724 361 4
                        ISBN-13: 978 1 84724 361 4

Printed and bound in China

10 9 8 7 6 5 4 3 2 1

Picture credits
The publishers would like to thank the following for permission to reproduce illustrations and photographs:
Corbis on pages 27, 68, 80, 88, 101, 109, 113, 121, 129, 141, 149, 161, 181, 193; © Lebrecht Music and Arts Photo Library pages 1, 4, 8, 12, 16, 20, 23, 35, 39, 44, 60, 64, 72, 76, 84, 97, 105, 117, 125, 133, 137, 145, 165, 169; page 56 © Lebrecht Music and Arts Photo Library/Alamy; page 93 © Mary Evans Picture Library/Alamy; pages 157, 173, 177, 185, 189, 197 © Popperfoto/Alamy; page 31 © Visual Arts Library (London)/Alamy; pages 49, 52, 153 © World History Archive/Alamy

Edited by Ben Dupré
Design by Austin Taylor
Picture research by Victoria Huxley
Index by Ingrid Lock
Project management and typesetting by Windrush Publishing Services,
12 Adlestrop, Moreton in Marsh, Gloucestershire, GL56 0YN